DE PROPRIETATIBUS LITTERARUM

edenda curat
C. H. VAN SCHOONEVELD
Indiana University

Series Didactica, 3

SHOLOM ALEICHEM

A Non-Critical Introduction

by

SOL GITTLEMAN

Tufts University

1974
MOUTON
THE HAGUE · PARIS

© Copyright 1974 in The Netherlands
Mouton & Co. N. V., Publishers, The Hague

No part of this book may be translated or reproduced in any form, by print, photoprint, microfilm, or any other means, without written permission from the publishers

LIBRARY OF CONGRESS CATALOG CARD NUMBER: 73-87373

Printed in Hungary

to Edna and Frank Gittleman

TABLE OF CONTENTS

Preface 7
   I. Adventure of a Language 11
  II. The Poet of the People 21
 III. The Town of the Little People 55
 IV. "With God's help, I starved to death": The Tevye Stories 103
  V. "What doesn't a Jew do for a living?": The Letters of
      Menachem-Mendel 131
 VI. Stories for Jewish Children 143
VII. Outside of Kasrilevke 161
VIII. The American-Jewish Writer: An Epilogue 177
Appendix 195
Bibliography 199
Index 201

PREFACE

How does one go about writing a book about a culture-hero whose language is scarcely known to the vast majority of Americans? Moreover, the culture with which this writer was so closely identified has disappeared, the former inhabitants are spread out all over the world, and their children are at a loss to understand what their parents are talking about when they reminisce about 'the old country'.

The culture-hero is Sholom Aleichem, the language is Yiddish, and that world is the world of the Jewish *shtetl*, the dilapidated Jewish townlet, in Sholom Aleichem's case, in the pre-Soviet Ukraine, which existed for centuries in a suspended state of medievalism, until the twentieth century shoved it into oblivion.

As if this did not suggest enough difficulty, the tradition has been established, at least in the minds of the vast majority of those interested or touched by Yiddish literature and culture in America, that one does not discuss critically either the major Yiddish writers or Yiddish literature. For the most part, we are confronted by anthologies of humor, anecdotes, definitions, generally quite sentimental and thoroughly rooted in the cultural heritage of the *shtetl*. In the case of Sholom Aleichem, the detached observer is running a considerable risk in taking on a literary subject who has almost transcended the normal status of even the traditional folk writer. The few highly professional Yiddishists in America are immediately offended by any attempt to broaden the perspectives of Yiddish and to place Sholom Aleichem in any context other than the Yiddish one; and the vast majority of his non-professional admirers prefer to hold to a romanticized nostalgia best represented by the Broadway success of *Fiddler on the Roof*. His works represent, after all, the ultimate expression of a people. It is safe to say that few writers in the history of world literature have so completely fused their art to their subject matter. Sholom Aleichem's complete works could replace any serious sociological-anthropological study of the Jewish world in the Russian Ukraine from 1850 to 1914. Indeed, Sholom Aleichem's world *is* the world of Yiddishkeit and as such almost defies critical objectivity. He is the personal property of Eastern European Jewry, his works are a private memoir of these people, most of whom died during Hitler's Third Reich.

Ironically, now that the *shtetl* world has almost disappeared, it seems time to re-examine the works of Sholom Aleichem, and to do so particularly from the American viewpoint. Sholom Aleichem is no longer the personal property of the remnants of Eastern European Jewry or their American descendants. He has emerged as a major influence in modern American fiction, and readers of Bellow, Malamud, the Roths, and others who may never have heard of Sholom Aleichem would do well to understand the themes and characters of this earlier writer, in order better to comprehend the nature of the current American literary movement.

This is not a book of 'higher scholarship'. It is a general, non-academic portrait of the most famous writer of the Yiddish language, as well as an analysis of as many of his prose works as is feasible within the scope of an introductory volume. Sholom Aleichem was a most prolific writer, completing over three hundred short stories and sketches, several full-length novels, as well as some fifteen plays. However, it is in the shorter prose works, vignettes, and monologues where his artistic greatness is most apparent. Like his mentor Anton Chekhov, Sholom Aleichem could not sustain his creativity in longer prose works; and in spite of the success of *Fiddler on the Roof*, the stage was not his medium.

In writing this book, I was faced immediately with a major dilemma: to what extent should I rely on the reader's knowledge of Yiddish? After considerable deliberation, I decided that future studies may well better serve the linguistically gifted, but that this work should aim itself at those very people who find Sholom

PREFACE 9

Aleichem's Yiddish no longer accessible. All quotations are given in English, and all references are to the English translations available to the general reader. Much had to be sacrificed as a result. In translation it is nearly impossible to discuss questions of style and other aspects of the writer's art which may be uniquely tied to his language. For those purists who may be offended, I apologize and suggest that you write the book you would like to have written. For the history of Sholom Aleichem scholarship in English has done little to make this writer more available to the non-specialist.

I have attached an appendix which gives additional information concerning Yiddish sources. There is no definitive Yiddish or English edition of the works of Sholom Aleichem, although twenty-eight volumes of a planned complete Yiddish edition have appeared.

I am indebted to a variety of people for a variety of reasons. Most particularly I should like to express my gratitude to the *Society for Religion in Higher Education* and to the Danforth Foundation for providing me with the time and the means to complete this work, and to the Faculty Research Fund of Tufts University.

S. G.

I

ADVENTURE OF A LANGUAGE

The world of Sholom Aleichem is no more. The fact is, for many readers this study must first attempt to re-create the atmosphere and environment of a culture which is dead and a language which, in spite of optimistic predictions, is dying.[1] Perhaps within the next three or four centuries a linguistic scientist will be sitting with a tape recorder of some futuristic vintage, taking down the final gasps of the world's last native speaker of Yiddish. When this event occurs, the world of Sholom Aleichem will be officially extinct. For the world of Sholom Aleichem is uniquely tied up with this incredible language, which Alfred Kazin describes as "the poor Jew's everyday clothes".[2] More specifically, Yiddish was the everyday language of millions of Jews, particularly in Eastern Europe from the Middle Ages to the present time. Thanks to Hitler, the number of native speakers of Yiddish in Poland and Russia is estimated today at no more than 3,000,000,[3] while a similar number can be found in The United States and Israel. However, the Russians are not eager to encourage the spread of Yiddish in The Soviet Union, and in the Western Hemisphere natural assimilation is cutting drastically into the numbers; in Israel, Yiddish is the hated language of a ghetto past, and runs a poor fourth to the official languages of Hebrew, English, and Arabic.

---

[1] The leading optimist is the Yiddish scholar Curt Leviant. See his introduction to *Some Laughter, Some Tears* (New York: Putnam, 1968), 12.
[2] *Selected Stories of Sholom Aleichem*, Modern Library Edition (New York: Random House, 1956), xi.
[3] For Russia's Jewish millions, there is one Yiddish journal, *Sovietish Heimatland*, and about 150 books published annually.

The Jews did not always speak and write Yiddish. After the Diaspora in the first century of the christian era, hundreds of thousands of Jews wandered across North Africa, speaking a Semitic dialect similar to Aramaic, not unlike the language spoken by Jesus himself. Of course, most Jews were also versed in Hebrew, the holy language of the Bible and of the many volumes comprising the Talmudic Laws. Along the way, many Jews dropped the use of Aramaic as their spoken language and absorbed the native languages of the particular region, but in general, they remained a linguistically unified people. The same thing occurred when the Jews crossed the Mediterranean and entered into Spain, although the incident of linguistic assimilation was even greater than had been the case. The fusion of the Jewish languages with Spanish produced the first of numerous hybrids, Ladino, a language still spoken today by many non-Yiddish speaking Jews of the Sephardic branch of the cultural tree.[4]

The Jews continued moving northward into Europe, and by the tenth and eleventh centuries had established centers of Jewish learning at Troyes in France – where the great Jewish scholar Rashi held forth – and in Worms, Speyer, and Mayence in the Rhineland of modern Germany. In Germany the spiritual climate was particularly free for the Jews, and they lived with their German neighbors in a remarkable state of peace and prosperity. During this period, a unique linguistic phenomenon occurred. The Jews gradually abandoned their spoken language and acquired the German spoken by their Rhenish neighbors. But the liturgical Hebrew still exercised a profound influence, to the extent that the

---

[4] "Early commentators identified the word *Sepharad*, which appears in Obad. 9 : 20, with the country of Spain. As a result, the Jews of the Iberian peninsula and their descendents came to be known as *Sephardim*, in distinction to the Jews of the Franco-German tradition who are known as *Ashkenazim* (*Ashkenaz* in Gen. 10 : 3 having been identified with Germany)... After the expulsion of the Jews from Spain in 1492 the word *Sephardi* was given wider connotation as the Jews from Spain imposed their culture and traditions upon the Jewish communities of North Africa and the Middle East. The word *Sephardi* today is thus frequently used for a Jew belonging to one of the Oriental communities which adopted the *Sephardi* rite, whether or not the community is originally of Spanish provenance." *The Encyclopedia of the Jewish Religion*, eds. Werblowsky and Wigoder (New York: Holt, Rinehart and Winston, 1965), 347–48.

Jews continued to write this newly acquired language from right to left, using the Hebrew alphabet! It was called, at various points in this early development, *Ivri-Teutsch, Judenteutsch*, and *Jüdisch*, all of which was intended to indicate that this was German, but the way the Jews spoke it and wrote it.

But, inevitably, the fast-progressing assimilation of Jew into German ended with the Lateran Council of 1215. The *ghetto* concept was established, and the amount of contact between Jew and Gentile diminished markedly. The development of Yiddish as a Germanic language based on Middle High German was arrested, and Yiddish was turned back onto itself, as well as to the Hebrew, Aramaic, Spanish, French, and Italian elements which the Jews had incorporated into their language earlier.

There are some remarkable literary documents from this initial phase of Yiddish development, documents which dramatize the extent to which the Jewish population identified with their German hosts. "The Jews", as Salcia Landmann notes, "read and loved the same songs and sagas as the Germans."[5] There was a Jewish troubador poet, Süsskind von Trimberg, who was a contemporary of the great German Minnesängers. The oldest extant manuscript of the famous German *Gudrun* saga is a Yiddish one, and there is also a Yiddish *Nibelungenlied*, as well as numerous literary adaptations in Yiddish of Arthurian romances and folktales of knighthood.

But the Jews did not remain in Germany and Western Europe. The persecutions intensified, as the crusades progressed, and the plague which swept Europe in the fourteenth century was blamed on the Jews. Large numbers of Yiddish-speaking Jews fled to the east, taking with them their language. The ghetto was now firmly established, and regardless of the relative amount of freedom which the Jews of Eastern Europe enjoyed, they remained alienated linguistically from their host countries. Yiddish remained the common, communal language of the so-called *Ashkenazi* Jews of

---

[5] *Jiddisch: Abenteuer einer Sprache* (Munich: Deutscher Taschenbuch Verlag, 1964), 22.

Europe.[6] From the 15th century on, the vast majority of Jews settled in Poland and Russia – often in areas limited by law – in ghettoes isolated from the Gentile world around them, picking up snatches of Russian, Ukrainian, or Polish, which managed to find their way into the everyday Yiddish of the streets.

Within the cultural heritage of the Jewish community, Yiddish was relegated to a second-class citizenship. It was the language of daily intercourse, 'the language of the week', of commerce and trade, a jargon, a 'mishmash' of words and gestures which in general enjoyed no respect as a serious language. It was not even socially respectable. Yiddish, at various times during the Middle Ages, was associated with the underworld of Europe, and to this day there is a remarkable high frequency of Yiddish words in the several underworld languages of Europe.[7] Moreover, Yiddish was associated with women; it was called the *Mame-loschen*, the mother's

---

[6] "Jewish communal and social life as well as Jewish scholarship developed in Christian Europe from the three Rhineland communities of Speyer, Worms, and Mayence in the 10th century. Thence they spread westward to France through Rashi and his descendants and eastward to Germany and Bohemia establishing a unity of custom, ritual, and law differing from the parallel tradition in what was then Moslem Europe – Spain. As a result, the word *Ashkenaz*, from having a purely geographic connotation became applied to a religious and cultural tradition of those who followed the custom which had its origin among German Jews. With the drift of German Jews over the eastern borders of their country into the Slavonic lands in the 16th century, and the adoption by the Jews in those countries of the traditions (and language, namely Yiddish) of the German Jews, the word *Ashkenazi* received an even wider connotation... The word *Ashkenazi* is generally applied to all Jews of European origin and customs, apart from the Jews of Spanish and Portuguese origins...*Sephardi* is generally applied to all Jews of oriental countries who follow the parallel Spanish tradition...The difference is marked in such spheres as religious customs, Hebrew pronunciation, synagogal cantillation", and the use of Yiddish, which is limited to the Ashkenazim. *Encyclopedia of the Jewish Religion*, 45.

[7] See Salcia Landmann, in *Jiddisch: Abenteuer einer Sprache*, "Geschichte des Rotwelschen", 75ff. There are numerous instances of the marriage of Yiddish and the demi-monde world. The Yiddish – actually Hebrew – word *Mesuse* means a small capsule which Jews place on their doorposts, in which is contained a portion from Deutoronomy. Pious Jews touch the object with their fingers, and then kiss the sanctified fingers. In the language of the German underworld, *Mesuse* means 'prostitute'. The analogy is quite clear. Prostitutes are normally found in doorways, and are also similarly caressed. For other examples, see Leo Rosten, *The Joys of Yiddish* (New York: McGraw-Hill, 1968).

tongue. In general, women were not educated in Torah or the more esoteric religious business of the Jewish community. They could not read Hebrew, as could almost every male. As a result, it was necessary to translate much of the Hebrew Bible into Yiddish, in order that the women could follow along, or study at home.

Hebrew remained the language of serious discourse. Whatever literature was written in Yiddish between the period of the fourteenth and nineteenth centuries was either imitation of romance meant for women or moralistic tract with a similar female orientation. No intelligent male would be seen reading a Yiddish book, for fear of humiliation. And certainly no serious writer, talmudist, or scholar would use Yiddish for any literary or scholarly work.

As early as the eighteenth century, Yiddish was identified as the language of the Jewish past and as an impediment to Jewish progress. In Germany, the enlightened Jewish philosopher Moses Mendelssohn (1729–1786) was determined to raise the level of life for his co-religionists and to bring the benefits of the Age of Reason to the ghetto. He translated the Bible into German, using Hebrew orthography. His followers were determined to eradicate Yiddish as the language of everyday speech and at least in Germany succeeded in uprooting Yiddish and in substituting German. Thus began the *Haskalah*, the Jewish Enlightenment. It spread eastward and northward across Europe, attacking the entrenched orthodoxy of the rabbis in Northern Russia and Poland.

At the same time, another phase of Jewish intellectual history was beginning. In Polish Galicia, a compassionate and saintly man, Israel Baal Shem Tov (1700–1760), was preaching a new doctrine of joyous piety and simple love of God. The movement which he founded, *Hassidism*, followed the southern route across Europe, and won to it the vast masses of wretched Jews living in the squalor of the still medieval Jewish townlet, the *shtetl*. Naturally, the language of the Hassidic teacher and master was Yiddish, the language of the *prosteh Yid*, the common, ordinary, down-trodden Jew. The Hassidic followers of the Baal Shem Tov spread the tales of his (as well as their own) miracles in Yiddish pamphlets as well as by word of mouth.

The Russian and Polish Jewish intelligentsia which had been

won to the Haskalah quickly saw that they possessed no ready means of communicating the ideas of the Enlightenment to the Jewish masses. With a considerable reluctance, in the mid-nineteenth century some of these men, who had previously only written in Hebrew, began turning, often anonymously, to the despised language of the masses, so as to make their ideas available to these very people whose language they detested. Ironically, to gain converts to religious reformation and Jewish cultural integration, these Hebraists were forced to revert to a mode of expression which to them represented Jewish isolationism at its worst.

It was inevitable that this social pamphleteering would soon take the form of literature. In the 1850s, a Hebrew scholar from Vilna, Lithuania – long a center of East European Enlightenment – "stooped to write tales in the despised vernacular" and found himself an unprecedented success.[8] Isaac Meir Dick (1814–1893) became an instant sensation, and his works were literally read to tatters by the hungry masses of the *shtetl*. Yiddish was now ready to join the other languages of Europe as a serious means of literary expression.

What was lacking was a major literary talent, and that emerged, as well. Sholom Yakob Abramowitch (1836–1917) was a modestly successful Hebraist, an identifiable *Maskil*, an enlightened, committed Jewish intellectual who searched for a means to reach the 16,000,000 of his co-religionists living in legal bondage in the Pale of Settlement. By law, the Jew enjoyed very limited latitude concerning his right to live in Czarist-ruled Eastern Europe. Abramovitch had seen the Jewish *shtetl* and what he considered its decadence, medievalism, and suffocating social restrictions and was determined to break through to these people. In 1863, he took a daring step. He submitted his first Yiddish manuscript to a publisher of a Hebrew journal, but in order not to damage his reputation as a Hebrew writer, he asked that the work be published under a pseudonym. Abramovitch and the editor agreed on a name: Mendele Mocher Sforim, and the work was *Dos kleine Menshele* (*The Little*

---

[8] See Sol Liptzin, *The Flowering of Yiddish Literature* (New York: Thomas Yoseloff, 1963), 17–18.

Man). In this tald o anersto fol soolowthn e, Mendele set the standard for much of the literature of Yiddish's Golden Age. Mendele was the moral satirist, a Swift of Naturalism whose devastating descriptions of Jewish life in the Pale were meant to elevate and inculcate. He created most of the motifs which Sholom Aleichem made famous a generation later. He conceived the mythical community of Jews, a device particularly effective for criticism and one that inspired Sholom Aleichem to the creation of the legendary Kasrilevke, the town of hilariously jolly paupers. In *The Little Man* Mendele presents a biting description of corrupt Jewish politicians and *negidim*, the rich men of the town, and advocates another of the major ideas of Sholom Aleichem: the need for reform in the Jewish school system and the brutality which Jewish children suffered from in *cheyder*, the Jewish parochial elementary school. In *Die Takse* (*The Meat-tax*, 1869), Mendele dramatizes the abuses of the rich in placing taxes on Kosher meats in order to gain wealth for themselves. After this it was necessary for Mendele to flee to Odessa, so harsh had become the outcry against his works from the people he was attacking. The common Jews of the *shtetl*, for whom no one had ever written seriously in Yiddish, devoured his works in paper pamphlets which were read to rags, as they circulated from house to house. *Die Klatshe* (*The Old Nag*, 1873), a poetic satire on Jewry, is one of his most famous works. It is an allegory of the Jews, as they stagger through life like an old horse, beaten, without the courage or determination to resist. In *Fishke der Krumer* (*Fishke the Lame*) Mendele presents the theme of the *lamed vav*. In the Talmud, the comprehensive compilation of Jewish law, there is a statement that asserts that the existence of the world is guaranteed by the presence of thirty-six (in Hebrew, *lamed vav*) righteous men who enjoy a particularly intimate relationship with God. In Jewish folklore this evolved into the legend of the *lamed vav*, thirty-six men of wretched and humble background whose true saintliness cannot be revealed. This tradition in Jewish life perhaps accounts for the unique position given to beggars, who are never refused, for fear of rejecting unwittingly one of these pious men. The type naturally evolved into the Jewish *nebbich*, the simple, honest, abused, impoverished fool. Fishke is such a man, wretched, yet completely compassionate. The gentile counterpart is the fool-in-Christ, a theme which impressed Dostoyevsky, Gerhart Hauptmann, and a host of western writers. Sholom Aleichem later consistently employed the same motif, and it became a standard in Yiddish literature. Peretz' *Bontsha the Silent* and I. B. Singer's *Gimpel the Fool* are two of the more notable illustrations.

Masoes Beniamin Haslishi (*The Wanderings of Benjamin the Third*, 1878), a Don Quixote-like mock epic, complete with a Jewish Sancho Panza, presents the prototype of the *luftmensh*, that "apotheosis of Jewish rootlessness"[9] the Eternal Jew in search of *parnosseh*, 'a living', and very rarely succeeding in finding it; the Wheeler-Dealer who carries his assets around in his pockets and conducts his business transactions in telephone booths. Sholom Aleichem was to turn him into the immortal Menachem-Mendel, *luftmensh* par excellence. In *Der Vinshfingerl* (*The Wishing Ring*, 1870–80) Mendele deals with the problem of Jewish assimilation and the inroads of the outside world.

There are endless variations in Mendele which Sholom Aleichem later orchestrated. In Mendele's writings we encounter pompous intellectuals, over-zealous Zionists, sadistic teachers, beloved rabbis, fake scholars, the hypocritical rich, as well as the happy poor, types which Sholom Aleichem did not have to create, because they had been created for him by Mendele. Yet, these two writers had to serve different functions within the development of Yiddish literature; Mendele had hardly anyone to imitate, so his shortcomings are more obvious. He dealt with his characters with a forthrightness which had never been seen in Yiddish writing before. Most often he created types he did not like personally, in order to condemn them and to teach his fellow Jews what they should *not* be like. Mendele was blunt, unabashedly moralistic, a relentless teacher of truth and honesty. This role of literary conscience of his people placed a considerable limitation on Mendele's art, because he often sacrificed literary integrity for moral integrity.

But most important of all, he had discovered the perfect setting for his message: the *shtetl*, the Jewish microcosm. In an age of

[9] Maurice Samuel, *The World of Sholom Aleichem* (New York: Schocken Books, 1943), 256.

realism, where the social novels of Dickens, Flaubert, and Tolstoy dominated prose fiction, this Jewish intellectual demonstrated that he came to his profession not as a naive and folksy primitive, but as a conscious craftsman who shows the impact of the literate European world around him. Mendele instinctively went to the heart of Jewish society, but he clearly understood the nature of fiction as a vehicle for social commentary. His descriptive mode, the imagery, the types, all reveal that Mendele deserves a most significant role in the history of Yiddish literature.

The stage was now set for even a more significant breakthrough. With Mendele's contribution, Yiddish literature achieved almost instant maturity. Within the next thirty years, Sholom Aleichem would give it immortality.

II

THE POET OF THE PEOPLE

Rarely in the history of literature has a writer come along who could be said to have captured the total identity of a people. Such a writer becomes a folk-hero in his own time, to his own people. This is the unique moment in literature when there is absolute, instant communication between artist and public to such an extent that it is difficult for the literary historian to imagine. After all, how many 'national' writers can we name who have achieved such a position? Did Dickens, or Thomas Mann, Balzac or Zola, even Hemingway or Faulkner, did any of these literary giants penetrate to the hearts of every single citizen of their respective worlds? Certainly not.

Sholom Aleichem, a Russian-Jew born Sholom Rabinowitz, is one of these rarities. In the twenty-eight volumes of his complete works we are given not only an unparalleled picture of life in the Jewish *shtetl* of the Pale of Settlement around the turn of the past century, but also an unerring account of the psychological, sociological, and economic forces which led to the breakdown of this *shtetl* world prior to World War I. Yet, he was not genuinely of this world; he was not, as one might initially suspect, an unlettered primitivist, an inhabitant of the *shtetl*. Sholom Aleichem was "a conscious artist thoroughly aware of literary form and tradition",[1] a sophisticated European who clearly shows the influence of Turgenev, Chekhov, Swift, Heine, and Dickens; a city dweller, Sholom Aleichem spent only a few of his fifty-seven years within the confines

---

[1] Curt Leviant, "Introduction", in *Old Country Tales* (New York: G. P. Putnam's Sons, 1966), 12.

of the *shtetl* which he described so meticulously. Through some extra-literary means, however, he developed into this folk-hero, a living legend, the most beloved of all Yiddish writers.

1. "A TATENS A KIND"

This phrase, like so many in Yiddish, has a peculiarly 'inside' meaning. It reflects the entire social hierarchy of Jewish life in Eastern Europe for centuries after the arrival of masses of Jews after the Crusades. It means 'the son of a somebody', the offspring of a particularly learned, pedigreed Jewish family which enjoyed the highest position of status in the Jewish community. It means, also, that this status gives you the privilege, indeed the obligation, of not associating with the less gifted and endowed Jews of the community. You possessed *yikhus*, a Hebrew word meaning lineage, breeding, station and status, generally based on the amount of erudition amassed by your ancestors and the prominence of your forebearers in Talmudic studies.[2]

Sholom Rabinowitz was born into such a family on March 2, 1859, in Pereyaslav, a medium-sized town in the Ukraine, Russia, but as an infant moved to a genuine Ukrainian *shtetl*, Voronko, where he spent the next ten years of his life. Sholom Aleichem describes his father's position in Voronko:

A tall man with a broad, white, wrinkled forehead, a thin beard which seemed to smile, and a constantly worried expression! A man of means and an amateur cantor, a scholar and a man well versed in the Bible, a pious man and a lover of Hebrew, a disciple of the Hasidic Rabbi of Talna, and a secret admirer of the more "worldly" writers like Mapu, Slonimsky, and Zederbaum; philosopher, arbiter, counsellor, chessplayer, and connoisseur of diamonds and pearls – this describes the hero's

---

[2] "*Yikhus*: Pedigree, lineage. High status based chiefly on scholarship or wealth of ancestors or relatives. *Yikhus atsmo*: Status acquired by one's own efforts. *Yikhus ovos*: Status based on geneology. (All Hebrew)". *Life Is With People*: *The Culture of the Shtetl*, Zborowski and Herzog, eds., introduction by Margaret Mead (New York, Schooken, 1962), 447.

father, Reb Nahum Vevik's (than is, Nahum, son of Vevik), who was considered the richest man in town.³

It was here in Voronko that young Sholom began storing the wealth of images which were to re-appear later in his stories. As a child his position in such a prominent family gave him a unique vantage point from which he could observe the world of the *shtetl*, even though he was, by tradition of this prominence, forbidden to do so. In his autobiography he tells of this social eminence:

> Looking at his tall father, dressed in a handsome silk coat with a broad belt and a tricornered hat on his head, which he wore on Sabbaths and holidays; or watching his little mother, Haya Esther, when she raised her delicate white hands to bless the candles in tall puffed silver candlesticks; or listening to his tall neat Grandma Minde talk with God as with an intimate friend; or hearing Uncle Nissel the strong man, gabble Russian like a real Slav – Sholom would feel proud and happy. He thanked the Lord for his good fortune in being born into such a family, in feeling contented as a prince and secure as in a royal fortress.⁴

Sholom's father, besides enjoying the status which his erudition gave him, was also the *nogid*, the town's rich man, which in the financially hazardous world of the permanently depressed *shtetl*, meant a great deal. He was the town aristocrat, its political leader as well as its social pacesetter, and as such a constant stream of townsfolk passed through the home of the Rabinowitz family. As for young Sholom Rabinowitz, he took advantage of the endless stream of rich and poor visitors – Voronko had its share of paupers – to search out, at considerable risk to himself, friends from among the

---

³ *The Great Fair: Scenes from my Childhood*, translated by Tamara Kahana, Noonday Paperback (New York, Noonday Press, 1958), 9. Abraham Mapu (1808–1867), author of the first Hebrew novel, *Ahabat Zion* (*The Love of Zion*, 1853), a highly romantic story set in the times of the prophet Isiah. Mapu was not really concerned with ideas, but his writing in Hebrew created a language of literature which until that time had not existed. Hayim Selig Slonimski (1810–1904), a scientist and inventor, was the first to use Hebrew to popularize science among Eastern European Jews. In 1862 he founded the Hebrew weekly *Ha-Zefirah*. Alexander Ossypovitch Zederbaum (1816–1893), a Hebrew journalist, was founder and editor of *Ha-Melitz* in 1860, which grew to become the leading Hebrew publication dedicated to raising the level of intellectualism among the Jewish masses. All three men were early Zionists.
⁴ *The Great Fair*, 69.

wretched of the town. He refused to allow himself to be isolated behind the walls of his well-built home, or to follow the dictates of his family's social position. As a result, Sholom was able to experience everything that this typical Hassidic community, living on the edge of Medievalism, had to offer.

His father, Reb Nahum, was a rarity, a pious Hassidic Jew who was not afraid to read the modern Hebrew masterpieces, such as Abraham Mapu's *Love of Zion*, one of his favorites. He read much of the writers of the Jewish Enlightenment, the *Maskilim* – radicals in Voronko! – who were urging modernization of Jewish life and an end to religious conformity in Judaism. As one of SholomAleichem's daughters describes her grandfather's home, "his house was perhaps the only place where orthodox and modern met".[5]

But given the precarious nature of economic existence in the *shtetl* it was not extraordinary that Reb Nahum Rabinowitz' fortunes should turn for the worse. After about a decade of living in the considerable pleasure of Voronko's 'high society', the family of Nahum Rabinowitz was shaken by financial disaster. His partner had swindled Rabinowitz out of most of his holdings, and Reb Nahum was suddenly and unexpectedly ruined. In Sholom Aleichem's memoirs, he recalls the catastrophic proportions which this episode took in his mind. Even as a young adolescent, Sholom was a creature of economics and well understood the financial situation of his family as well as his own monetary situation. When he came to write about Jewish children many years later, he imbued in them a sense of materialism which one normally would attribute only to an adult, but which Sholom Aleichem clearly intends to be representative of Jewish children. When they talked together among themselves, they talked 'money' as often as not. As a child Sholom remembered the words that his friend Pinneleh uttered as he left Voronko the year before his own departure:

'"What is Voronko? A wilderness, a ditch, a mudhole, a tiny village! The people! They're paupers. beggars, ragamuffins! All the Jews of Voronko taken together, even counting the wealthy ones, don't earn

---

[5] Marie Waife-Goldberg, *My Father, Sholom Aleichem* (New York: Simon and Schuster, 1968), 33.

as much as Ephrati earns in Odessa!' Sholom asked him, 'Who is Ephrati?' Pinneleh replied, 'He is a relative to us on mother's side. He's a wealthy man, a capitalist, a millionaire! I've already told you, dumbbell, all that the Voronko Jews earn together won't add up to what Ephrati keeps in one coat pocket.... Money will simply roll into our pockets.'"[6]

It is obvious from the one volume of autobiography that he wrote before his death that a considerable amount of his attention was devoted to financial matters. After his mother's death, he spent a good deal of time with his maternal grandparents, who were pawnbrokers and moneylenders. Sholom's attention became riveted on the moneybox which his grandmother kept constantly under her pillow. Family life seemed to gravitate around this moneybox, as Sholom watched his "Uncle Itzie smiling maliciously, smoothing his earlocks, glancing at the pillow under which lay grandmother's fortune."[7] In Voronko and later on, Sholom Aleichem describes a sort of *Lord of the Flies* children's world of mercantilism, where the youthful capitalists outstrip their parents in hard-nosed business sense. They borrowed from each other at interest, traded, made deals for goods, acquired wealth. Interestingly, one finds parallel situations in the memoirs of other Yiddish writers, such as the situation described by Isaac Bashevis Singer in *My Father's Court*. As a pre-teenager, he says, "there were times when I was forced to borrow money from a cheder classmate, a young usurer who demanded interest – for every four groschen, I paid a groschen a week".[8]

In Voronko, meanwhile, the situation grew impossible for Reb Nahum and his family. The patriarch decided finally that there was no future for him and his family in the *shtetl* and that it was time to return to Perayaslav. Leaving the children behind for the summer, the Rabinowitz' left for the city, to look over prospects and to prepare the way for the family. Soon after, Sholom and his brothers and sisters were sent for. There was considerable shock when the children discovered that their dignified and respected parents had been forced to go into business as innkeepers in Perayaslav. For

---

[6] *The Great Fair*, 75–76.
[7] *The Great Fair*, 224–225.
[8] *In My Father's Court* (New York: Farrar, Strauss & Giroux, 1966), 109.

Sholom, this was a tremendous disappointment and embarassment for such an illustrious man as his father, but there was little choice. From now on, life was economically precarious. Soon, another disaster struck, when Sholom's mother died of cholera in an epidemic, and the father, after an appropriate period of mourning, re-married. The stepmother proved to be a shrewish, brutal creature who abused her own as well as her step-children. She took particular pleasure in harassing Sholom, who seemed to enjoy a special place in his father's affections.

Sholom was showing signs of great precociousness. In spite of the normal dismal existence in the Jewish *cheder*, or parochial school, with its beatings and narrow scholasticism, Sholom proved to be an outstanding student. He had impressed his city relatives in Pereyaslav with his considerable Talmudic learning as well as his knowledge of Hebrew grammar and writing. He had taken advantage of his father's library to delve into the more modern Hebrew classics as well, and after reading Mapu's *Love of Zion*, Sholom tried his hand at imitation. He produced *The Daughter of Zion*, a romance in Mapu's style, with slight variations.[9] His stepmother discovered the manuscript and dragged Sholom before his father, who read it and instructed his wife to henceforth leave this young writer alone. He was not to do household chores, nor to be punished.

Reb Nahum realized that his son was something special, and he had to make a momentous decision. He would not send Sholom to Yeshiva, the traditional Jewish religious academy for advanced studies, but would apply to the Russian County School. For a religiously orthodox Hassidic family, this was an extraordinary step, one guaranteed to cause considerable family friction. Reb Nahum prevailed, and Sholom, in spite of his inability to communicate in Russian, was enrolled in the Russian District School at Preyaslav. The commitment had been made. Nahum Rabinowitz was taking his son, his most gifted offspring, into the Enlightenment.

[9] This novel was actually Sholom's second literary effort, his first being *A Dictionary of Curses*, which he gathered from the abuses heaped upon him by his step-mother.

Already at that time, the elder Rabinowitz as well as his closest friends were convinced that Sholom would be a writer. While in school, after reading Defoe's *Robinson Crusoe*, he did still another Hebrew adaptation, *The Jewish Robinson Crusoe*, completed when he was about fifteen years of age. The argument in the house, however, raged as to what language Sholom should write in. The choice was Russian or Hebrew. His father preferred him to emulate the classical Hebrew writers of the century, while his friends urged the young boy to read Gogol, Pushkin, and Turgenev. He did both, and soon developed a passable Russian style. At the age of seventeen, in 1876, he graduated with highest honors.

2. DIE WANDERJAHRE

With a diploma fresh in his hands, Sholom set out to discover the world around him. He considered himself at that time already a young Jewish intellectual, 'a somebody' of the Haskalah. He read all the novels of the German writer Friedrich Spielhagen, at the time one of Germany's most popular social chroniclers. Sholom was particularly impressed by the German-Jewish writer Berthold Auerbach, as well as by Buckle's *History of Civilization in England* and John Stuart Mill's *Essay on Liberty*. In short, he had 'liberated' himself from the customs and ways of his elders. He wore short coats, unlike the Hassidim, spoke fluent Russian, had a secular education, and could not wait to leave the family home. No sooner had he graduated than he began looking for employment. The threat of military service kept him from enrolling in a teacher's program at an institute, because there was the distinct possibility that he would be inducted in the middle of the course. So, Sholom decided to look for a position as a tutor, and his good fortune took him to the estate of a rich, distant relative in Sofievka.

Elimelech Loyeff was a different kind of Jew. He lived in the style of the grant gentile landowners of Russia, in the country with the peasants, a man of great stature in the community, admired by gentile peasants and gentry alike. Sholom Rabinowitz was employed as a tutor for Loyeff's young daughter, a thirteen-year-old child of his second marriage. Loyeff, who was in his late fifties when Sholom came to Sofievka, took an immediate liking to the bright, young tutor. He gave him the run of his library, which had considerable holdings in Talmudic as well as modern literature, much translated from the Russian, French, and German masters.

Sholom's relationship with his pretty pupil could scarcely have taken a more predictable turn. Olga Loyeff was attracted to the eighteen-year-old teacher quite naturally, and together they read through her father's library: Shakespeare, Dickens, Tolstoy, Goethe, Schiller, Gogol, as well as the current heart-pounding romances. Inspired by this youthful Platonic affair, Sholom wrote incessantly, almost compulsively, but destroyed all of the manuscripts. Quite naturally, they fell in love. Sholom remained three years at the Loyeff estate, in complete contentment. He had matured into a man of twenty-one, and his secret beloved was now a young woman of sixteen (a considerable age for marriage among Eastern European Jews).

It all ended very suddenly. No doubt Sholom had miscalculated old Loyeff's feelings for him. When the master discovered that his daughter and the tutor were seriously involved with one another, the aristocrat rose up in him; his daughter was not going to marry a pauper. After having been informed by his sister of the affair, Loyeff became enraged, and without saying good-bye, left an envelope of money for Sholom and instructions to catch the first train. He left Sofievka in the winter of 1879, arriving in Kiev soon after. The big city treated Rabinowitz harshly. As his daughter writes, "He arrived in Kiev in 1879 with illusions about the great good intellectuals of the new age and with a considerable amount of money in his pocket – and he was to lose both."[10] He found the Hebrew writers dull and insipid, was fleeced by a confidence man, and found himself broke and despondent in a matter of weeks, without means of employment.

Suddenly, a livelihood appeared, albeit a dubious one. A near-by town, Louben, was looking to fill the position of Rabbiner, the Certified Rabbi appointed by the Russian government to oversee

---

[10] *My Father, Sholom Aleichem*, 77.

Jewish affairs. This is not to be confused with the town's own Rabbi, who was the leader in matters of faith and law. But the Russian government felt that it was essential to have some means of control over the independent Jewish community. The post of Rabbiner was established for this purpose. For the Jews, he was the lowest form of traitor, a Jew who worked for the Czar, elected by necessity by the Jews themselves, paid for out of their pockets, but answerable to the state. Maurice Samuel sums up his position in the community: "His Jewish learning was exiguous, his standing nil, his function despised."[11] This was the position for which Sholom Rabinowitz applied, and the status of the Crown Rabbi gives us an idea of the desperation of the young man trying to survive in the big city. He hated himself for taking on such a challenge, and when he actually received the appointment, he was determined to make something useful out of this position. Later on he was to write a short story with a Rabbiner as the protagonist, and his own experience no doubt had a profound influence on this particular story, for the only genuinely compassionate character in the tale is the young Crown Rabbi, who rises above the petty squabbles of the town.[12] The story is, moreover, written in the first person.

Meanwhile, Sholom, now a government official, began writing earnestly in Hebrew. Articles on educational and liturgical reform began to appear, particularly in the prestigious Hebrew publication *Ha-Melitz*. The main positive result of this literary activity was that through it his former pupil discovered his whereabouts. Olga Loyeff, now nineteen, could not forget her love for the articulate young tutor; she discovered through a relative that he was writing for Hebrew journals, and contacted him. After a considerable correspondence she came to Kiev and secretly married Sholom, in a private ceremony, on May 12, 1883. The enormous nature of this step – to marry a Jewish girl without her father's consent – must have been clear to Rabinowitz at the time. He was breaking every rule of the traditional Jewish courtship, and his father-in-law would have been justified in taking any number of actions approved

---

[11] *The World of Sholom Aleichem*, 236.
[12] "Tit for Tat", in *Selected Stories of Sholom Aleichem*, 212–228.

under Talmudic law. Instead, he did not appear angry. After a brief period in Louben where Sholom was still Rabbiner, the couple was invited back to Sofievka, and old Loyeff urged Sholom to give up the position of Crown Rabbi, and to live on the estate. After a few efforts at independence, the young couple acceded to the wishes of the old man, and Sholom settled in as a traditional 'kept' Jewish son-in-law.

This custom, ironically, was most prevalent among the orthodox Jews, who considered a life dedicated to learning as the best of all possible existences. A man should not taint his hands with labor if possible. So for hundreds of years, whenever it was economically feasible, the Jewish father-in-law-to-be would look for a prospect for his daughter among the most intelligent Yeshiva students of the neighboring towns, arrange the marriage, and then provide for as many years as necessary for the couple's sustenance, while the young scholar devoted himself exclusively to his learning. This was the ideal state for the typical and traditional Jewish family of Eastern Europe. Now, Sholom Rabinowitz, emancipated Jew that he was, found himself a 'kept' son-in-law, and he did not seem to mind at all. Indeed, his prospects were excellent, since he was heir to a considerable fortune. He had done what so many of his own literary types of dubious reputation had done: he married money. And for the first time in his young life he could indulge himself in his major concern: his writing.

But Sholom felt a compulsion to try something else as a writer. He saw the endless number of hacks and pseudo-intellectuals working away in Hebrew, writing for the relatively few who could understand the *loshon hakodesh*, the sacred tongue. Mendele Mocher Sforim had had a considerable success by that time, but it was still risky for a serious writer to consider using Yiddish for literary expression. Rabinowitz knew instinctively that there was a ready-made public out there in the *shtetls* of Russia waiting for a Jewish writer to speak to them, and when the Hebrew journal *Ha-Melitz* began publishing a Yiddish supplement in 1883, Rabinowitz took the plunge into Yiddish. But, like Mendele before him, he tried to protect his identity by assuming a pen-name. In 1883, with a story entitled "Two Stones", the Yiddish writer Sholom Aleichem appeared in print. The name itself was an inspirational choice. It is the common everyday Hebrew greeting between Jews, "Peace Be Unto You". Alfred Kazin best describes the significance of the phrase:

...He found in the phrase, an image of the sweet familiarity, the informality, the utter lack of side, that is associated with the Yiddish-speaking masses of Eastern Europe. A Yiddish writer who calls himself *Mister* Sholom Aleichem tells us by this that he has chosen cannily to picture himself as one of the people – and modestly to be a register or listening post for his people.[13]

Almost as if by instinct Sholom Aleichem, by the choice of this name, assumed the most intimate and guileless relationship to his subjects. He would write as if he were one in their midst.

3. HOMO ECONOMICUS

But the outside world was to intrude rudely into the personal literary ecstasy of Sholom Aleichem. Suddenly, in 1885, father-in-law Elimelech Loyeff died, and Sholom, as the sole male relative available, was required to take over the administration of Loyeff's considerable land holdings. The family decided that without the agricultural wisdom of the old man it would be senseless to continue, and the decision was made to liquidate and to divide the capital among the remaining relatives.

As a result of all these transactions, Sholom became the administrator of a fortune of over 200,000 rubles, since the wife's property, according to Russian law, reverted to the husband. It was now necessary to figure out some profitable way to use this capital, and Sholom's choice took him and his family to Kiev in 1888, where he had already engaged in high finance. He chose the world of the Kiev stock exchange, a fateful and ironically – at least from the point of his future as a writer – useful choice.

Meanwhile, he continued writing in Yiddish, and in 1886 Sholom Aleichem received the critical acclaim he had been waiting for.

---

[13] "Introduction", *Selected Short Stories of Sholom Aleichem*, x.

The appearance of "The Penknife" almost immediately established the writer as something quite different on the Yiddish literary scene. Here was a writer of such sensitivity to Jewish life that his readers marvelled at his insights. In this first major story Sholom Aleichem probes particularly into the family structure, from the perspective of a young Jewish boy living in a typical Jewish home. The story concerns the boy's perpetual and perfectly normal preoccupation with having his own penknife and the complete lack of understanding of his needs on the part of his parents, particularly his father. The patriarch is perhaps the most devastating characterization in the story. The father is constantly studying, indifferent to the youthful enthusiasms of his son, whose interruptions and flights of fancy are met with beatings. It seems as if Sholom Aleichem suggests that the father sees in the son's desire to possess a knife a threat to his own existence at the hands of his son. The mother protects the boy whenever possible from the Talmudic zeal of her husband who beats the son into studying. The picture of the *cheder*, the child's school, is devastating. Sadistic teachers whip the students gleefully, in an effort to pound the teachings of the Talmud into them. The boy possesses a series of makeshift knives, until one day he steals a magnificent pocket knife from a German-Jew who is staying at his parents' inn. The guilt which riddles the young lad causes him to hallucinate, and for two weeks he is bed-ridden in a feverish state of semi-consciousness. Finally, he awakens to the joy of his parents, who have tried every conceivable superstition available in Jewish folklore to ward off the evil spirits which possessed their child. He was so happy to have recovered, "that he could have kissed his father. But how can one possibly kiss one's father?"[14]

From the point of literary form and technique, this story far surpasses anything written in Yiddish before it. The father's constant coughing echoes like a Dickensian leit-motif through the conflict. Sholom Aleichem gives himself the added detachment by placing the narrative body of the story in the pluperfect, told from the point of view of an adult looking back on the psychic effects of

---

[14] "The Penknife", in *Some Laughter, Some Tears*, translated by Curt Leviant (New York: G. P. Putnam's Sons, 1968), 128.

his childhood, one dominated by a perpetually angry father and a protective mother. This reminiscence of a Jewish childhood became Sholom Aleichem's most familiar form, eventually. He developed variations on it, as his narrators demonstrated more complex personalities. Indeed, in his most mature writings, one is apt to be more interested in the peculiarities of the person telling the story than in the story itself. In this sense, Sholom Aleichem's irony, much like that of Thomas Mann, found its expression in the narrative form and technique.

Although he now found himself in the position of having to manage the family fortune with its considerable complexities, Sholom Aleichem felt compelled to find time for his Yiddish activities and literary efforts. After the success of "The Penknife", he began writing longer fictional works and from this period derived the three major novels of Sholom Aleichem, *Sender Blank*, *Stempenyu*, and *Yosele Solovey*. In these works he moves out beyond the familiar environment of the *shtetl* to explore what for him was the equally familiar world of the citified Jew, the Jewish middle-class and its newly-found pretentions. Jewish lawyers, doctors, artists, actors appear in these longer social novels, but away from the coziness of the *shtetl* world, Sholom Aleichem apparently could not sustain plot and characterization sufficiently to succeed in the novel form. A series of fairly stereotyped lovers, villains, and heroes parade before the reader with predictable passions. Sholom Aleichem appears to be strongly under the influence of his German contemporary Friedrich Spielhagen, who wrote a host of similar social novels. In any case, these novels of Sholom Aleichem do not represent the best of his literary efforts.

Perhaps the continuous pressure of the stock market had a debilitating effect on his writing; in any case, Sholom was unhappy with the necessity of having to live a sort of dual existence. His daughter quotes a letter written during this period:

I am pregnant with so many thoughts, so much imagery, that I must be made of iron that I do not come apart at the seams, and ah me, I have to run after a ruble! The stock market be damned! The ruble be damned! That a Jewish writer should not be able to live on his writing alone, but have to run in search of a ruble! Those who know me, who see me every day, ask me when do I write? Truly, I do not know myself. This is how I write – walking, running, sitting in someone's office, riding on the trolley; and just when they bother my head about timber land, a plantation, a plant somewhere – just then the most beautiful imagery emerges and the best thoughts come to mind, and I can't wait a minute, a second, to put it down on paper. Damn the business! Damn the world![15]

It was quite clear that his first concern was for his literary profession, even beyond merely his involvement as a creative writer. Sholom Aleichem was emerging as a leading intellectual spirit of the Yiddish community, an arbiter of taste. His initial success as a writer led him into an attack on the prevailing tastes in Yiddish literary circles for overly romantic and melodramatic love stories. The most prolific and successful of these formula writers was N. M. Shykevich, who wrote under the name of Shomer. Sholom Aleichem, in order to establish the legitimacy of Yiddish literature, attacked him in a highly polemical pamphlet called *Shomer's Mishpot* (*Schomer's Trial*) in which he tried and condemned the entire school of sentimentalists. Meanwhile, he continued to explore what he considered the serious aspects of Yiddish. Besides editing an anthology of Yiddish folksongs, in 1888 he founded *Di Yidishe Folks Bibliothek*, the first Yiddish literary annual, devoted exclusively to Yiddish writers. Sholom Aleichem was determined to make writing in Yiddish respectable and even profitable. Besides himself and Mendele, there were few serious Yiddish writers. In order to strengthen the ranks, he induced the noted Hebraist I. L. Peretz to write for his journal, a move which unified the Polish and Russian Yiddish intelligentsia. Peretz, generally recognized as "the supreme literary artist of Eastern European Jewry", contributed a Yiddish poem to the annual in its first year, a work which represented his first published work in Yiddish.[16]

From that point on, Peretz was destined to join Mendele and Sholom Aleichem in the triumvirate of Yiddish classical literature. In terms of Yiddish literature, by 'classical' is meant these three men and the role they played in the further development of Yiddish

---

[15] *My Father, Sholom Aleichem*, 86.
[16] *The Flowering of Yiddish Literature*, 98.

literature and literary criticism. Together, they had brought Yiddish out of its simplistic origins and away from its trivial accomplishments with astonishing speed.

But in the fall of 1890 Sholom Aleichem was rudely shocked back into the world of the *homo economicus*. The Kiev stock market crashed, the family fortune was lost, and the writer-turned-businessman found himself in a situation similar to that of one of his later creations, Menachem-Mendel, Sholom Aleichem's fictional *schlemihl*: he kept one step ahead of the authorities. His daughter's recollection concerning this episode is somewhat vague: "This was a crushing disaster. The family moved to Odessa, and my father went abroad for a while, a desolate traveler in Paris, Vienna and Czernowitz, while Babushka [Sholom Aleichem's mother-in-law] paid off the creditors from her portion of the estate."[17] Apparently the writer fled from his debts. Soon after, in 1892, Sholom Aleichem began writing his Menachem-Mendel stories, the correspondence between an eternally optimistic failure of a Jewish business-type trying to squeeze a living out of the Kiev and Odessa stock markets, and his impatient wife, living back in the *shtetl*, mystified by his business terminology and prepared always for the worst, which inevitably transpires. In the letters of Menachem-Mendel and Sheinch-Sheindel we see Sholom Aleichem parodying his own life's situation, his own business follies. For the next few years, the Rabinowitz family lived in a fashion similar to the fictional couple. The head of the family moved from position to position, from deal to deal, first as a commission agent, then as a broker, as he searched for the secret to *gesunt und parnosseh* 'good health and a good living'. The Rabinowitz' lived illegally in Kiev, without work or residency permits. Olga Rabinowitz, who had acquired some training as a dentist, set up practice with a local dentist and treated patients illegally.

Life for them was very tentative at this point, and their existence could be jeopardized at any moment. For the next few years the family moved between Kiev and Odessa, with Sholom Aleichem writing and publishing stories, taking notes for future ones, in

---

[17] *My Father, Sholom Aleichem*, 85.

between trips to the stock exchange, where he continued to gather with the crowds of Jewish traders on the street in front of the main building, to which he and his fellow Jews rarely had access. Even in his literary career now there appeared a certain desperation that led to less than total candor with his publishers. He was accustomed, as his reputation grew, to send the same story to several different periodicals, with minor changes, in an effort to increase his royalties and to shore up the family's financial structure.

Life in the mid-nineties did manage to stabilize sufficiently so that the growing Rabinowitz family – there were several children now – could return to some of the more amenable middle-class comforts it had previously enjoyed. They began to take extended summer vacations in Boyarka, a resort town not far from Kiev; and once again Sholom Aleichem found his own experiences most suitable for his literary purposes. This summer village became the Boiberik of many of his tales, the prototype of the Jewish vacation resort which has provided Jewish writers in both Europe and America with an endless amount of types and characters. It was in Boyarka one summer that Sholom Aleichem met a delightfully honest Jewish dairyman who made regular deliveries to the family all summer. His name was Tevye. The first of Sholom Aleichem's 'Tevye' stories appeared in 1894, and the most recent phase of these nine tales is still a growing part of Broadway folklore.

Gradually, Sholom Aleichem the writer began to gain some measure of control over Sholom Aleichem the unfortunately not-so-successful businessman. Within a few years after the initial successes of the Menachem-Mendel series and the Tevye stories, the financial situation grew sufficiently stable so that Sholom Aleichem could give up business in order to devote himself completely to his writing.

4. WRITER IN EXILE

In the fifteen years since the appearance of *The Penknife*, Sholom Aleichem's reputation had experienced an unprecedented change. Even he had not been prepared for the voracious appetite of the Yiddish-reading community of Eastern Europe. His stories sold in every conceivable edition, from elegant leather-bound to the cheapest paperbacks, which traditionally circulated through the poorer homes until only a paper rag remained. Yet, in spite of this extraordinary fame, Sholom Aleichem remained financially insecure. Very early in his career he bartered his copyright to several unscrupulous publishers, and only much later, as he lay near death in Italy, was he able to secure once again these copyrights, and then only through the personal appeal of many other literary notables.

Still, there was fame. Yiddish Literature, through Sholom Aleichem predominantly, and Mendele and Peretz as well, had established itself as a national, identifiable literature. Sholom Aleichem was being translated into all the languages of Western Europe, and he personally was in great demand for speeches, readings, and lectures. Politically, he had emerged as a champion of Zionism and was an active supporter of Herzl. Jewish life in Russia was flourishing, in spite of the ever-present anti-Semitism. Yiddish cultural activities were expanding and reaching Jews in ever-greater numbers. In 1903 the first Yiddish daily newspaper opened in St. Petersburg. Literary journals, newspapers, reviews both in Europe and abroad began springing up. Although the Yiddish theatre was still banned in Russia at the time, Jewish theatre groups where being activated in Poland, and Sholom Aleichem, in order to take advantage of this new medium, began adapting some of his short stories for the stage. Around 1903 a four-volume edition of his works appeared in Warsaw, in Yiddish. At the zenith of his career, Sholom Aleichem could be counted among the prominent intellectuals of Russia; in his correspondence were letters to and from Chekhov, Tolstoy, and other members of the elite of Russian *belles lettres*. His acquaintances included Gorki, Andreyev, and Kuprin.

But, as swiftly as he had risen, just as quickly came the great tragic events which swept him and his family from Russia. In many of his stories of this period, the Kishinev pogroms play a prominent role. Kishinev was a major center of Jewish life in the Ukraine, and in 1903 pogroms of extraordinary violence erupted which left many thousands of Jews killed and wounded. The most ominous aspect of the outbreak derived from the apparent inspiration for it which from all indications came from the local and provincial authorities. It was a well-planned, co-ordinated riot which later proved to be government-inspired. Sholom Aleichem perceived the intentions of the ruling forces: divert peasant dissatisfaction from the rulers to an appropriate scapegoat, namely the Jews. Blood accusations followed the events in Kishinev. Jews were accused of murdering gentile children in order to use their blood for *Passover matzohs*.[18] The following year saw the outbreak of the Russo-Japanese War, and the armies of the Czar suffered humiliating defeat. Once again, Sholom Aleichem chronicles the events of Russian and Jewish history in order to frame his stories. In an unusually patriotic and nationalistic tone, he created several war stories which showed Jewish patriotism and loyalty to the Czarist regime and attempted to offer an alternative to the characterization of the Jew usually found in both Jewish and non-Jewish literature as cowardly or at least dubious about dying for a country which did not really concern him. This theme will be dealt with in a later chapter, but a cursory look at "The First Passover Night of the War" would clarify this point of the Jewish stereotyped soldier. The seriousness of the issue for Sholom Aleichem is eminently obvious, because the writer's hand is quite heavy, even propagandistic, in his efforts to show the brave and loyal Jewish soldier. Even the setting is something quite novel for the author: "A thin black ribbon consisting of two threads stretched over a broad white field in ancient Manchuria: the great Siberian railway winding its way downhill over the wild expanse of Asia toward Kwantung, Port Arthur, and the sea."[19] On the first night of Passover, two Jewish soldiers are sitting among the others. Again Sholom Aleichem deviates from his normal narrative style of providing an intermediary story-teller to allow himself to tell the story: "One could immediately tell by their pale faces, white hands and black eyes that they were our brethren, fellow Jews." The younger Jew is

---

[18] The most famous of these blood accusations was the case of Mendel Beiliss, accused in 1911 in Kiev of having murdered a Christian child for Blood Ritual purposes. The trial started in September, 1913. Beilis was cleared, and emigrated to Tel Aviv in Palestine. In 1924, he came to the United States and died in Saratoga Springs, New York, in 1934.

[19] In Sholom Aleichem, *Old Country Tales*, translated by Curt Leviant (New York: G. P. Putnam's Sons, 1966), 259.

frightened, never having been away from home. He feels alienated among the gentiles and fears for his life. But the older soldier explains to him the importance of the struggle. Upon leaving home, he had spoken to his family: "He told them that now that the enemy had attacked his land, as a true-blue soldier who had already served his Czar for five years, he had no alternative than to go and fight for the last drop of his blood...For he was going to war. 'For Czar and Fatherland'"[20] As later stories will demonstrate, this was not the typical image of the Jew's involvement with the Czarist military system. But at this particular time of his life, Sholom Aleichem felt compelled to assert Jewry's loyalty to the nation.

It was to no avail. In 1905 The Treaty of Portsmouth ended the war ignominiously for Russia. Even before the end of hostilities demonstrations of dissatisfaction with the government had broken out in Saint Petersburg. The armed forces mutinied, and by October, Petersburg was paralyzed by a general strike. On October 20, the Czar capitulated to the demands of the people and granted major constitutional reforms. The October Manifesto of 1905 promised great relief for the Russian Jews as well. But no sooner had the decree been made public than a wave of reactionary repression swept the promised reforms aside, and left Russia's Jews at the mercy of some of the worst barbarisms up until that time. The Russian peasants were stirred up, the Jews were blamed for the failures of the Russian government, and over six hundred Jewish communities in Russia were plundered and hundreds of Jews murdered. Again, Sholom Aleichem reflected the times in his fiction. The last of the Tevye stories, "Get Thee Out", shows Tevye at the mercy of the peasants with whom he had lived for many years, as they explain to him why they must smash his windows and wreck his house. In the blackly humorous epistolary story "Otherwise, There's Nothing New", the pogroms are graphically described by a Jew who has remained in Russia as he writes to a more fortunate friend in America:

---

[20] "The First Passover Night of the War", 261.

Dear Yenkel, I can only report one thing – I'm still alive! I've looked the Angel of Death in the face three times. But never mind. How does Getzi the dressmaker – remember him? – put it? 'Who by earthquake and who by plague'. In other words, if you're destined for lots of suffering, then at least God spares your life... My heart went out for my wife and children, so I sent them away. They hid in the attic of a kindly peasant and lay there in all their glory two days and two nights without so much as a drop of water, a crumb of bread, or a wink of sleep. Things only quieted down, thank God, on the third day, when there was no longer anything to rob or anyone to beat. Then everyone slowly crawled down from the attics, alive and well, praise the Lord. No one from our family was hurt, except Lipa, who was killed along with her two sons, and Noah and Melekh, two workers with golden hands, and poor Moishe-Hersh who was dragged down from an attic, and Perl-Dvora, who was later found dead in a cellar with her tiny infant, Reyzele, at her breast... Otherwise, There's nothing New..."[21]

This posture of the Jew during a pogrom is typical of the characterizations of Sholom Aleichem, and most likely an accurate picture of Jewish reaction. The Jew did not defend himself, as a matter of principle, a reaction to violence which no doubt helped strengthen the image of the cowardly Jew. But cowardice was not the motivating force in his reaction to attacks on his life:

In this sense pogroms are treated also as acts of God. There is usually no defense organization. If organized resistance is attempted... it is criticized by the very orthodox as 'un-Jewish'. One pleads with God for help and mercy. Perhaps one sends a delegation to the leader of the attacking group. But to fight back is the exception rather than the rule. This passivity cannot be attributed simply to fear of death. There are too many instances of Jews who have accepted death rather than to violate the Sabbath.[22]

However, in other Yiddish writers, an effort was clearly made to show a more militant, zestful Jew, eager for a fight. The Polish-Yiddish writer Sholem Asch particularly favored this image. In "Kola Street", a powerfully violent story of the Jewish lower classes, the Jewish tradesmen and laborers "were not in the Diaspora, as it were: there no Jew was ever beaten. If it happened that

---

[21] In *Some Laughter, Some Tears*, 240.
[22] *Life is With People*, 224.

recruits passing through the town in the fall began to riot, members of the congregation would take matters into their own hands: armed with shafts and iron bars, they would go out into the streets and teach the hooligans a lesson."[23] Yet, in this story as well, such self-defense is looked upon by "the street of the scholars" with great contempt, even though they depended on the brutish yet pious Kola Street Jews:

> The scholars lived entirely on the festival money contributed by Kola Street; and whenever they were in trouble – whenever, for instance, a shepherd set his dog on a Jew or a drunken peasant started a row in the street – Jews, young and old, would run to Kola Street, crying for help. Nevertheless, at heart, the scholars condemned the Kola Street crowd. 'Not at all like Jews', they would say to one another, 'and when the Messiah comes, they will come to us for help... Savages with no manners at all! But we need this rabble sometimes, to keep the recruits quiet and to stop them from smashing our windows.'[24]

Asch's blood-stirring idealization reflects the author's particular impatience with those pious Jews who preferred to allow themselves to be beaten, rather than defending themselves. His stories are filled with Hassidic students cringing under tables and chairs before a wave of drunken peasants, while outside Jewish workers take on the attackers with a gusto usually reserved for more belligerent people.

The actual case was undoubtedly closer to Sholom Aleichem's descriptions, and given his generally unerring ability to capture the genuine scene of Jewish life, we can be fairly certain that the reaction to the pogroms which he chronicles can be found in *his* stories, rather than in those of Sholem Asch. In Sholom Aleichem's works the reaction of the Jews was to hide – or to run, and to places as far away as America. The wave of Jewish immigration was destined to hit its peak soon after the 1905 pogroms, and in December of that year, Sholom Aleichem, together with his family, left Russia, crossing the border into Austrian Galicia. Now began a period of

---

[23] "Kola Street", translated by Charles Angoff, in: *A Treasury of Yiddish Stories*, edited by Irving Howe and Eliezar Greenberg (New York: Viking Press, 1953), 261.
[24] "Kola Street", 262.

wandering from town to town, as this prominent Yiddish writer reflected the plight of hundreds of thousands of homeless Jews.

Why did not Sholom Aleichem immediately move himself and his family to America? Again, the answer can be found in the stories. The image of America in Sholom Aleichem's fiction is somewhat surprising, especially when considered in the light of the more traditional visions of the Land of Freedom and Opportunity, A Haven from Russian Oppression, etc. In the world of Sholom Aleichem, America turns out to be the place for runaway husbands, crooks hiding from the authorities, a home for the wheeler-dealers of the *shtetl*; and finally, a place of sanctuary for the homeless. In a sketch called "A Predestined Disaster" the narrator of the story bids goodbye to his ward with the blessing "Off to America with the rest of the bums!"[25] In "The Story of a Greenhorn" the effect of America on a Jewish businessman is to create one of the few genuine Jewish villains in Sholom Aleichem. Mr. Baraban, the narrator, is a business broker who hates newly arrived Jewish immigrants and with an Iago-like glee goes about ruining them financially.[26] In the *Adventures of Mottel*, in which Sholom Aleichem traces the travels of a Jewish Huckleberry Finn from *shtetl* to Second Avenue, the arrival of Mottel's family at Ellis Island is a nightmare of mismanagement and cold-hearted authoritarianism. Finally, in the vignette "On America" we get the most devastating of these pictures. One Berel-Ayzik, a Kasrilevke native, has returned from a brief visit to America and "is filling in" for his neighbours, in order to tell what America is all about. "It's a free country. You can swell from hunger, die in the street, and no one'll bother you, no one'll say a word...Jews don't wear beards or earlocks. Their faces are as smooth as glass. It's hard to tell who's a Jew and who isn't."[27] Beral-Ayzik goes on to describe the costs of various types of funerals for Jews in the United States. The impression is one of business as usual; money is everything, and get it while you can.

---

[25] In *Old Country Tales*, 152.
[26] *Some Laughter, Some Tears*, 243–248.
[27] In Sholom Aleichem, *Stories and Satires*, translated by Curt Leviant (New York: Thomas Yoseloff, 1959), 232.

Of course, there was the other side to Sholom Aleichem. Although it is quite clear that he had certain reservations about the climate of life for a Jew in America, he was undoubtedly aware of the obvious advantages in terms of genuine freedom. One of the most stirring moments in all of his works comes when Mottel's friend Pinney arrives finally in New York City, after spending several miserable days in "Ellie's Island". In spite of the wretchedness he had felt only a few hours before, Pinney now has another vision of the new home. He turns to face the abandoned land of his birth and shakes his fist, crying:

Listen, you asses, brutes, drunken sots! Listen, you hooligans, you murderers! We have to thank you for having reached this haven, this refuge, this great and blessed land, the land of the free. If not for you who persecuted us with your evil edicts and your pogroms, to this very day we wouldn't get to know Columbus, and Columbus wouldn't get to know us. You'll have to wait a long, long time until we return to you... Someday you'll awake to the fact that you've lost a treasure – the people of Israel. The treasure was once yours, and you let it slip through your fingers. Yours will be the fate of Spain. Someday you'll wake up and start howling for us. You'll start searching for a Jew in all the corners of your land, but you won't find a single one. You'll start begging us to return. You'll plead, but nobody will be there to reply, and nobody will come to your call...[28]

Sholom Aleichem moved his wife and children to Lemberg, and from there, began a series of lecture tours to support himself, since he was cut off from his publishers. The tours took him to all points of Austrian Galicia, Rumania, Paris, London, and Switzerland, where he finally settled, in Geneva, in the summer of 1906. Plans were being made for the first American tour later that fall. In spite of the success of these reading engagements, Sholom Aleichem felt that he had to contact the new Jewish communities of the New World, and so, the voyage to America was undertaken. There was no intention of a permanent stay. He travelled only with his wife and one daughter, leaving his other children behind in Switzerland. They sailed on October 13, 1906.

[28] Sholom Aleichem, *The Adventures of Mottel, the Cantor's Son*, translated by Tamara Kahana, Collier Paperback (New York: Collier's, 1961), 62–63.

5. THE *SHTETL* ACROSS THE SEA

The trip was arranged by a Jewish committee of leading citizens, and from the very beginning, Sholom Aleichem was confronted by most of the riotous characters and situations encountered in the Jewish communities of his fiction. It was one gigantic Kasrilevke. All three religious groups – Orthodox, Reform, and Conservative – had to be represented on the committee, as well as the editors of the four Jewish daily newspapers of New York and the directors of the three leading Yiddish theatres. The German-Jews from 'Uptown' had him to one reception, the Eastern Jews from 'Downtown' had him to another. Although for the most part the Jewish community of New York pulled together to greet Sholom Aleichem on his arrival in the city on October 20, cracks appeared soon afterwards. It was socially impossible for the wealthy 'our-crowd' German-Jews to co-operate with the 'disgracefully' active and noisy goings-on on the East Side. In any case, with some anxiety, Sholom Aleichem took an apartment in the Bronx and got down to the 'business of literature' in New York.

There are two aspects of Jewish intellectual life in New York which need some development at this point, in order better to understand the situation into which Sholom Aleichem entered. Both the Jewish press and the Jewish theatre were involved in deep-seated rivalries, internal struggles which in their bitterness and self-destructive impulses caught up many an innocent bystander who by chance got caught in the middle.

The major newspapers in New York City for Jews attached themselves to particular religious, political, and ethnic prejudices. *The Hebrew American* was assimilationist and catered exclusively to the Reformist German Jews. It was this paper, a weekly, which first sniffed at the fantastic excitement which Sholom Aleichem's visit caused among the inhabitants of the East Side. The oldest successful daily was *Tageblatt*, founded in 1885, and by 1900 enjoying a circulation of 70,000. Its audience was the orthodox immigrant, and it held to orthodoxy in every aspect of Jewish life with complete single-mindedness. In 1897, after several failures by labor groups in an effort to establish a paper closer to their interests, the *Forverts* was created, under the editorship of a man who was destined to become one of the great names in Yiddish journalism, Abraham Cahan. The main cause of the daily was trade unionism within the framework of American democracy. Its editorial policy, dictated by Cahan, was socialist. Today, it is the last of the great Yiddish newspapers of New York, and it still maintains a certain historical glory, as in the days when Leon Trotsky was a contributor, when I. B. Singer's stories appear in the original Yiddish under the *Forverts* masthead.

The *Morgen Journal* was also an orthodox paper, but the first in the morning. In appeared in 1901 and was the first item read in the morning by thousands of newly arrived immigrants in search of a job. Politically and editorially, it was allied with *Tageblatt*, and in 1928 *Morgen Journal* absorbed the older paper.

In 1901 the enterprising journalist Louis Miller began the first liberal-intellectual newspaper with a distinctly non-religious orientation. If anything, there was an inclination to Reformed Judaism, but that might have seemed the case because few Orthodox or Conservative leaders would write for the *Wahrheit*. After Sholom Aleichem's first visit, a rival liberal paper arose, *Tog* (*The Day*), and by 1918, *Wahrheit* ceased publication.

The Jewish press in New York was a tremendously vital and exciting force. Daily circulation in 1914 was estimated at 646,000 copies. Liptzin notes that "since each copy was read on an average by about three readers, it may be assumed that about two million Jews felt the impact of the Yiddish word every day."[29]

The Yiddish theatre in New York was dominated by two figures. Jacob Adler was America's greatest Yiddish actor and had his own theatre company. Boris Thomashevsky was the first impresario to bring Yiddish theatre to the United States. In 1882 he successfully produced three musicals in New York, and when Czarist Russia banned all Yiddish theatricals in 1883, Thomashevsky brought a horde of talent over to act in his productions, which were primarily musical comedies of a highly stylized Yiddish type. Thomashevsky

---

[29] *The Flowering of Yiddish Literature*, 61.

himself was an outstanding actor, and he and Adler began a tradition of Yiddish acting which led to Maurice Schwartz, Jacob Ben-Ami, Paul Muni, John Garfield, Luther Adler, and others too numerous to mention. At its peak the Yiddish theatre in New York could boast of twenty regular playhouses.[30]

Jacob Adler and Thomashevsky were great rivals, and each was presented with a different play of Sholom Aleichem's to produce soon after his arrival in the United States. For Thomashevsky's theatre Sholom Aleichem had dramatized his earlier novel *Stempenyu*, which he had written and published in 1888. It is the story of a small-town musician-turned Don Juan and his love affair with the beautiful and innocent Rokhele. For Adler, Sholom Aleichem had an adaption of a previous play, which he now called *Samuel Pasternak*, the story of a similar small-town operator, this time a broker who engages in dangerous speculation. The openings of both plays in New York were typical of the rivalries between factions which we encounter all through Sholom Aleichem's works, and the description of which makes him one of the major social critics of any period. Adler and Thomashevsky raced to see who would have the privilege – and the glory – of being the first to present a play by Sholom Aleichem in America. Finally, an agreement was reached: they opened on the same night! Sholom Aleichem wrote home to Geneva describing the event:

My dears: Well, I passed the examination, and I believe gloriously. The trouble was that it was impossible to obtain a complete impression because I had to split up into two. I attended two acts at one theatre and two acts in the other... The audience seemed to me to be satisfied... As far as the press is concerned, I am confident about the non-Jewish press, since it is more honest than the Yiddish; the Yiddish is partial, and I expect nothing good from it...[31]

His perception of the Yiddish press was unerringly accurate. The critics split on party lines. The orthodox papers gave it a warm reception, and the Socialist-Labor group struck hard at the play's

---

[30] For a definitive study of the Yiddish theatre in the United States, see David S. Lifson, *The Yiddish Theatre in America* (New York: Thomas Yoseloff).
[31] *My Father, Sholom Aleichem*, 214.

lack of social reality. Abraham Cahan, the *Forverts* editor was the most influential Yiddish drama critic of his day and to a major extent could make or break a play. His harsh cirticism certainly helped to make both productions failures.

And both productions did indeed fail. Within two weeks their performances ceased, and Sholom Aleichem's first America trip was, financially at least, a disaster. He had hoped to enjoy enough royalties from these productions to support himself and his family in Geneva. The reasons for the collapse of the productions are somewhat complicated. The nature of the Yiddish theatre, particularly in New York, had to be taken into consideration. It was primarily a folk theatre, with main emphasis on remembrance of the homeland, ritual, and old habits. There were numerous musicals, and in almost every play a dramatist had to incorporate two events guaranteed to win the approval of his audience: a wedding and a kaddish, or mourner's recitation. The wedding made them cry for joy; the kaddish prayer, traditionally a prayer for the dead, made them cry out of sadness. These two essential ingredients in a Yiddish production indicate in many ways the level of literary acceptance of the *shtetl* audience of New York's Yiddish theatre. Marie Waife-Goldberg is quite correct when she describes the plays' reception as a casualty in the collision between two cultures:

My father came from a country where the theater had reached artistic heights. Kiev, as I have said, had the best of Russian and continental drama, classic and modern. In these plays it was the psychological insight, rather than plot, that mattered... The American theatre was in a temporary decline, the Yiddish theatre in America had not come into its own. Yiddish actors were only one generation removed from minstrels and mummers...[32]

Although Sholom Aleichem's reputation will never rest on his credentials as a dramatist, his plays were nonetheless ahead of the times, at least insofar as Yiddish theatrical audiences in New York were concerned. He concentrated on subtle psychological motivations, while the often raucous Jewish audiences wanted

[32] *My Father, Sholom Aleichem,* 217–218.

action. There was no meeting of the minds here at all, and Sholom Aleichem was forced back to his fiction to make a livelihood.

He wrote feverishly for the New York papers and managed to produce some of his best material. Some of the Tevye stories are from this period, as well as several of the episodes from *The Adventures of Mottel*, Sholom Aleichem's most delightful child character.

But he was unhappy, felt unwanted, and missed the rest of his family desperately. After eight months of a disappointing visit, Sholom Aleichem borrowed enough money to return to Europe and to unite his family. He was in Geneva by June of 1907.

6. MORE WANDERINGS

Immediately Sholom Aleichem had to find some means of providing for his family. Besides the meagre royalties which the Yiddish publishing houses provided grudgingly, there was no other income. He decided to arrange another lecture tour, this time to his native Russia, in the hopes of gaining some financial security for his family. The largest audience was still the ordinary Jew for whom he had become a folk hero, *their* Sholom Aleichem. After sell-outs in Warsaw, he undertook a series of one-nighters in cities all over western Russia. The frantic pace took its toll, and in August, 1908, during a reading in Baranovici, Sholom Aleichem was struck by fever, and soon after he was hemorrhaging from a lung. Doctors diagnosed the illness: acute pulmonary tuberculosis. For almost two months he remained in Baranovici, unable to be moved to a more hospitable climate, although the people of the town opened up their hearts to the stricken writer. By late September, the semi-invalid could be moved sufficiently to enable the family to move to Nervi, Italy, a resort town not far from Genoa.

The family was now in serious financial difficulties. It was difficult for Sholom Aleichem to write, yet the expenses of his convalescence were tremendous, and his income slight. With his works being read by literally hundreds of thousands of enthusiastic followers, Sholom Aleichem was near bankruptcy. He had sold his copyright to publishing houses years ago, and only a steady stream of new material could keep the household from going under. Something dramatic was needed, and it was provided. A friend of the family, Moshe Weizmann, undertook a campaign to celebrate the twenty-fifth anniversary of Sholom Aleichem's literary career. The idea gained momentum, and before long gifts and donations were pouring in from all over the Jewish world. An account was opened up in the writer's name, and the Anniversary Committee for Sholom Aleichem gave the writer financial independence. And most significant of all, the conscious-stricken publishers who had held almost total control of the royalties returned them to Sholom Aleichem as a final gesture of gratitude for all the money he had earned for them. With this one dramatic stroke, by the spring of 1909 Sholom Aleichem had at last gained financial independence as a writer.

Soon after, the crest that Sholom Aleichem was riding grew even more impressive. His works were translated into Russian, and for the first time his audience was no longer exclusively Jewish. He became a recognized international literary figure, for the Russians a sort of Jewish Chekhov, who was his favorite Russian author and the single literary figure who had the greatest influence on Sholom Aleichem's writing. His letters were prized by literary museums, critics praised the translations and the writings. Russian intellectuals such as Gorki and Kuprin wrote directly to Sholom Aleichem; the critical reception in the press was unanimous: here was a major writer, born in Russia, and portraying most accurately one of Russia's national peoples.

But the recuperation had to continue. The family moved in a constant search for warmth, and the year was divided between Nervi, Swiss resorts, and southern Germany. Ironically, in the Black Forest, Sholom Aleichem stayed at Badenweiler, the very same spa where Anton Chekhov, only a few years earlier, had died of tuberculosis. Sholom Aleichem kept writing all the while. Stories of Kasrilevke, his mythical town of happy 'losers', of Mottel, of Menachem-Mendel kept coming out. His illness gradually diminished to the point where in 1913, the doctors declared him fully recovered.

Now, in the years immediately prior to the outbreak of World War One, Sholom Aleichem's popularity was at its zenith. His presence at the tenth Zionist convention in Basel in 1913 was a great occasion and lent to the Zionist cause a considerable significance. In 1914 he undertook a twenty-city tour of Russia which resulted in his greatest personal triumph. His daughter's account is typical of the reception he received:

Although, in keeping with his request, my father's arrival in a town was kept secret, each time his train pulled in not only the railway station, but all the streets around, would be filled with people. His appearance would evoke an outpouring of Hurrahs and *Heydods* and he was not only presented with bouquets but literally sprayed with them... Once my parents took a stroll in the city park of Warsaw. Word spread that Sholom Aleichem was in the park, and people began flocking there from all sides... My father retired to a nearby restaurant to prevent an incident. The people massed around the restaurant for so long that he had to stay there until dark, when he went through the back door into a waiting carriage.[33]

7. HELLO, COLUMBUS, AGAIN

In the midst of all this success and triumph came, as most of Sholom Aleichem's philosophical nearly-rich paupers would have expected, disaster. Sholom Aleichem returned from his Russian tour on July 22, 1914, ten days before the outbreak of hostilities. The family was vacationing on the Baltic coast of Germany, when they were caught up in the confusion of the first days of the war. Aliens and subjects of a country at war with Germany, their plight became suddenly desperate, and it was essential that they flee Germany immediately. In Berlin the family broke up and travelled separately to Copenhagen, where once again Sholom Aleichem was stricken with an illness, this time diabetes. He was quick to realize, in spite of the pre-occupation with his sickness, that in Europe there was no longer a place for him or his family. Four months after their arrival in Denmark he took his wife and children to America, this time to stay.

---

[33] *My Father, Sholom Aleichem*, 264.

Once again, soon after his arrival Sholom Aleichem was caught up in the intrigues of the Jewish press. He had offers to join the staff of the three leading papers, *Forverts*, *Warheit*, and *Der Tog*. When he accepted the offer from *Der Tog*, his name was banned from the other papers! But at least there was more financial security than during the first visit, and in addition he enjoyed the presence of most of his close relations. Sholom Aleichem's second coming to The United States was considerably more pleasant than his first sojourn there. The Jewish community, although still at times provincial, had matured sufficiently to enable Sholom Aleichem to live contentedly with his eminent reputation. These last years of his life were marred only by the tragic death of his son Misha in Copenhagen, in 1915.

In that same year *The New York World*, New York's largest newspaper, serialized the Mottel stories in English, giving Sholom Aleichem his first major in-put and exposure to American audiences.[34] Also, as if sensing the time of his approaching death, he began work on his autobiography *Funim Yarid* (*From the Fair*), the first volume of which was completed.

When he died on May 13, 1916, a part of Sholom Aleichem's world died with him. It was as if the Jews of America realized that they were burying their heritage, for hundreds of thousands paid their respects to the writer at his apartment in the Bronx, where he lay in state, as well as at the cemetery in Brooklyn where he was buried. The wealthy uptown Jews, the pushcart peddlars, Zionists, Socialists, rabbis from all persuasions, Hassidim, the wretched, and the worse-off, appeared to say goodbye to their apologist. In the history of western literature one could scarcely find a better example of a Folk Poet who was both a major literary figure as well as a genuine chronicler of his people. The Jews mourned him as they would one of their family. As Maurice Samuel, who attended the funeral says, "Why, then, should they not mourn? Who was to speak for them now that Sholom Aleichem was dead, and who was to remember them if he was forgotten?"[35]

---

[34] Serialization began December 26, 1915.
[35] *The World of Sholom Aleichem*, 330

Sholom Aleichem was not forgotten. Today, he is more widely read than ever before, but, ironically, in English translation! At the time of his death, although some of his stories were appearing in English, the family could not find a publisher sufficiently interested in an English edition. Today, a new volume of the stories appears every six months. Almost the complete works are currently available. After five years, *Fiddler on the Roof* continues to be a major success on Broadway as well as in every town across the breadth of Jewish and gentile America alike. The phenomenon of Sholom Aleichem's popularity fifty years after his death can be traced to a variety of sources. But the most significant reason, I might suggest, is the impact of the cultural memory of Sholom Aleichem's world on two generations of Jews: the first being that generation which left the *shtetl* decades ago, became sufficiently Americanized to lose its *shtetl* identity, and now, as it approaches old age, looks once again to establish a connection with its roots. This group of people are the *Fiddler*-goers in particular, who sentimentalize and romanticize Sholom Aleichem's world and the world of the *shtetl*. The second group are the offspring of the *shtetl*-born. Thoroughly Americanized, never speakers of Yiddish, they sense the cultural memory, although they know little first-hand of that world. They read Sholom Aleichem's stories, and the specter of generations of Jews before the Nazi destruction appears before them. And to the gentiles, it presents us with a world devoid of Hitler, the death of 6,000,000, a pre-holocaust world empty of collective human guilt.

It is to this world we should now turn, in an effort to better understand this culture which no longer exists.

8. IN THE EUROPEAN CONTEXT

Before turning to the works finally, just a brief word about Sholom Aleichem's traditions as a writer. Of course, he writes as a Jew, steeped as he is in four thousand years of a religious tradition, as well as a half-millennium of Russian Jewry.

But Sholom Aleichem is above all a European writer. In terms of form and content, we constantly see the influence of western literary developments and the translation of these elements into a language comprehensible to Sholom Aleichem's Jewish audiences. It is only natural that Russian literature should have the most pronounced influence. Particularly Gogol and Chekhov have exerted the major impact on Sholom Aleichem's art. The whimsical and often grotesque humor of the former, coupled with the subtle and ironical characterization of the latter gave to Sholom Aleichem a singular vision which, when joined to the folk traditions of Yiddish literature, created that monumental product which is Sholom Aleichem's hallmark. Perhaps the favorite form of Sholom Aleichem was the monologue, in which a character is permitted to reveal to the reader his psychological inner world, without being aware of the revelation. In these short yet striking vignettes, Sholom Aleichem's characters unburden themselves of the anguish of their lives, yet present their plights in such a humorous light that we still do not take them so seriously so as to view them in bathos or sentimentality. The hilarious is never far behind the tragic. The grotesque is never outdistanced by sentimentality. A hero never takes his heroics seriously.

There are also hints of the Kafka to come. Franz Kafka, an avid reader of Yiddish literature and devotee of the Yiddish theatre, seemed to incorporate in his uneven world the same combination of humor and grotesqueness that we encounter in some of the more Gogol-inspired stories of Sholom Aleichem.

III

THE TOWN OF THE LITTLE PEOPLE

Sholom Aleichem's career as a writer was uniquely tied up with an early decision that he made: to chronicle Jewish life within the frame of reference of a popular folkloristic device, the mythic community of bumbling townsfolk, in whom are concentrated every excess, foible, weakness, and imperfection of the collective conscience. The Greeks had Abdera, the Swiss Seldwyla, even the Jews had Chelm before Sholom Aleichem.[1] Almost every national literature indulges itself in this scapegoat self-criticism, generally well-intentioned, satirical, and non-destructive. Indeed, the Jewish community seemed ready-made for this sort of literary treatment, since the overwhelming majority of Jews were living in hamlets already. Moreover, a strongly moralistic and critical tone had become the hallmark of the first major Yiddish writer, Mendele, whose writings were veritable diatribes against Jewish weakness.

Mendele's biting criticism and the phenomenon of the *shtetl*: these were the two midwives present at the birth of Sholom Aleichem's creation, Kasrilevke, the imaginary town of jolly, hilariously daffy Jewish paupers who dominate a major portion of Sholom Aleichem's writings.

Who were the inhabitants, the Kasrilevkites? First of all, the name of their town ("better it should be called a glorified slum") tells everything about them. Maurice Samuel describes the Kasrilevkite as "the jolly pauper", the wretched yet humorously reflec-

---

[1] To mention just a few variations: the Wise Man of Gotham in English folklore; and in Rabelais, the inhabitants of the Abbaye of Thélème are viewed by the surrounding folk as fools, while in reality they are very wise indeed.

tive Jewish poor who populated the *shtetls* of the Pale.[2] The Jewish Everyman, crying out for a champion, starving with dignity and with his faith, yet vulnerable to forces both within the ghetto walls and without, because of centuries of enduring an existence which literally froze the Jewish people of Eastern Europe at a particular moment of their history. For hundreds of years these Jews had lived in a state of feudal isolationism, keeping themselves as much as possible removed from the threatening non-Jewish world around them, totally involved with the most minute details of their religious life. Speaking Yiddish, these Jews used Hebrew in their religion, only when utterly necessary using the gentile languages of their host country, usually Polish, Russian, or Lithuanian, as the case may be.[3] Sholom Aleichem had seen this world in Voronko, and he had never forgotten it. The unbelievable squalor, the misery of the poor, the fear of the outside world, the indestructible good nature of the people, the desperate search for a living, the total commitment to faith, the fights, the petty pretentions, all of these are part of Kasrilevke, of Sholom Aleichem, and of the world of the Jewish *shtetl* which he chose to immortalize.

Unlike Mendele before him, Sholom Aleichem could not indulge in the hard-hitting moral criticism of his people. What will emerge, it is hoped, in this study will be a sense of Sholom Aleichem's unique gift of portraying his characters in a way which gently, yet devastatingly, characterizes them. When the mood gripped him, he was capable of a more mordant wit, one which stung. But this sting was usually reserved for 'the city people', for the assimilated, elegant Jews who had left the *shtetls*, who had, as it were, abandoned Kasrilevke. In each case, one must stand back for a moment to question Sholom Aleichem's own posture concerning both himself and his subjects. Philosophically, as an emancipated, enlightened, urban Jewish intellectual, Sholom Aleichem looked at the *shtetl* as a monument to a world better left abandoned. The Jews of Russia, so felt the emancipated, deserved something better than

---

[2] *The World of Sholom Aleichem*, 25.
[3] These same habits were carried over into the New World, when the Jews came to the United States. See Hutchins Hapgood, *The Spirit of the Ghetto*, copyright 1902, Schocken paperback edition (New York: 1966), 3–52.

this half-life existence, and it was up to the *Maskilim* to bring the modern world, with its Jewish pride, to the ignorant. Yet Sholom Aleichem was torn by the ambiguities of his emotions, as he saw the traditional Jewish world disappearing; his heart yearned for the *shtetl*, while his mind urged its destruction. His own commitment to progress was honest enough. He was a Zionist, a liberal with a socialist orientation, and adventurous enough to have travelled twice to America. Yet in his Kasrilevke stories, more often than not he pays homage to 'the good old days' and to the people of the *shtetl* who hold to the old ways. He chastises those who flee to the big city and give up their heritage (There is not one thoroughly admirable big-city Jew in all of his stories!); his image of America is decidedly negative.

What were, then, Sholom Aleichem's feelings toward *shtetl* life? To say the least, they were mixed. He describes with real nostalgia this world in the premier story of Kasrilevke, "The Town of the Little People": "Stuck away in a corner of the world, isolated from the surrounding country, the town stands, orphaned, dreaming, bewitched, immersed in itself and remote from the noise and bustle, the confusion and tumult and greed, which men have created about them and have dignified with high-sounding names like Culture, Progress, Civilization."[4] This is one side of Sholom Aleichem's love affair with the *shtetl*. It is clearly anti-intellectual, emotional, nostalgic, and dominated by a distinctly "know-nothing" attitude in regard to the outside world, which is contemptible. "None of them are gloomy, none of them are worried little men of affairs, but on the contrary they are known everywhere as jesters, storytellers, a cheerful, light-hearted breed of men. Poor, but cheerful". Their frame of reference is their religion: "To provide for the Sabbath – that is their goal in life". Their orientation is to the past, not to the future: "The real pride of Kasrilevke is her cemeteries...It is of the old cemetery that the people are especially proud...For this is not only the place where the ancestors lie, but also the only piece of land of which they are the masters."

---

[4] In *Selected Stories of Sholom Aleichem*, Modern Library (New York: Random House, 1956), 28–34.

The description of the *shtetl* which Sholom Aleichem offers in this vignette is to a certain extent typical of his approach. With all of its poverty and aching misery, the *shtetl* was for Sholom Aleichem and for many other 'modern' Jews a world to be seen, whenever possible, through rose-colored glasses. In fact, the *shtetl*, over several hundred years, produced an inordinate amount of suffering for the Jews. At times, of course, Sholom Aleichem deals directly with this suffering, and one can sense the honesty of his presentation. But in a large number of stories and anecdotes dealing with Old Kasrilevke, one encounters a sentimentality which is at best moving, at worst banal and regressive in its criticism of modernity.

At his best in this type of story, Sholom Aleichem is a sort of Jewish Damon Runyon. In "The Merrymakers: Sketches of Disappearing Types",[5] he describes a typical *shtetl* celebration of one of Judaism's most festive holidays, *Simchas Torah*, when Jews indulge in a vice which is not a normal part of their traditional life style: drunkenness. But in this case, the drunkenness is religiously authorized! Sholom Aleichem portrays several members of the community under the influence of a modest amount of wine which they are otherwise too poor to possess: "Ordinarily they are timid, unpretentious folk, but when *Simchas Torah* comes they become jolly and full of life. You wouldn't believe that God-fearing pious Jews would do such things, would you?" Sholom Aleichem parades forth, with obvious satisfaction, his "disappearing types": Aleck the Mechanic, "not a mechanic at all, but a tailor, and a little bit of a tailor at that, a dwarf with short legs, tiny hands and a scrap of a beard", but with a magnificent bass voice. Like his fellow merrymakers, Aleck is a pauper, but Sholom Aleichem uses his poverty to make some social protest: "He has a houseful of children to support, but as for work, every year there is less and less. And it's all because of Lazer Ready-to-Wear, may the plague take him." Lazer is modern, and does business the modern way, with ready-to-wear clothes and credit accounts. Worst of all Lazer is one of Kasrilevke's own,

---

[5] In *Tevye's Daughters*, translated by Frances Butwin (New York: Crown, 1949), 162–171.

one of our own people, a former tailor, a pious 'holier than thou' sort of fellow. In the synagogue he has the best seat right up front. He is always being called to read the juiciest portions of the Law. He finds matches for his children among the best families. He has entirely forgotten that he was once a poor tailor himself, in fact the word 'tailor' is distasteful to him. He won't look at an ordinary workman. Poor people are chased from his door with sticks. And the good Lord sees it all and does nothing about it!

Here we have a microcosm of the world of Kasrilevke, with all the laughter, bitterness, happiness, and misery. In telling us about Aleck the Merrymaker, Sholom Aleichem explains, as a Kasrilevkite himself, the reasons for Aleck's poverty, and in passing criticizes a Jewish type, indeed, a Jewish archetype: the wretch who has made good in business, and who now possesses a status in the community while at the same time losing his humanity. Lazer Ready-to-Wear has committed, to Sholom Aleichem, the greatest crime of the *shtetl*: he has forgotten the poor. But on *Simchas Torah*, Aleck gets even. He makes the rounds of the houses, and no one dares deny him a holiday drink, not even Lazer Ready-to-Wear:

Listen to me, Brother Ready-to-Wear! Though you hate a poor Jew worse than a Jew hates pork, still because we are celebrating a holiday over the whole world today, and since you treated us to cake and wine, let us now drink each other's health and pray that we live until next *Simchas Torah* and remain as good Jews as we are now. Now let us kiss each other tenderly, and may the world never learn that you are a tailor and the son of a tailor as well as a scurvy knave and a low-down cur and an enemy of all Israel!

Thus, on this holiday, the low-down, common Jews of Kasrilevke have their day, and return to the rich a full measure of humiliation, reminding them of their humble origins. This is a Sholom Aleichem calling card.

Kopel the Brain is so named because of a gigantic forehead, "a forehead like a prime minister's, but Kopel is not a prime minister. He is only a poor workman. He is a shoemaker." For three hundred sixty-four days out of the year, Kopel's existence is a grim disaster. He lives and works with his family in a cellar, without light, except for that which shines dimly through a greenish-yellow pane in the single window. On top of this awesome poverty, Sholom Aleichem complicates Kopel's life by burdening him with a horror of a wife, a shrewish woman who badgers, humbles, and constantly reminds Kopel of his failure in life. Sholom Aleichem, interestingly, seemed to be unable to create female characters of lasting interest to himself. His major heroes – and villains – are inevitably men. Certainly Tevye the Dairyman, Menachem-Mendel, the "wheeler-dealer", and Mottel the Cantor's son are his three major creations. Sholom Aleichem created many female characters, but none of endurance. Tevye's wife Golde is the long-suffering Jewish matriarch, bitter and complaining. Kopel's wife is, characteristically for Sholom Aleichem, a not particularly sympathetic creation: "And perhaps his melancholy stems from the fact that God has blessed him with such a terror of a wife who, aside from the fact that she makes life miserable for him, never stops talking; her mouth doesn't shut for a moment. The neighbors call her Sarah the Speechmaker... Her speech is as bottomless as the ocean, as long as the Jewish exile, as endless as Kopel's misery." Under the guise of merryment, Sholom Aleichem probes several major characters of the Jewish community: the wife-mother, or at least his peculiar image of it; the timid, pious *schlemihl*, and his unique, quite special relationship with the Almighty; the Jew who can worship his God at the same time that he chastises Him for treating His people so badly. As for the Jewish *schlemihl*, his roots can be found both in the folk mentality as well as in the religious lore of Judaism. In kabbalistic writings since the Middle Ages a special place of honor was reserved for the *lamed-vav*. Traceable to Talmudic passages, the legend of the *lamed-vav*, or thirty-six, concerns the thirty-six saints whose piety sustains the world.[6] These holy men must remain obscure and anonymous, and their importance to the world must never be revealed. Their work must be of a menial nature, and they must be indistinguishable from the most miserable wretch of the community. For this reason, the beggar, the pauper, the poverty-stricken have never been forgotten by their fellow Jews. There is a strict obligation

---

[6] This tradition served as the theme for André Schwartz-Bart's prize-winning **nov**el of 1959, *The Last of the Just*. See also Chapter 1, 17.

on the part of all Jews to pay a kind of homage to any beggar, lest he insult unknowingly a saint and thereby bring upon himself and the Jewish people the wrath of God. Out of this ancient tradition Yiddish literature fashioned the *schlemihl*, the down-and-outer, the born 'loser' with an eternal smile on his lips, a man whose just rewards come only in the afterlife.

This is Kopel the Shoemaker,

'gloomy and sad, unhappy and depressed. But he doesn't utter a word of complaint. He bears his lot in silence; he carries his sorrow quietly within himself. A man has to be a philosopher to keep so much within himself. Kopel the Brain is a philosopher, and a potential saint. But on *Simchas Torah*, all the pain is forgotten: There is one day when he is cheerful. Did I say cheerful? He is like a new-born soul, beside himself with joy, mad with happiness, literally mad... Then Aleck begins to sing and the 'Merry Crew' joins in. 'Louder, men, louder', Shouts Kopel the Brain, and his forehead runs with sweat. 'Don't worry, brothers, the main thing is not to worry. Just keep on singing, keep on dancing, rejoice and make merry!'.

The other point implicit in an earlier passage – "God blessed him with a terror of a wife" – underlines the lovers' quarrel aspect of Jewish religious life. In Jewish proverbial literature are endless examples of a people's effort to communicate with a God whom they fervently worship, in spite of extraordinary suffering which they have experienced for His sake. As a result, one encounters a tone of "Look, you know how much we honor and respect You, but give us a break!" throughout Jewish writings. Yiddish sayings such as the following provide us with examples of what becomes a way of discourse between the Jew and his God;

'Thou hast chosen us from among the Nations' – Why did you have to pick on the Jews?...Only one God and so many enemies...God loves the poor and helps the rich...God will provide; if only he would provide until he provides...Lord of the universe, don't lift me up and don't throw me down...Lord of the universe, glance down from heaven and take a look at your world...What makes God happy? To see a poor man find a treasure and return it.[7]

---

[7] See *Yiddish Proverbs, In Yiddish and English*, ed. Hanan J. Ayalti (New York: Schocken Books, 1963).

1. KASRILEVKE AND THE HOLIDAYS

It would only be natural for Sholom Aleichem to use the Jewish holidays as a point of reference in a great many of his stories set in Kasrilevke. For any Jewish community, life was a long series of dismal periods in between the glories of the holy days of the calendar. *Simchas Torah* represents both the end of a festival year and the beginning of the next. The last lines of Deutoronomy are read, followed by the reading of the first lines of Genesis. The complete reading of the Pentateuch having been accomplished, the Jewish community breaks out in joyous celebration. It was the unrestrained joy of this holiday which Sholom Aleichem took as his excuse in "The Merrymakers". In numerous other stories, Sholom Aleichem, while apparently focusing on a particular holiday and its characteristics, digs beneath the surface to analyze particular characteristics of the people. "Two Shalachmones" is a Purim story, and the *Shalachmones* are the traditional gifts of sweet platters which families send to one another on this holiday which commemorates the victory of good Queen Esther over the wicked Haman. The story centers on an exchange of such gifts between two neighbours. The giving of these platters is closely tied to the social status of the giver and the receiver. An extra piece of cake, a missing cookie, any sort of oversight in the arrangement and quantity of the gift could cause a scandal within the community. Sholom Aleichem takes off from this particular pettiness in the *shtetl* to make his point. Two servant girls on their way to deliver the platters to their opposite number's household, meet and nibble away at the sweets. After making considerable inroads on the assortments, they say goodbye and continue on their journey. Sholom Aleichem describes the impact of the decimated *Shalachmones* on the recipients:

'Good *yom-tev*, my mistress sends you *Shalachmones*', said Black Nechama, walking in and handing her the covered plate. 'Whom do you work for?' said Zelda, smiling graciously and taking the plate from her. 'I work for Zlata, Reb Isaac's-may-his-tribe-increase', said BlackNechama, and waited for Zelda to take the *Shalachmones* and return the plate.

Zelda put one hand into her pocket to give the girl a *kopek* for the trip and with the other she uncovered the plate. She took one look and stood there as if turned to stone. 'Look at this *Shalachmones*', said Zelda, folding her arms over her stomach. Zelda threw the plate with the napkin back at Nechama and said to her, 'Tell your mistress that I hope she lives until next year and isn't able to afford a better *Shalachmones* than this.'[8]

Meanwhile, the following scene is taking place at Zlata's, Zelda's neighbor, business competitor, and erstwhile bosom companion:

'Good *yom-tev*, my mistress sends you *Shalachmones*', said Red Nechama, bringing in the covered plate of *Shalachmones*. 'Whom do you work for?' asked Zlata, smiling sweetly and taking the plate out of her hands. Zlata reached one hand into her pocket to tip the girl and with the other she uncovered the plate, and almost fainted on the spot. 'Of all the black, ugly, miserable nightmares that anybody ever had. Of all the bad luck that I wish to my enemies. Look at this *Shalachmones*. She's insulting me, the slut.'

A monumental battle erupts as the former friends confront each other with the insulting platters. Reason goes out the window, and the screaming mob – almost the entire community has become involved – marches off to the Jewish town clerk to lodge complaints, which are then brought before the ultimate authority, the gentile Magistrate. In Sholom Aleichem's works, the general image of the gentile is not particularly positive. It is more or less the traditional Jewish characterization of the *goy*, one filled with suspicion built on centuries of distrust. The gentile is usually the Russian peasant, slow-witted, drunken, and a brutal tool for those who are conscious anti-Semites. These are also usually stereotyped as vicious, hate-filled fanatics determined to destroy the Jewish communities through organized pogroms. The specific examples will be treated in a later chapter, but this brief general statement is necessary at this point, because of the unusual characterization of the Kasrilevke Magistrate, Pan Milinewsky, in this story, "a portly squire with a long beard and a high forehead. He had been magistrate for so long that he was acquainted with the whole town, was on good terms with everyone,

[8] In *Tevye's Daughters*, 192–202.

and especially with the Jews of Kasrilevke. He knew each one's weaknesses and peculiarities thoroughly and spoke Yiddish as well as any of them. 'He has a real Jewish head on his shoulders,' they used to say about him in Kasrilevke." The characterization is all the more striking because of the narrowness and petty stupidity of the Jews, as Sholom Aleichem portrays them: "In autumn, around the time of the high holidays, he was deluged with written complaints, all of them from Jews. They were not, God forbid, reports of thefts or robberies or serious crimes. No! They were all concerned with petty quarrels, and fights over precedence in the synagogue and interpretations of the Law over the privilege of closing and reopening the reading of the *Torah*." The litigants appear before him, hurl horrendous insults at one another, and finally out of despair, Pan Milinewsky throws the case out and passes the decision to the venerable Rabbi Yozifl, an ancient and wizened spiritual leader who appears in more Sholom Aleichem stories than the more famous Tevye. Rabbi Yozifl is both loveable and laughable. Whenever he makes a verdict, "it's not a sentence, but a discourse". He dearly loves to embellish his judgments with parables, allegories, and tales of the Hassidim. But he is sublimely kind and learned, and the people heed his every word. He admonishes the disputants, shames them into forgetting their squabble, and urges them "to forgive and forget". The husbands are the first to make the effort:

On the first day of Passover, after the services at the Synagogue, Reb Yossie Milksop (he was the younger of the two) went to the home of Reb Isaac-May-his-tribe-increase, for *kiddush*. He praised the Passover wine which had turned out exceptionally well this year and licked his fingers after Zlata's *falirchiks*. On the second day of Passover, after services, Reb Isaac (he was the older of the two) went to Reb Yossie's house, praised the raisin wine to the skies and smacked his lips over Zelda's *falirchiks*. And that afternoon, after dinner, when the two women got together and talked over the *Shalachmones*, the truth rose like oil on the waters and both girls, Red Nechama and Black Nechama, got their just deserts. Right after Passover they were both sent packing.[9]

[9] *Kiddush*: a ceremony or prayer in which the holiness of the Sabbath is proclaimed; *falirchik*: a dough-like confectionery.

A favorite motif of Sholom Aleichem's was that of Rabbi Yozifel as mediator and interpreter of the Law. In "The Inheritors", twin brothers Maier and Schnaier inherit their father's seat of honor in the synagogue. At least, the older had inherited it, but since no one in town could be certain who was the first-born, "they became enemies at once, ready to tear each other's beards out" for the seat next to the eastern wall of the house of worship.[10] Once again Rabbi Yozifel settled the argument with his unique mixture of wisdom and humility: he will offer his own seat, adjacent to the contested one, to the brothers, "for where is it written that a rabbi or any other man, for that matter, must have his own seat and especially at the east wall...The important thing is to come to the synagogue and to pray." Of course, Maier and Schnaier reacted in typical Kasrilevke fashion: they refused to occupy any of the seats! Thus the narrator, who is very rarely Sholom Aleichem himself and more often a Kasrilevkite native, chuckles to himself with mild frustration:

If there is anyone who would like to have his own seat by the east wall in the old, old Kasrilevke Synagogue, the seat next to Reb Yozifel, the Rabbi, at a reasonable price, let him go to Kasrilevke and see the children of Reb Shimshen Beard, either Maier or Schnaier, it does not matter which. They will sell it to you at any price you say, because neither of them uses the seat anymore. It stands there – unoccupied. What a waste!

For the Jews of the *shtetl*, the year reaches its climax in the Days of Awe, the high holidays of Rosh Hashonah, the Jewish New Year, and Yom Kippur, the Day of Atonement. Yom Kippur is the holiest of the holies, the most solemn occasion of the Jewish Calendar. The day is strictly observed as a twenty-four hour fast and is accompanied by sincere repentence and prayer for forgiveness. Most orthodox Jews will remain in the synagogue for the entire period, and in Kasrilevke, this would be the general case. Sholom Aleichem uses these High Holy Days as background for two types of stories, one humorous, the other tragic. For Kasrilevke's paupers, Yom

---

[10] In *Selected Stories of Sholom Aleichem*, 35–46. —

Kippur is a particularly sad time, since each man looks within himself to examine the state of his existence, and what the poor discovered annually was prolonged wretchedness on this earth. Yet, in true philosophical fashion, Kasrilevke's poor enjoyed the Day of Atonement, at least more than the rich, since they had relatively little to atone for. In fact, as the title of a story indicates, a poor man on Yom Kippur was "Someone to Envy": "In all of Kasrilevke's history, there was no finer funeral than Reb Melekh the Cantor's. Reb Melekh was a pauper, the poorest of the poor, just like the rest of the Kasrilevkite villagers."[11] Yom Kippur becomes for Sholom Aleichem the perfect background for the *schlemihl*, the wretched individual, or wretched village, or wretched folk, who spends his years in misery only to garnish the most beautiful reward: a blessed death: to die while fasting on Yom Kippur, like Reb Melekh: "Rabbi Yozifl quoted the Bible and the Midrash and showed that Reb Melekh the Cantor's death was not that of an ordinary mortal. Only saintly, very saintly, men died that way. Such saints went straight to paradise. Everyone ought to envy a man as saintly as he, for not all were worthy of dying at the pulpit during the closing *Yom Kippur* prayer, when God has forgiven man's sins." Yet, as in almost all of Sholom Aleichem's tales, one senses the irony, gentle but pressing, which emerges from the description supplied by the narrator: "For a long time thereafter, the Kasrilevke folk talked about Reb Melekh the Cantor's death and about the fine funeral he had. Mentioning it, they sighed: 'Ah, yes. There was someone to envy!' "Here is not the standard romanticizing of the holiday. In Kasrilevke, where poverty had found a home, Sholom Aleichem concentrates on the grinding burden of existence which for the Jews of the Pale can only be removed with death.

And yet, funny things can occur on Yom Kippur, as well. Funny, at least, for the reader, but not necessarily for the participants. "The Search" represents still another category of Sholom Aleichem's narrative form, the railroad story. In several dozen stories he used

---

[11] In Sholom Aleichem, *Stories and Satires*, translated by Curt Leviant (New York: Thomas Yoseloff, 1959), 171–174.

a technique which in that day was as familiar to Jewish life as the Sabbath. Toward the end of the nineteenth century the Jew had 'discovered' the railroad, and to a significant degree the railroad helped free him from the confines of the *shtetl*. It provided relatively cheap transportation and gave him access to the larger cities (to be sure, illegally); it provided him, moreover, with an opportunity to mingle with Jews from all over Russia, Poland, and even from Germany. Whenever possible, he avoided the gentiles, or was avoided by them. A Jewish salesman typically would search through the cars of a train until he was able to locate 'his crowd', and there he would sit, swapping hard-boiled eggs, home-made wine, and stories. The railroad story, of which more will be said later, is the *Canterbury Tales* of Sholom Aleichem, his excuse for more stories, yet as a framework as revealing and as detailed as the story itself. In "The Search" we find a Kasrilevkite on the road. The frame is not as elaborate as in many of the other railroad stories, but its brevity is in this case part of its merit: '"Now listen to *me*', said a man with round bovine eyes, who had been sitting in a corner by the window, smoking and taking in stories of thefts, holdups, and expropriations. 'I'll tell you a good one, also about a theft, what happened in my town, in the synagogue of all places, and on Yom Kippur, too. You'll like it."' Whereupon our friend launches into a tale about a visitor to Kasrilevke, a *Litwak*, a Jew from Lithuania, who arrives just before Yom Kippur and is therefore unable to reach his home in the north. A stranger spending some time – and money – in Kasrilevke was no minor event, and it caused considerable excitement in town:

He arrived in time for the evening prayer and ran into the trustees with their collection box.
'Sholom Aleichem!'
'Aleichem Sholom!'
'Where are you from?'
'From Lithuania'.
'And what's your name?'
'What difference does that make to your grandmother!'
'Well, after all, you've come to our synagogue!'
'Where else do you want me to go?'
'You surely want to pray here?'

'Have I any choice?'
'Then put something in the box.'
'Of course. Did you think I was going to pray for nothing?'"[12]

The generous donation gave the stranger a place of honor in the synagogue, and our narrator reports that the piety of the guest impressed everyone. He refused to leave his place, and did not sit once during the entire day of fasting:

To stand on one's feet on a day of fasting without ever sitting down – only a Litwak can do that! Suddenly, in the middle of a prayer, the stranger screams for help and falls into a dead faint: What had happened? A fine thing! He had on him – the Litwak, that is – eighteen hundred rubles; and he had been afraid, so he said, to leave his money at the inn. You think it's a trifle, eighteen hundred rubles? To whom could he entrust such a sum in a strange town? Nor did it seem right to keep it in his pocket on Yom Kippur. So, after thinking the matter over, he decided quietly to slip the money into his stand – yes, a Litwak is quite capable of such a thing! Now do you understand why he didn't leave his stand for a minute?

The entire congregation was thrown into a panic. Reb Yozifl, the ever-ready wise man of Kasrilevke, ordered the doors of the synagogue locked when he discovered the cause of the stranger's fainting: his money had somehow been stolen in the midst of the holiest shrine of Kasrilevke, on the holiest day of the year! The rabbi orders a search of everyone, with no one, not even himself to be spared. When the rabbi himself submitted to the search, no one in good conscience could refuse, and the entire congregation of men allowed themselves to be examined, until it came to Laizer Yosl: "He turned all colors and began to argue. The stranger, he said, was a swindler; the whole thing was a Litwak's trick, no one had stolen any money from him." But the community insisted that he be searched, in spite of pleas accompanied by tears and oaths that he had not stolen the money. For some strange reason, Laizer Yosl did not want to be searched. At this point, the narrator deems it

---

[12] In *A Treasury of Yiddish Stories*, 182–187. The traditional Jewish greeting of "Sholom Aleichem", peace unto you, is returned inverted normally: "Aleichem Sholom".

urgent to explain something about the relationship of Laizer Yosl and the town:

But wait a minute, I have forgotten to tell you who this Laizer Yosl was. He was not a native of Kasrilevke; he came from the devil knows where to marry a Kasrilevke girl. Her father, the rich man of our town, had unearthed him somewhere and had bragged that he had found a rare gem, a real genius, for his daughter, a man who knew by rote a thousand pages of the Talmud, who was an expert in Scriptures, a Hebraist and a mathematician who could handle fractions and algebra, and who wielded the pen like nobody's business – in short, a man with all seventeen talents ... His father-in-law bought him.

So, there is additional significance to Laizer Yosl, "the gem" of a son-in-law, in not wanting to be searched. In Kasrilevke, he was something apart from the community, an import intended to underline the importance of his father-in-law. What Sholom Aleichem is writing about in this conflict is once again a classical *shtetl* motif: the envy by the town of the *nogid*, the community's residential rich man, who is generally thoroughly unadmirable. In this case, Sholom Aleichem depicts the wealthy man in search of *yikhus*, or status, which can be easily acquired in a good match with a learned son-in-law. This particular rich man is still sufficiently tradition-bound so that he searches for his prospective son-in-law in the *yeshivas*, the Jewish academies of learning, rather than in the stock markets of Kiev and Odessa. He already possesses wealth; learning must be bought. It is this notion upon which Sholom Aleichem comments in setting up the tensions between poor Laizer Yosl and the community. In him the town sees the vulnerable spot of the *nogid*: "No one ever saw him do anything wrong; nevertheless it was whispered that he was not a pious man – after all, no one can have all the virtues!" This brings the story back to the synagogue and Laizer Yosl's refusal to be searched. It also accounts for the enthusiasm with which the members of the congregation grabbed the wretched young scholar, "laid him on the floor by sheer force, and began to feel him all over and shake his pockets. And then they shook out – guess what? – chicken bones and a dozen plum pits; everything was still fresh, the bones had recently been gnawed, and the pits were moist. Can you imagine what a pretty sight it was, all that treasure shaken out of our genius's pockets? You can imagine for yourselves the look on their faces, he and his father-in-law..." In Sholom Aleichem's world the price one pays for Jewish *hubris* is a particular brand of Jewish disgrace, in this case, having your prized son-in-law caught in the synagogue on a holy fast day with fresh chicken bones and plum pits in his pockets. The only person who felt any genuine remorse is Reb Yozifl who "walked alone, with bowed head, unable to look anyone in the eyes, as though the remains of food had been shaken from his own pockets". For the pious rabbi, the shame falls to the entire community for its envy of the rich man, and to all the people of Israel, for the disgracing of Laizer Yosl.

Back in the railroad car, the narrator sits back with some satisfaction after having told what he considered an excellent story: "'And what about the money?' we all asked in one voice. 'What money?' the man said with an uncomprehending look as he blew out the smoke. 'What do you mean, what money? 'The eighteen hundred' 'O-o-o-oh,' he drawled, 'The eighteen hundred? Vanished without a trace.' 'Vanished?' 'Without a t-r-a-c-e.'" A true son of Kasrilevke, the story teller had forgotten the apparent main thrust of his narrative. For him, by far the most significant aspect was the defection of Laizer Yosl and the come-uppance of his father-in-law, who next time maybe shouldn't be so smug and boastful. In the vast majority of his stories, Sholom Aleichem employs the intermediary narrator, and often this narrator becomes the central character of the story, as the presumed tale fades into insignificance and the narrator reveals his own personality and peculiarities in the form of a Chekhovian monologue, much in the tradition of "On the Harmfulness of Tobacco". The monologues of Sholom Aleichem will be discussed later, but one sees in the narrator of "The Search" a hint of the self-revealing irony of Sholom Aleichem's outer-frame characters. By removing himself further from the action through this intermediary Sholom Aleichem gains additional maneuverability as well as perspective. It enables a typical Jew – which Sholom Aleichem was not – to describe typical Jews. This narrative technique, later favoured by Hermann Hesse and Thomas Mann, created some of Sholom Aleichem's most memorable characters.

2. KASRILEVKE AND THE OUTSIDE WORLD

The last five decades of the nineteenth century represented a revolution for the *shtetl* as well as for the rest of Europe; and Kasrilevke was, in its own happy, poor, and muddling way, right in the middle of things. For the Kasrilevkites, this last half of a century was a period of 'isms': Socialism, Zionism, Capitalism, and Anti-Semitism. Sholom Aleichem, enlightened and intellectual, viewed with considerable interest the effect of these ideologies on the Jewish community of the Pale, which because of its isolation was affected in a different fashion than were the Jews living in the cities or in other countries. In some cases, Jews in the *shtetl* world were totally unaware of outside activities. In "Hodel", one of the Tevye stories, Tevye's daughter has fallen in love with a young Jewish revolutionary and Tevye is mystified by his ideological commitment. In another Tevye story, Chava tries to convince her father of the merits of her beloved Fyedka, a gentile boy who has hopes of becoming a writer. Chava describes him as "a second Gorky". Tevye replies: "And who may I ask was the first Gorky?"[13] In the midst of extraordinary social and political change, Tevye had never heard of the Russian revolutionary writer who most clearly represented the hopes of the Russian radicals. That his daughter should be familiar with Gorky, and Tevye not, also indicates the extent to which a generation gap of gigantic proportions existed in parts of the Jewish world prior to the Russian Revolution.

Sholom Aleichem dealt with the outside world in non-Kasrilevke stories, but in this chapter we are concerned with the effect of this change on our Kasrilevkites, with their peculiar penchant for pauperism and human frailty.

Modernization of communications in the nineteenth century brought considerable outside news to Kasrilevke that fifty years earlier would never have gotten to town. For the Kasrilevkites, it was a matter of considerable pride in their Jewishness when word came to them of Jews on the outside who were making a name for

---

[13] "Chava", in *Tevye's Daughters*, 96.

themselves. Particular affection and esteem was held for those who 'were doing alright', and none was doing any better than the Rothschilds. "Rothschild": the name was on the lips of every Kasrilevkite. It represented a way of thinking, several ways of thinking, and in Kasrilevkite parlance, the name had a significance all its own. For example, in a story called "Two Dead Men" Sholom Aleichem describes the poorest man in town: "If you asked him if he was hungry he never answered...he would rather die than hold his hand out to beg."[14] The town called him Rothschild. For want of a concrete definition, this might be given as an example of Jewish humor.

Yet, in reality, every Kasrilevkite dreamed of being Rothschild. Sholom Aleichem expressed this wish in a brief monologue, "If I were Rothschild", and uses the Rothschild-motif as an opportunity to expand on some of his own moral and philosophical positions, a temptation which Sholom Aleichem rarely fell prey to. He almost exclusively limits his social commentary to the role of the Jew, within the Jewish community, and then within the gentile world. But in this interesting anecdote, he permits himself this wider framework. To be sure, Sholom Aleichem begins inside the smaller world. His narrator begins,

If I were only Rothschild, guess what I would do? First of all, I would pass a law that a wife has always to have a three-ruble piece on her, so that she won't have to start nagging me when the good Thursday comes and there is nothing for the Sabbath...Then I would take my Sabbath garbardine out of pawn...and my wife's squirrel coat. Let her stop whining that she's cold...Then I would buy the whole house outright... Let her stop grumbling she hasn't enough room...[15]

Here once again we find the Jewish Everyman's material paradise. Enough for the Sabbath, and enough money to keep his wife from nagging. This Jewish mother-wife is for Sholom Aleichem at least – and one suspects for the Jewish male in general – a fixation, and in his works she looms larger than life, a matriarch who can dominate the entire social order of community life.

[14] In *Selected Stories of Sholom Aleichem*, 74–88.
[15] In *Tevye's Daughters*, 16–19.

Once his home life is settled, our friend moves with his fantasies to other areas. Like Tevye, he dreams of his daughters all being married off ("Woe to the poor Jew who has only daughters for which he must provide dowries"). Now that all material needs have been met, he is prepared to turn to more spiritual matters. A new roof for the synagogue; a new bathhouse; a new hospital for Kasrilevke; a home for the aged and infirmed; a Society for Clothing the Poor; another for Lending Money to Needy Jews; A Society for Outfitting Brides. But soon his imagination takes him even beyond Kasrilevke, to every community where Jews can be found: "This Board of Charity would keep watch over all of Israel and see to it that Jews everywhere had enough to live on, and that they lived together in unity...Everything would be run with a view to the common welfare." From there, it is only a brief step to the salvation of all mankind; and the first step in this direction which Sholom Aleichem has his *pintele Yid*, his little Jew, take, is directly toward the heart of the Jewish ethos: "Ah, the wars, the wars. The terrible slaughters. If I were Rothschild I would do away with war altogether. I would wipe it off completely from the face of the earth." How does he propose to do this? By abolishing that factor which has governed his own destiny as well as the destinies of countless other nations: the desire for wealth. He would hand out his billions to all the greedy nations of the world: "Here, you Englishmen with the long legs and the checkered trousers, take a billion. Here, you stupid Turks with the scarlet caps, take a billion. And you, Aunt Reisel, that is Russia, take another billion...What do we need armies and cannons and military bands for and all the other trappings of war...? There will be no more envy, no more hatred, no Turks, no Englishmen, no Frenchmen, no Gypsies, and no Jews."

At the end, the imaginary Rothschild who might have solved all the problems of the world sighs, as he realizes that he does not have the means to provide for the next Sabbath, and that his wife will remind him of this in a not particularly pleasant fashion. But, for an exhilarating moment, this Jewish Walter Mitty allowed himself the indulgence in what for him and his fellow Jews was paradise on earth: to be Rothschild.

There are several other prominent Jewish millionaires who received the admiration of Kasrilevke: the Wissotsky tea merchants, who had a representative in almost every Jewish community; the Brodsky sugar kings. Their names were known to every inhabitant of the *shtetl*. But, ironically, it was a relatively poor Jew from the outside who *really* captured the imagination of the Kasrilevkites. Most ironic of all, he was a Jew in a military uniform: Captain Alfred Dreyfus, whose treason trials even penetrated the medieval iron curtain of Kasrilevke. Sholom Aleichem uses the Dreyfus affair as a means of showing just how Kasrilevke reacts to the outside, especially Jews on the outside. In "Dreyfus in Kasrilevke" we see the *shtetl* amidst the political intrigues of Europe in the last decade of the nineteenth century, and the agitation is considerable: "I wonder if the Dreyfus affair made such an impression anywhere in the whole world as it did in Kasrilevke...the agony, the pain, and despair that Kasrilevke lived through from all this...Paris will never match, not until the coming of the Messiah."[16] Sholom Aleichem's tone, obviously, will be humorous. Again, he creates a Kasrilevkite narrator:

How, in Kasrilevke, did they ever find out about Dreyfus in the first place? Don't ask me! How did they find out about the war of the English against the Boers? How do they know what's going on in China? What kind of alliance does Kasrilevke have with China? Are they drawn together because of the great commerce that Kasrilevke carries on with China? No, tea Kasrilevke imports, not from China, but from Wissotsky in Moscow...

In this case, as in all cases where the news comes from the outside, the town found out from Zaidle, the only one in town who receives a newspaper. Zaidle rose in the synagogue one day to tell of Dreyfus's treason. The reaction to Dreyfus's defection was negative: "What a Jew won't do for business! It serves him right! A Jew who tries to crawl all the way up there to the highest places and mix with the royalty!" But soon after Zaidle rose with his newspaper and told of a plot against the captain because he was a Jew, "that

---

[16] In *A Treasury of Yiddish Stories*, 187–192: and *Selected Stories of Sholom Aleichem*, 269–273.

the Jewish Captain, Dreyfus, the one who had been imprisoned, was the soul of innocence, and that the whole business was just a plot ...Then the entire little village instantly took Dreyfus to heart. He became one of theirs, a Kasrilevker. Wherever there were two, Dreyfus was the third." Soon the crowds of Jews grew impatient waiting for Zaidle to arrive at the synagogue, so they went straight to his house, and soon, not even waiting for Zaidle, they went right to the post office to get the paper without Zaidle, "and there discuss it over and over, scream, disagree, and argue, everyone at the same time, exactly as usual". When the trial came with Zola and Lambori leading the defense of the imprisoned officer, Kasrilevke went beserk: "When the trial began a frenzy broke out in Kasrilevke. They tore Zaidle's newspaper to pieces; they choked over their food; at night they couldn't sleep – would they live through the night to see the next morning?" After Lambori had been shot, the town became even more hysterical, until the trial came to its final day, "and this final day worked upon Kasrilevke like a seizure of epilepsy. They quaked, they shook, they twitched...When Yarmo, the janitor, unlocked the gates of the post office they all rushed inside at once." The gentile janitor, while cursing out the dirty Jews, drove them out the door, until Zaidle came to get his newspaper and read them the guilty verdict: "There arose such a roar, such a protest, that the very heavens must have split. And this protest was not against the judge who had judged so badly; it was not against the generals who had covered themselves with so much shame. No, this protest was against Zaidle, who read to them." Zaidle was held personally responsible for the unpopular decision of the French court, and he was forced to defend himself from the charges that he was lying to them: "'Idiots! Here! See what it says here in the paper!' 'Paper!' cried Kasrilevke, 'and if you stood here with one foot in heaven and one foot on earth we still wouldn't believe you!'" Sholom Aleichem is at his very best in "Dreyfus in Kasrilevke", and the nature of his unique humor comes through very clearly. He is not a wit nor a satirist, at heart. The characters are not subtly individualized, yet their personalities are at the heart of Sholom Aleichem's humor. He sees his characters, at least the natives of Kasrilevke, "through lenses of love" which are the unique property of a Jewish writer of his generation, studying 'types' of Jews, and reactions of Jews which were as familiar to him as his own reactions.[17] In this story he is not criticizing the passion of the Jews of Kasrilevke for coming to Dreyfus's defense. If anything, he is criticizing the futility of their passion in a gently ironic way. What, after all, he is saying, will be the effect of Kasrilevke's outrage on world public opinion? There is also a hint at more significant problems. A stereotyped anti-Semitic Polish postmaster represents the most disruptive aspect of the outside world to penetrate Kasrilevke, an aspect which Sholom Aleichem dealt with in considerable amount.

In almost every respect, Sholom Aleichem is an accurate literary sociologist of the Jewish people of his generation. As has been mentioned previously, to read his works is to know the Jews of the Pale. Most graphically one grasps the nature of the relationship between Jew and gentile, and in particular we see the growth of the new relationship which grew out of the nineteenth century's own virulent form of anti-Semitism. The entire panorama of Jew-gentile history comes across in "The Great Panic of the Little People", one of Sholom Aleichem's longest stories, and, written toward the end of his life with himself quite clearly acting now as chronicler, he seems quite consciously to want a summary of the state of anti-Semitism in Russia prior to World War I.

The story is sub-titled "Wherein the Author Confides in His Readers" and Sholom Aleichem deals first in general terms about the Jews and what in the outside world has stirred up Kasrilevke: Dreyfus, of course; the Boer War (Russian Jewry was strongly anti-British on this issue); the assassination of Archduke Ferdinand. But now comes what for most Jews in Russia seemed a conscious anti-Jewish policy in the government, beginning with the restrictive May Laws of 1882 and marked by well-organized pogroms during the next twenty years, culminating with the massacre of Keshinev's Jewish community in 1904 and the anti-Jewish riots of the next ten years. The Jews of Kasrilevke were, to say the least,

---

[17] Curt Leviant, "Introduction", in Sholom Aleichem, *Some Laughter, Some Tears* (New York: G. P. Putnam's Sons, 1968), 13.

nervous. So, when a town *shokhet* – a ritual slaughterer of animals – received the following letter, panic ensued:

With trembling hands and quaking knees do I write these words to you. Know that the *weather* here has undergone a severe change. No pen can possibly describe it. All I can say is, God be praised, we are all alive and well. The hail and tempest that struck this place just scared us a bit, but thank God the storm has passed and we are no longer afraid of anyone. My wife, children, and I beg you not to worry for, glory to God, we are all well. Be sure to write us immediately a lengthy detailed letter, telling us what's new with you, how the *weather* is, and if you're all in good health.[18]

The letter, according to the Jewish savants of Kasrilevke, meant that the *shokhet's* son and family had survived a terrible pogrom. Zaidle's newspaper – the same Zaidle of Dreyfus fame – confirmed the cryptic letter's implication: there were pogroms throughout the land. At this point Sholom Aleichem takes the reader back into Kasrilevke history to show what exemplary Jewish-gentile relations should be like. The peasant couple of Fyodor and Pockmarked Hapke had served the Jews faithfully for years, extinguishing Friday night lights, emptying slops, and performing menial tasks. A perfect understanding grew between them and their employers, the Jews of Kasrilevke. Sholom Aleichem attempted as detailed a characterization of Fyodor as he had done on any of his other creations, and what emerges is a fairly stereotyped gentile peasant, as one-dimensional as the stereotyped Jews created by nineteenth-century German writers such a Gustav Freytag or Wilhelm Raabe. Sholom Aleichem imbues Fyodor with the standard ingredients: stupidity, dullness, and drunkenness, which dissipates his normal good humor when sober:

On those occasions, he would smite his chest, weep bitterly and bellow: 'What do you want from me? Why do you keep sucking my blood and eating my flesh? I'm going to turn Kasrilevke upside down. Yids, anti-Christ Yids, dammit a hundred demons and a blasted witch'. He would continue shouting and raising a fuss until he fell asleep. After

---

[18] In *Old Country Tales*, Sholom Aleichem, translated by Curt Leviant (New York: G. P. Putnam's Sons, 1966), 98–135.

a good long snooze he would get up, return to the Jews, and once more be the same old honest and even-tempered 'Fyodor-dear', as though nothing at all had happened.

The attitude of the Jews toward him is demeaning, and Sholom Aleichem does not spare his countrymen, either. They curse the couple in Yiddish, abuse them, and in general, the picture one has of the traditional rapport between peasant and Kasrilevkite is somewhat depressing: "The rest of the peasants in Kasrilevke were also in constant contact with the Jews. They knew that since time immemorial the Jews were destined to be storekeepers, merchants, and middlemen. For no one could do business or bamboozle you like the Jews, a people created for this very purpose. Or as the peasants put it: 'Business deals, that's what the Jews were made for'." Hapke is dealt with by Sholom Aleichem in an equally stereotyped fashion: You could scarcely tell she wasn't Jewish: "She talked Yiddish as though it were her mother tongue...She went to the rabbi with a question concerning ritual...helped to salt the meat, koshered the chickens, brought in the Passover dishes...For a long time the Kasrilevke constable refused to believe that Hapke wasn't Jewish." She is paid the supreme compliment by the Jewish image of the 'goy': she is accepted as a Jew. Almost without exception, Sholom Aleichem's characterizations of gentiles, especially peasants, are disappointingly limited. Most generally they fall into the categories of Fyodor and Hapke, or similar stereotypes. There is also the malicious priest, outspokenly anti-Jewish, ignorant, and totally intolerant; and, of particular importance to this story, the 'professional' anti-Semite, the town official, also fundamentally ignorant, uneducatable, fanatical, and relentless. Of course, there are a few exceptions to Sholom Aleichem's normal treatment of gentiles in his works, and these will be dealt with. But for the most part, he stuck to the traditional prejudices of his readers in this respect. Makar Khalodne, the gentile municipal clerk of Kasrilevke, is the virulent anti-Semite of this story. He grew up in Kasrilevke hating Jewish children who taunted him and his gentile friends. But Makar did not remain a child forever: "Before they had a chance to turn around, Makar had already grown up, tall and strong. He sported a pair of thick black mustaches and wore a red band and a gold button on his cap." Makar was a town official now, and a threat to the Jews. His anti-Semitism now becomes institutionalized and supported by the rhetoric of the national anti-Jewish movement. He subscribes to *The Flag*,

a noted Jewish newspaper; that is, it took Jewish interests to heart. Its editors were constantly concerned about the welfare of the Jews and explored ways to be rid of them – for their own good, naturally... *The Flag* made Makar a top-notch specialist in Jewish affairs, a mastermind of Talmud, the Code of Law, and the entire range of Jewish customs and ceremonies, such as – usury, deception, flimflam, and especially the use of Christian blood for matzohs.

In the course of characterizing Makar Sholom Aleichem spends some time on another of his pet targets, the *nogid*, the *shtetl*'s wealthy Jew. Kasrilevke's "Rothschild" is Mordecai-Nossen, who "like all other men of means, held the town under his thumb and did with it as he wished. For he was the tax agent, the synagogue trustee, the communal leader, the town's big wheel. In a word, he was everything: he was the Rich Man in Town." Mordecai-Nossen was also a sycophant who fawned over the likes of Makar, who was a regular visitor: "Mordecai-Nossen and Teme-Beyle rose in honor of their guest. They accompanied him to the door... They bowed and scraped and begged him: 'Don't forget now, be sure to come next Friday night...In a lead coffin', hissed the hostess at her guest once the door had slammed, furious with her husband for spending all of his time with the authorities." Mordecai-Nossen's friendship with the anti-Semite does not prevent Makar from hinting at a charge of ritual murder against the Jews; a panic sets in; rumors fly about that peasant villagers are on the road to Kasrilevke, prepared to plunder and burn. The townsfolk panic: "In Kasrilevke one store after another closed. The Jewish villagers looked at, and hid from, one another...They began renting any available means of transportation..., their haste nearly matching that of their ancestors' departure from Egypt." The Jewish town was completely deserted, except for the two old attendants at the ritual bath house, dubbed Adam and Eve by the local wits, and the venerable Rabbi Yozifl, who refused to abandon his native village and was prepared to die there. The old couple stayed behind because of their love for their rabbi. The rest of the village, the entire population of Kasrilevke, set out on the road out of town, frightened and terrorized. They are stopped dead in their tracks when they see a mob coming toward them – which turns out to be the entire Jewish population of the village of Kozodoievke, archenemies of Kasrilevke who for generations have been carrying on a senseless Martin-and-Coy feud over the most trivial matters: "It began with a few blows and ended up with all sorts of false denunciations, as well as a continuous display of boorishness, intrigue, and mutual recriminations. In a word, it was a nasty, revolting affair." So, two groups of Jews, fleeing for their lives, hating one another, meet on a dusty road between their towns:

Kasrilevke: Where are you off to, fellow Jews?
Kozodoievke: Where are *you* off to?
Kasrilevke: Who us? We're just traveling...On business.
Kozodoievke: What? An entire community on the move for business?
Kasrilevke: What about you? Aren't you an entire community?
Kozodoievke: With us it's a different matter. We're not traveling, we're running.

Out of this discourse comes the revelation that each is running from danger in the direction of the other. From their mutual embarassment emerges first an understanding of their panic, then a confession of their stupidity in this ancient feud: "Then they began to confer, chat, babble. They talked themselves hoarse. They unburdened their hearts", separated friends, returned to their respective villages and resumed their daily tasks.

In this panoramic story Sholom Aleichem jumps from issue to issue, until he settles on what becomes for him the dominant theme: the Jewish people and their enemies, real and imaginary. In Sholom Aleichem's mind, aware as he was of the political climate in Russia at the time, there could be no doubt that antiSemitism was rampant throughout the Czarist empire, but it is equally true that he was less than contented with the reaction of most of the Jewish communities like Kasrilevke, whose instinct was to panic and flee from the attackers. As a group, the Jewish intellectuals have always demonstrated their dissatisfaction with Jewish collective behavior in times of stress. From Sholom Aleichem to Hannah Arendt, these intellectuals have scolded Jews and what they considered this stereotyped reaction to violent attacks on them, which usually found the Jews either fleeing or hiding in attics and basements, or, still worse in Miss Arendt's eyes, willingly going to their deaths. Some writers took it upon themselves to create a new image. Sholem Asch's "Kola Street" with its street-fighting Jewish workingmen defending their synagogues and the cowardly Hassidim is one example. The great Russian writer Isaac Babel, himself a Jew, created in his Odessa stories a whole Jewish underworld of rough-and-ready types, who terrorized police and 'respectable' people alike. On the other hand, the reaction of the Kasrilevke community, while exaggerated by Sholom Aleichem, was sufficiently representative of Russian *shtetl* Jewry, and it was against this instinct to flee from panic that Sholom Aleichem directed the story.

The other major thrust was against the traditional conflict of Jew against Jew. The rivalry of the two very similar towns had its historical model in Jewish life down through the past two hundred years prior to the Russian Revolution. The Hassidic movement saw villages develop almost fanatical allegiances to the great teachers and mystics of the Hassidim, so that not only did it become common for a Hassidic community to attack a non-Hassidic one; it also came to pass that the rival Hassidim exploded in often violent altercations with one another. This kind of factionalism within the Jewish community of Poland and Russia found an expression in popular folklore in the 'Litwak-Galiciana' confrontation, with the Litwak-Lithuanian being considered the non-Hassidic, rabbinical, rational wing of Judaism, while the Galiciana-Southern Jew belonged to the fervent Hassidic tradition. Today, in Jewish humor, it is no more than a mild joke when a 'Litwak' marries a 'Galiciana'. In the eighteenth and nineteenth centuries, it was a matter of deadly seriousness for the Jews, and sufficient grounds for riots. Sholom Aleichem places the enmity of the two villages toward one another in, for the Jews, a realistic enough frame of reference:

The Jews of Kozodoievke did not resemble those of Kasrilevke. They were the same Jews, of course; they had the same bellies and souls; they even shared the same shred of poverty. The only difference between them was a prayer in the morning service. The Kasrilevke Jews recited 'Blessed be He who spoke' *before* 'Give thanks to the Lord', whereas the Kozodoievke Jews, on the contrary, reversed the procedure. What possible difference could it make whether one or the other was recited first? After all, both were prayers to God. But don't you dare suggest such a simple explanation.

The result was a bitter feud which is made light of in the story because of the satisfactory outcome, but which was at the very core of internecine struggle among Jews.

For those critics who have suggested that unlike Mendele, Sholom Aleichem was not a moralist, "The Panic of the Little People" represents a challenge.[19] Although he demonstrates considerably more wit and good humor than his earlier contemporary, Sholom Aleichem is here the critic of his people. There is no detachment as he takes off after the *negidim* who ignore their own poor in order to gain favor with the anti-Semitic government officials; nor does he spare the Jews for their hysteria, small-mindedness, and their own particular brand of anti-gentile racism. In the meantime, he never loses focus of the primary point of the story: the increasing threat of institutionalized anti-Semitism. Throughout there is a commitment on the part of the author to instructing his fellow Jews how they should 'behave'. However, much less than Mendele, he does not admonish so much as he points out. He himself thrusts less into the story; he allows the characters to demonstrate their foibles, and the point gets driven home just as clearly. Although he was not as pre-occupied with social criticism of his fellow Jews to the extent that Mendele was, Sholom Aleichem never avoided making his point whenever possible.

---

[19] See Liptzin in *The Flowering of Yiddish Literature*, 88–97; "Introduction" Julius and Frances Butwin, in *The Old Country*, Sholom Aleichem (New York: Crown Publishers, 1946): "Introduction", Alfred Kazin, in *Selected Short Stories of Sholom Aleichem*; Howe and Greenberg state in their introduction to *A Treasury* of Yiddish Stories, p. 53, that Sholom Aleichem was "without didactic intentions or social ideology".

The two 'isms' for which Sholom Aleichem felt the most sympathy were Zionism and Socialism, both of which seemed to offer the greatest hope to the Jewish masses, and which played a role in the modernization of Kasrilevke. In "Homesick", Kasrilevke hears of Zionism for the first time: "The Kasrilevkites have one good quality – once they laugh, they keep laughing. But, having had their fill, they start thinking about the topic, mulling it over until they begin to understand. That's exactly what happened with Zionism."[20] After some debate, the town pooled its money, and sent for a share in the Holy Land, via a Jewish bank. The anti-Semitic postmaster ridicules their efforts, and it appears that he might have been justified, when after several months no word is received from the Zionist headquarters. The pro-Zionists are stung, the anti-Zionists jubilant: "The whole business played right into the hands of the anti-Zionists, that is – the devout and the pious Jews and the *Hassidim* who didn't think much of Zionism." But nine months later old Rabbi Yozifl receives the package in the mail with the certified share in Zionist Palestine, and the local Zionists are vindicated.

Although in his personal life Sholom Aleichem was anything but a Socialist – he spent most of his adult life on the stock markets of Kiev and Odessa –, in his Kasrilevke stories he leans clearly toward this ideology. He is both bitter and sweet. On the negative side he shows the exploitation of the Jewish masses. "An Easy Fast" is the story of a proletariat Jew surrounded by wretched poverty; Chaim Chaikin is a Jew alone with his God, who fasts because there is no food and because "my investment in heaven gets bigger".[21] He cannot work, because there is no work. His daughters are the sole breadwinners, making cigarettes in a local factory: "This one earns a *gulden*, another half a gulden a day. And that, not every day. Sabbaths are not included. Nor holidays. Nor the days on which they are out on strike. For everywhere, God be thanked, and even here in Kasrilevke, we have learned how to strike. And out of these earnings they have to pay rent for the

---

[20] In *Stories and Satires*, 222–229.
[21] In *Tevye's Daughters*, 172–179.

damp corner of the cellar in which they live." The scene is one of abject poverty. So, Chaim Chaikin makes the best out of a bad situation by declaring fast days. He invents, he improvises, he passes his meagre piece of bread to one of his scrawny children: "It's a fast day." At the synagogue he was always the first to arrive, and he prayed with greater fervor than anyone else. Sholom Aleichem describes a vision of his children which came to Chaim Chaikin while he was praying at the altar: "He wanted to ask their forgiveness, to explain that he wasn't to blame. Was it his fault that there were people who found it necessary to exploit others and to suck their blood? Or that human beings hadn't yet attained such a high degree that they didn't have to drive others to work as they might drive a horse?" With these last thoughts, the little wretched Jew dies of starvation on the altar of the synagogue.

In "The Passover Expropriation" the unseen villain becomes visible. Benjamin Lastechka is the blood-sucker of "An Easy Fast", the *nogid* with no mercy for his fellow starving Jews, and Sholom Aleichem's outrage is tempered only by the humorous treatment which to be sure is characterized by righteous indignation, plus a measure of irony: "The rich people of Kasrilevke have such tender hearts that they cannot bear to look upon the plight of the poor man. They keep their doors locked and a lackey stationed outside to turn away anyone who is not respectably dressed."[22] As the town's most important *nogid* Lastechka is in charge of gathering donations for *Passover matzoh* for the poor, a task which he fulfills with no particular hardship for himself, for he makes only a token donation, in spite of his wealth. He tells himself that it is not his fault that this year some will have to do without: "With a clear conscience, bathed, and dressed in holiday clothes, Benjamin Lastechka sat down to the *Seder* with his wife and children the first night of Passover. He felt tranquil and at ease..." Just as the family is about to attack the sumptuous Passover feast, there is a knock on the door, and the *nogid* and his family are greeted by a band of young men. Sholom Aleichem introduces for the first time in his story the Jewish working proletariat in rebellion!

---

[22] In *Tevye's Daughters*, 273–280.

Under the leadership of one Samuel Abba Fingerhut, the young unemployed Jews rise up in revolt against

the bourgeois exploiters!... The spokesman stepped out from the rest of the group and began a speech in mingled Russian and Yiddish as was his custom: 'Here you sit, all of you, in a bright warm room with the wine glasses in front of you, observing the holy *Seder*, while we poor proletarians are perishing of hunger outside. I consider this a great injustice. I hereby command you to have the dinner served to us instead. And if anyone of you lets out so much as a peep or opens a window, or dares call the police or – *tomu podobniu* – it will be the worse for you. *Tovarisch* Moishe – where is the bomb?' The last words were enough to turn the family into graven images right where they sat.

Frozen with fear, the family stares at a tall, round object which one of the swarthy young Marxists places gingerly on the table. They remain immobile while the meal is served to the happy intruders. After eating up the last crumb, Samuel Abba Fingerhut addresses his host: '"Every year we recite the *Hagadah* and you eat the dumplings. *Wnastojatcheie wremie* – this time – you recite the *Hagadah* and for once we are eating the dumplings.' He raised his wineglass. 'Lchaim – long life to you – my bourgeois friend, may God grant that you become a proletarian like the rest of us. Next year may we celebrate the Constitution!'"[23] The Lastechkas sat in their places for two hours without moving, after the uninvited guests had left. Finally, gathering up enough courage, Benjamin examined the bomb – to discover a tin container, filled with matzoh meal!

What kind of revolutionary is Samuel? Above all, he is still a Jew. He maintains his Jewish identity regardless of his ideological commitment. Sholom Aleichem, in this characterization, seems to be aiming at a specific goal, that of showing how a revolutionary could still be a good Jew, and even lean toward some assimilation. The mixing of Russian phrases in with the Yiddish is the author's way of saying that Samuel is a Jew who considers himself also a Russian. For Sholom Aleichem, this is no minor fact of life, since

---

[23] *Hagadah*: Hebrew, 'narration'; the set form which the Passover stories takes in the retelling during the first two nights of that holiday.

he himself spoke mostly Russian in his own home as an adult. Still, his main purpose in expropriating the dinner of the *nogid* is to enjoy a proper Passover *Seder*. He toasts the Lastechka family in Hebrew, yet his language is peppered with the rhetoric of the radical. He looks forward to the freedom and emancipation of the Constitution, while celebrating a parochial Jewish holiday dating back almost three thousand years. This is how Sholom Aleichem chose to view the Jewish revolutionary, as if one could not take him too seriously, or at least as a revolutionary who still had his roots in a cultural heritage, and therefore less of an anarchic threat. As for the *nogid*, Sholom Aleichem's triumph of the proletariat does not extend beyond the loss of a *Seder*. The author morally reprimands, points an accusatory finger, but lets this Jewish *homo economicus*-without-a-heart off with nothing more serious than ridicule.

3. KASRILEVKE IN DECAY

"The Passover Expropriation" begins with a sentiment which, in regard to the Kasrilevkites, represents a new feeling on the part of Sholom Aleichem vis-a-vis his beloved little people:

Kasrilevke has always been known to ape Odessa. But since the recent disturbances began, Kasrilevke hasn't deviated from Odessa by a hair's breadth. Is there a strike in Odessa? Then there is a strike in Kasrilevke. A Constitution in Odessa? Then there is a Constitution in Kasrilevke. A pogrom in Odessa? Then there is a pogrom in Kasrilevke. Once a certain wag broadcast the news that in Odessa people were beginning to cut off their nose. Right away the people of Kasrilevke began sharpening their knives. Luckily, in Kasrilevke itself, one person apes another, so that each one waited for the next person to cut off his nose first. And they are waiting to this day.

A tone of bitterness, of satire creeps into the description of the townsfolk. It seems as if the events described – strikes, governmental reform (which never took place), pogroms (which did) – caused a severe enough disruption for Sholom Aleichem and *his* world for it to effect his Kasrilevke. There is no doubt that the Jewish *shtetl* itself was shaken to its foundations. Modernism, the outside world, various forces where penetrating to remote regions of Czarist Russia that had not been touched for centuries. Nowhere was life more disrupted that in the *shtetl*, and Sholom Aleichem, although an advocate of progress and enlightenment, looks with some resentment and nostalgia on the cost of progress for Kasrilevke.

By decay, Sholom Aleichem meant the metamorphosis of the *shtetl* and the *shtetl's* traditional Jewish values into something which he himself might describe as 'modernity'. The old world was changing, and the emancipated Sholom Aleichem did not like the new product; he did not approve of what the Jews did with their emancipation, and in Kasrilevke he began to express this disappointment. In fact, he expresses his profound personal involvement with this problem in that he dispenses with his usual intermediary narrator, and quite obviously thrusts himself into the role of story-teller. The jolly or sad, the haughty or down-trodden, the rich or impoverished Kasrilevkite who usually acts as narrator disappears, and in his place steps Sholom Aleichem; the narrator comes to visit his ancient home, and is saddened: "A month before *Rosh Hashona*, I returned to Kasrilevke to visit my parents' graves. The ancient Kasrilevke cemetery was much nicer and livelier than the town itself. Here you found little tombstones finer than the nicest of Kasrilevke houses. Here, at least, you saw some green growth. You heard the twittering birds hopping from branch to branch, talking to one another in their own language. Here, you saw the round, blue, skullcap-shaped dome of the sky and the bright warm sun..."[24] This appears perhaps as a very modest nature description, but for Yiddish literature, and for Sholom Aleichem, it is utterly uncharacteristic. But the author allows himself the luxury of serving as his own narrator, and the poet takes over from the Kasrilevkite. In this story, "There's no Dead", Sholom Aleichem is not yet ready to take on the New Kasrilevke. He is simply looking with sadness at the end of the Old Kasrilevke:

---

[24] In *Stories and Satires*, 156–159. Rosh Hashonah: the Jewish New Year, which traditionally falls in the autumn and is one of the holiest holidays of the Jewish calendar.

"Here, at the cemetery, the dead all lay in one spot. In town, they still walk around. Here, they were at rest and knew of no troubles. In town, they still had troubles and who could tell how many more there were yet in store for them in this world." The narrator describes his meeting with ancient Reb Arye, the caretaker of the cemetery, who recalls him and his relatives, and then goes on to explain that business is terrible: "Sure, they still die, but who? It's either children, babies, or poor men. You can't make a thing on them, unfortunately." In lamenting the fact that the town no longer has anyone in it who can afford to die, Reb Arye ironically shows the state of existence in Kasrilevke at that stage of its history. It is a dying townlet, abandoned by those who once lived there.

Where did the people go? Many went to Yehupetz (the fictional name given to Kiev, the Jew's dream of the big city), and their fates will be discussed in another chapter. A great many went to America, and quite consistently, Sholom Aleichem was very outspoken in his scepticism about the Jew's American Dream. No doubt his first bitterly disappointing trip to the United States had some effect on his attitude. Also, he saw America draining off the cream of Kasrilevke, as well as every Jewish bigamist, embezzler, and *gonev* (an all-around Jewish crook) who could manage boat fare to the New World. Of course, the Kasrilevkites who stayed behind might be accused of unfair criticism, and perhaps envy, but Sholom Aleichem paints them rather sympathetically. Berel-Ayzik, a native of Kasrilevke, is a rarity: a returnee! He spent several years in America, found it not to his liking, and returned voluntarily (much like Sholom Aleichem himself!) to his native town, glad to be back. He talks with the Kasrilevkite's own delicious irony: "'It's a free country. You can swell from hunger, die in the street, and no one will bother you, no one will say a word... But you ought to see how healthy they are. They fight just for fun. They roll up their sleeves and slug away to see who beats who. Boxing is what they call it." As far as traditional Jewish appearance is concerned, that too is quite different in America: "Most of the Jews don't wear beards or earlocks. Their faces are as smooth as glass. It's hard to tell who's a Jew and who isn't. You can't tell by the beard and by the language, but at least you can recog-

THE TOWN OF THE LITTLE PEOPLE

nize him by his hurried walk."[25] Berel-Ayzik concludes with a commentary on what it is like to die in America. The first-class funeral, "that's what I call a funeral!" The second-class funeral "can't compete with the first-class affair", but is acceptable, only that the liturgical singing "befits the five hundred dollar rate". The third-class funeral is dismal, costs only a hundred dollars, and there is no singing at all. "What can you expect for a hundred dollars?" The implication is that America is the *ne plus ultra* of materialism, where a major decision of a family is to determine the size of the family plot at the cemetery, and a considerable amount of status is gained by flashy funerals. The *homo economicus* triumphs even in death in America.

However, Sholom Aleichem did not restrict his criticism to those who abandoned Kasrilevke. He also directed numerous barbs at those who stayed in town and changed the character of it. A considerable number of stories deal with this "New Kasrilevke", Kasrilevke without the paupers, a town of middle-class, capitalist Jews who have 'made' it. In this phase Sholom Aleichem has a new society to portray, a new, modernized, emancipated Jew, who emulates the gentile world around him and creates a new set of values which are thoroughly alienated from the cultural-religious heritage of Reb Yozifl's Kasrilevke. Although there is some self-revelation, for the most part these Kasrilevke stories are in their narrative form much more personal statements of Sholom Aleichem, less exposure of the people by themselves. In fact, Sholom Aleichem throws off all pretense at being anything but what he is – a writer, identifiable as such by the Kasrilevkites, who comes home to visit, and discovers, like many a writer or returning son, one simply cannot come home again:

Where did the famous little people with their little ideas disappear to? Where were all those know-it-all bearded Jews who poked fun at everything? Where were those young people with canes who used to wander around the marketplace looking for business in vain, who out of depths

---

[25] "Earlocks", or *peot, peos*; Hebrew, 'corners',. According to the Bible (Lev. 19 : 27), it is forbidden to remove the hair at the corners of the head. Orthodox Jews allow their earlocks to grow, then, and generally they are quite elaborately curled and are a distinct sign of orthodoxy.

of despair robbed one another and then the whole world? Now, I saw dandies strolling through the streets, staid people with homburgs and pince-nez. Of the once slovenly women with their white stockings and red garters, and of the girls with their colorful kerchiefs – not a trace remained. Ladies with chapeaus now walked past me. Matrons with parasols. Chic young ladies wearing gloves. New people. A new world. What's more – and this is a good one – the village had even paved its streets and put up lamp-posts. They had phonographs, they had movies. They really enjoyed life![26]

This is the strange paradox of Sholom Aleichem the writer-moralist during this elegiac, reminiscing period of his writing, as he looks back longingly on "the good old days" of the *shtetl*. He genuinely is torn apart by the loss of Old Kasrilevke, which nonetheless in terms of progress for the Jewish people, was a dead end, of which he was thoroughly aware. He romanticizes the *shtetl*, says in effect "Give me back the old days of poverty, starvation, and misery, because we have become corrupt". Kasrilevke was admittedly poor, but at least it was good-hearted, suggests Sholom Aleichem: "There used to be clubs..., societies like the Free Loan, the Free-Kitchen, the Visit-the-Sick, the Clothe-the-Poor, the Help-the-Needy, the Medical-Aid, the Relieve-the-Oppressed. It seemed that all these groups had gone the way of their founders. They passed on like most of the little people, like lonely old Rabbi Yozifl, may the fruits of Paradise be his. Thinking of him brought tears to my eyes."

In dealing with the New Kasrilevke, Sholem Aleichem distinctly shifts to outright satire, one with considerable charm but with more bite than is normal for him. The numerous stories which deal with this changed world formed an entity in his own mind, because he collected and revised them in the form of a mock guidebook, *Inside Kasrilevke*: "My book will serve as a guide to strangers visiting Kasrilevke...For Kasrilevke is no longer the town it used to be. The great progress of the world has made inroads into Kasrilevke and turned it topsy-turvy. It has become a different place."[27] The chronicle is told in the first person by Sholom Aleichem

---

[26] "Progress in Kasrilevke", in *Stories and Satires*, 17–67.
[27] English translation by Isadore Goldstick, with drawings by Ben Shahn (New York: Schocken Books, 1948).

himself, who identifies himself with his manuscripts and papers which the hotel hustlers grab out of his hands as he arrives by train. Like a Jewish Dante in his own grobian inferno, he wanders through the town, makes "a triumphal entry into Kasrilevke" on the back of a wagon after the Toonerville trolley of a tram breaks down, spends the night in a Marx brothers hotel ("A room with or without music?", i.e., next to a cantor or not), where he is confronted with bedbugs, salesmen bursting into his room, and finally bandits, *Jewish* bandits, who demand his money or his life: "We'll give you two minutes to think it over and one minute to say your prayers."[28] The author tells them that he is just an impoverished writer: '"Where are you from?' 'From Yehupetz.' 'What's your name?' 'Sholom Aleichem.' Mistaking my name for the customary Yiddish greeting, they returned the compliment by saying 'Aleichem Sholom', adding, 'Your name, please.'" Finally, the theft ends up as a conversation, with cigarettes handed back and forth, when they discover that the wretch of a writer is as poor as they are. Sholom Aleichem stays in town long enough to observe Kasrilevke's culture ('"Don't miss this play, even if you have to pawn your silverware!"'), fire department ('"This looks like a put-up job...the House was insured...It wouldn't be burning if it wasn't insured...Say Yankel, isn't it burning beautifully? Isn't it just lovely?"'), and restaurants. As he was about to attack a herring in a local eatery,

a woman came in. She was lanky and had only one eye. She kept one hand in her bosom and was scratching her ear with the other. 'What'll I do, Reb Moishe Yankel? What's your advice?' she asked the old man. 'My Shmulik's ear is running again...' Rochel returned with the bread and began to prepare the herring for me. All the while the lanky, one-eyed woman didn't let up describing how Shmulik's ear was running. She was afraid she'd have to call in the doctor's assistant again...Just try and give a doctor in Kasrilevke less than fifteen kopecks, he'll throw it in your face. It's not enough for the famous specialist.
'Give a sick man a handout', a livid-faced Jew said to me, holding out a small shriveled hand, expressly fashioned for begging. 'Help a miserable cripple', wailed a creature walking on his hands and feet, for both his

---

[28] *Inside Kasrilevke*, 98

lower limbs seemed grown together and twisted under him. 'Have pity on a man with the falling sickness...' I interrupted my 'feast', paid my bill and ran out of the restaurant as if pursued by a hundred demons.[29]

Finally, a disastrous fire consumes the town, and the inhabitants of Kasrilevke form a committee, to go out into the world for loans, donations, money of any sort, to help re-build. Kasrilevke's best take the train to the big city in order to find the wealthy Jews. What good will and humor there was in Sholom Aleichem's description of his visit to his hometown now disappears, as he expands the description into a travel journal, with a Heine-like sense of moral criticism. Jews travelling by train – railroad stories – was one of his more comfortable frames for storytelling, but in this episode, Sholom Aleichem, consistent with his own feelings about the new Kasrilevke, shows a harshness and bitterness not characteristic of him. The delegation finds itself in a car where they are harassed by gentiles and denied even the available seats: "The select men of Kasrilevke simply had to stand on their feet, huddled together in a corner like sheep, crowding and squeezing one another, all the while talking at the top of their voices as well as with their hands, and all together, as usual."[30] The abuse between the two groups grows, until a new passenger enters the car: "'Sholom Aleichem!' he exclaimed, 'Where are you men coming from and where are you going to? And why on earth have you gathered here of all places, among this kind? Join us, come to our coach. There at least you'll be among our people, among our own.'" The Jews joyfully leave the car and enter another, filled with only Jews, where they are royally greeted. Is Sholom Aleichem suggesting that Kasrilevkites can only live among themselves and are not tolerable enough to learn to live in the gentile world? Partly, to be sure, although the gentiles are at least as ugly and bigoted as are the Jews in Kasrilevke.

In Yehupetz, one finds an extension of these prejudices: "Thus you will read that such a number applied for admission to the university and were not taken in; such and such a number were

---

[29] *Inside Kasrilevke*, 56–57.
[30] *Inside Kasrilevke*, 155–164.

caught in a nightly raid and *were* taken in; the reverse has never been known to happen: that Jews seeking admission to the university should be accepted and those caught in a raid should be rejected."[31] The reference to the nightly raid is significant in explaining the nature of Jewish existence in Yehupetz-Kiev: almost all of the Jews were living there illegally, without permits; for the big cities were barred to the Jews, by law. This situation and the plight of the Jews of Kasrilevke who came literally to beg had, however, little softening effect on Sholom Aleichem's Yehupetz Jews. They are a hard-hearted lot of *negidim*: "Reb Yozifl was surprised not to find a single one among the big men to give him an ordinary homely welcome. There wasn't one among them who inquired after Kasrilevke or who cared to listen to the story of their misfortune." Jew and gentile, both demonstrate an inhumanity to one another which Sholom Aleichem finds distasteful to say the least. The only person who stands above it all is the ancient spiritual leader of the community, and the man selected to head the delegation, Rabbi Yozifl, the only holdover from the warmly remembered days of Old Kasrilevke.

In Old Kasrilevke, excess was not unknown, nor was debauchery a stranger. But Sholom Aleichem shows considerably more patience with Old Kasrilevke's brand of degeneracy .In this world of the *shtetl*, this had nothing to do with sexual licentiousness or uncontrollable drunkenness, both of which were so far outside of the Jewish moral code as to be inconceivable in Yiddish literature, where these themes are almost non-existent. A Kasrilevke degenerate was someone who played cards on the Sabbath, and nobody played cards like Velvel Ramshevitch and his wife Chayela, Old Kasrilevke's resident epicureans.[32] In the story "Cnards" we see the town libertines running an allnight card game. Velvel was "a free soul: he had shaved his beard and sidelocks, smoked on Saturdays on his front porch where all could see, and ate pork sausage – even on fast days! And he dared anyone to criticize

---

[31] *Inside Kasrilevke*, 115.
[32] The word "epicurean" in Hebrew and Yiddish, "apikoyres", has a particular connotation of skeptical freethinker, almost heretic. It implies a falling-away from the Laws of Judaism.

him."[33] Worse than he was his wife Chayela, daughter of a cantor, and the picture of delightful debilitation: "I cannot imagine Chayela Ramschevitch without a cigarette in her mouth. Add to this the powdered pockmarked face and the uncombed blond hair, with the tired, puffy eyes." But just so as to remind us and themselves of their heritage, on Hanukah the Ramschevitchs and their card-drugged friends light the menorah, the traditional candle-holder. Still, the entire town is in danger of being corrupted. 'Kept' sons-in-law, those precious scholars whose minds were permitted to delve only in Talmud, were losing their wives' dowries and hocking the family jewels to keep up with their gambling debts. Even the holiest of Jews appear to fall prey to this Jewish curse: the card game. During one of these all-nighters, two pious, bearded Jews in long traditional caftans appear at the door. There are solicitors, grandchildren of that great saint and founder of Hassidism, the *Baal-Shem-Tov*, who are wandering around the countryside collecting money for *yeshivas*, the academies of Jewish learning. They ask for a donation – and get taken into a card game! The two seemed like easy prey; they had never played cards before, and could not even pronounce the word properly. But miracle of miracles, they cleaned out the entire bunch, and, sat triumphantly, amidst outbursts of prayer behind a huge pile of money. Out of meanness and revenge, Velvel tricked the pious men into eating non-kosher food, indeed, pork, and gleefully informs them: "Before Velvel could finish the sentence our two visitors clutched their heads in terror, opened their mouths wide as if to spit everything out, and then with a bitter groan sprang for the door and swept out of the house like a cyclone. "Later, while laughing over their joke and lamenting their lost money, the group discovered that the deck they played with had an abundance of aces, as well as a wealth of everything else. Out they went, searching for the holy men, and they found them at the railroad station, on the train:

Both were clean-shaven, both wore short tailored jackets and derby hats. And yet they were familiar. The first to recognize them was the

---

[33] "Cnards", in *Selected Short Stories of Sholom Aleichem*, 410–425. In the original Yiddish, the impostors show their apparent innocence by mispronouncing "Kertl", cards.

pampered son-in-law, Eli Rafalski. As soon as he saw their smiling faces he pointed straight at them. But the train was already moving. And for Eli Rafalski, who had been so acute as to recognize them, they had a special farewell. Together they raised their thumbs to their noses, and made a broad arc with their outstretched fingers.

Here we have the spectacle of Jewish non-believers coming to grips with Jewish confidence men, and still everything takes place within the framework of traditional Jewish life. Where else would two crooks appear disguised as the grand-children of the founder of Hassidism?! Where else could they find an all-night card game in the middle of Hanukah? Sholom Aleichem lets them all off without a rebuke.

In New Kasrilevke, however, he finds the excess distasteful, because the entire community is tainted by the vices which Sholom Aleichem found most distastfeul in the Jewish people: greed and pretense. The two were inextricably tied together. After hundreds of years in the poverty of the ghetto, it was the singular desire of almost every Jew in the *shtetl* to be better off than every other Jew. Even within the narrow frame of reference of economics, where everyone was poor, the social hierarchy considered some less poor, and these people became the recognized *negidim*, and therefore deserving of an added measure of esteem, or *yikhus*. There were two roads to economic advancement: the short one which led right back to the *shtetl* and left one the richest among the poor; and the one to the city. Kasrilevke, as Sholom Aleichem often said, was no more than a slightly exaggerated imitation of the big city; but the signs of decay were just as clear.

How did the Kasrilevke *nogid* indicate how rich and prominent he was? By the quality of his sons-in-law and the size of his summer home! In "The Joys of Parenthood" we are given a first-person account of this new (for Kasrilevke) value system. The new Kasrilevke hero is, first of all, a businessman, "not really rich, but he makes a good living. A businessman, a conniver, a manipulator, may the Lord forgive him. He manipulates so long that he gets both himself and the other party all tangled up. But somehow, he always squeezes out himself, the scoundrel."[34] Of course, he is

[34] In *Tevye's Daughters*, 109–113.

bound to his faith, to his heritage, but something has corrupted this. He admires learning, but only for what it can give him in reflected glory: "For believe me, I have such sons-in-law that the wealthiest man could envy...I have one son-in-law who comes from a very superior family. He is really something to brag about – a young man of refinement, talent, education, a great scholar. Day in and day out he sits and studies. I have been keeping him with us ever since the wedding, for if you knew him you would admit it would be a sin to let him out into the world." The second son-in-law is "of not quite such a good family, but he's just as intelligent as the first". What constitutes a "good" family is either learning, money, or better yet, both. A third "has a good head, a fine handwriting, knows the *Gemorah*, can quote you Scriptures".[35] These three live with the *nogid*, never work ("God forbid!"), sit at home, coughing, "together with a wheeze", and study. There is also another-son-in-law: "This one is very plain, but a hard-working fellow. Not, God forbid, an ordinary workingman, a tailor or a cobbler, but not a student either. He is a fish peddlar. The whole family knows nothing but fish and fish and more fish. They're honest people, you understand, respectable people, but very common, ordinary people." The entire system of values is supported by the abused individual himself, the hard-working fish peddlar: "I can even say that almost all the work he does is for us. He has great respect for us too. He understands well enough who he is and who we are. He is what he is and after all we are something else. You can't dismiss *that* with a shrug...It's only right that he should be proud to have such brothers-in-law and he should be glad to labor in their behalf. Don't you agree?" The monologue concludes with the boast that has been at the core of the story: "A rich man, you understand, I am not. But one thing I can really boast of – my children! In that respect I am wealthier than the wealthiest man in Kasrilevke." This rich man reveals the nature of his values both through his language and his attitudes. His is not the liturgical and moral grandeur of a Rabbi Yozifl. In fact, the morality of the man

---

[35] Or *Gemara*. An Aramaic word meaning 'study', or that which is learned. It represents a large body of commentary on Jewish law.

is revealed early in the self-revelation when he urges, in fact, demands that one of his own sons divorce his wife because she cannot produce a child. The distraught daughter-in-law begged her husband not to divorce her, and the son went to his father: "'What do you mean, she doesn't want it?' I asked my son. And he tells me 'She loves me.' 'Fool', I say, 'Are you going to listen to that?' But he says 'I love her too.' Now what do you think of that smart boy? I tell him *children*, and he answers me *love*. What do you think of such an idiot?" He is totally lacking in the humanity of a Tevye, of the common, ordinary *shlemihl* who Sholom Aleichem loved. He is not even a learned Jew, for nowhere does he himself indicate any great theological understanding. What is he? He is a former common, ordinary *shlemihl* who 'is making a living', who, like Lazer-Ready-to-Wear forgets his origins and becomes the ultimate villain of Sholom Aleichem's Jewish Everytown: the *nouveau riche*, who can buy esteem.

This society was for Sholom Aleichem unappetizing from one end to the other. The children of Kasrilevke's newly rich are no better than their parents. In a highly autobiographical story, "My First Love Affair", Sholom Aleichem tells of how he was hired as a tutor for one of these children, "born and bred in lies". The tutor's first meeting with the father is a classic:

Let me tell you, young man, with no exaggeration, we have about twenty rooms. What am I saying, twenty? There are more than thirty! I don't know myself why we have so many rooms, although we often have company. What am I saying, often? Every week. Every day. In fact, a day doesn't go by without one, two, or three guests coming. And what guests, too! a nobleman, a police commissioner, a bailiff, a justice of the peace. Me? I get along with all of them...And my garden's worth seeing. It's more a forest than a garden. Wait until you see my apples, my pears, my plum trees...[36]

The employer turns out to be a practiced liar, and the mansion no more than an ordinary house. But the son, the young man to be tutored by Sholem Aleichem, is a model of dissipation. "He liked three things: eating, sleeping, and laughing." A match is arranged by

---

[36] In *Stories and Satires*, 129–146.

the parents for the young man, and a correspondence develops between the betrothed couple, with the tutor writing the letters for the indifferent fiance. These letters create some excitement at the young lady's home, because, although she has never met her intended husband, she replies with considerable passion. The exchange continues unabated, with eloquence from Sholom Aleichem and equal expressiveness from the fiancee. Finally, on the day of the wedding, Sholom Aleichem is almost consumed with passion for the unknown woman whom he had begun to love through this strange correspondence. He was prepared to confess the truth to her, beg her to run away with him, until the reception, when "I noticed another lost soul wandering around as if he too didn't belong. When he looked my way, I had the feeling that he saw right through me; he saw my heart, my secret, my sacred secret." The two young men found themselves sitting next to one another behind the betrothed pair, and the stranger speaks to Sholom Aleichem:

'She's an ass, a run-of-the-mill domestic animal. Can't even write her name. And she's a hellcat to boot. And look at the fine husband she's getting. You're his tutor, right?' The bespectacled young man – he was the bride's tutor – told me hair-raising stories about the bride.' 'All right. But her letters', I cried out. 'For God's sake, her letters.' Hearing this, the young man held his sides and laughed hysterically. 'Her letters,' he laughed, 'oho! Her letters! Oh, I can't take it any more. Her letters!' 'Then whose were they?' I thought that this young man had surely gone crazy and would soon throw a fit. He grabbed both my hands, walked around the house with me, slapping my shoulders, laughing without a stop.

So, Sholom Aleichem comes to the shocking realization that he had fallen in love with the tutor, who had been writing the letters. "The darkness in every corner of my soul", however does not cause the reader to lose sight of the two young people about to be married, nor of the environment in which they received their education. On the day of his wedding, our young couple was supposed to be fasting, as is the custom, but the groom helped himself to half a duck. "Born and bred in lies, he had to lie even on his wedding day."

The vulgarity of the nouveau riche in Sholom Aleichem's prosperous Kasrilevke emerges at its funniest, most critical, and grossest, when the Kasrilevkites decide that it's time to take a summer vacation. Status-seeking Jews rent cottages illegally from gentiles in the country, where the Jews are not permitted to reside; Jews bribing officials; spoiled and lazy children, adults solely interested in improving their social position through marriage or other means, a desire to identify with the new at the expense of the old: this is the world of Kasrilevke on vacation. In a rambling collection of anecdotes entitled "Summer Romances", Sholom Aleichem presents this Jewish menagerie in a hearty parody that reveals his sense of pain beneath the surface. The two wealthiest Jewish families of town, "our Brodskys and our Rothschilds", have young children, "bluebloods", fit, in the eyes of their parents, only for marriage with each other; yet the two families detest each other because of the rivalry over who is indeed the wealthiest in town. On a streetcar, the mother and daughter of one family find themselves seated opposite the son of the other; it is up to mother to get a conversation going:

Then she had a brainstorm (good old dependable mother). She started fanning herself and said (in good old, world-renowned Kasrilevke Russian): 'Oh what a heated day is it.' The daughter looked at the aristocratic young man and corrected his mother's grammar. 'Yes, what a *hot* day it *is*.' Now the young man had the opportunity to break in. So he turned to the young lady and said in Russian: 'Is the air at your place good, too?' But, nevertheless, the matron did not let her daughter answer. She had a mind to answer herself (that's a mother for you) and turned melodiously to the young man and said in Russian: 'What do we need the air for? We have money!'[37]

With this one exchange, Sholom Aleichem lays bare many of the follies of Kasrilevke's new values. The efforts to eradicate the past reaches the point where a Jew refuses to speak Yiddish, preferring imperfect Russian. Indeed, as Sholom Aleichem points out, "that was a yardstick of aristocracy", this lack of knowledge

---

[37] In *Stories and Satires*, 68–108.

of Yiddish. "For instance if a Rothschild said he had difficulty with Yiddish, a Brodsky would say that he didn't even know a single word of Yiddish."

The rivalry of the "Brodskys and the Rothschilds" spread to the summer resort, as well. The poorer part of the resort area where the Jews vacationed was called *Israel*: the elegant part, *Palestine*:

Palestine opened its door to the residents of *Israel*, and the down-and-out guests had themselves a time. How did this happen? Like this. One summer, our Rothschilds built their own summer villa in *Palestine* – under a gentile's name, of course. And what a villa it was! With a veranda, and a green picket fence, and a garden filled with gooseberries, currants, and cherries. They opened the garden for all of the Kasrilevke vacationers – free of charge. Anyone in *Israel* was welcome to stroll there on Sabbath afternoons. But only on the sabbath. Weekdays – beware! The next summer, the Brodskys decided to put up an even nicer villa, with a bigger veranda and a larger garden, also under a gentile's name, and also with gooseberries, currants, and cherries. They announced specifically in all the little synagogues that their garden was open to the public, not only on Sabbath afternoons, but on every day of the week.

The story, with the rivalries and the children, has the makings of a Jewish *Romeo and Juliet*, but the appearance of the famous matchmaker, Soloveytshik of Kasrilevke, puts aside any possible tragic overtones. The Matchmaker, the *shadchan*, is a serious business in the Jewish community, where it was considered unseemly conduct for your people to do their own courting. It was considered an honorable activity, and the commissions for arranging these transactions were fixed often by rabbinical action. The position, as much as the community rabbi or ritual slaughterer, the *Shokhet*, represent a part of the traditions of a Jewish town; it forms a tie to the past. But, in Kasrilevke of Today, in the New Kasrilevke, even the matchmaker's posture had changed, alas:

Soloveytshik was a modern Jew. He already wore a derby, a white shirt-front, and a tie. The hat was a bit tattered, the shirt-front none too white and the tie – no offense meant – well, a sort of shiny rag. Add to this a well-worn undersized jacket, a pair of ill-fitting, loudly checkered trousers which had seen better days. But all that was nothing compard to the beard and earlocks. What beard? What earlocks? The beard, at least, wasn't that bad. If it wasn't a full-fledged beard, it was a tiny Vandyke. Who says a man must sport a broom on his face? But earlocks? Not a hint of them! Cut off and rooted to the last hair. Not to mention his way of speaking! He never came out with a good old Yiddish 'Good Morning'. It was always 'hello' and 'goodbye' in Russian. He'd never use homey Yiddish to say 'I have a good match for you'. He always said it in a hodge-podge of German, French, and Russian phrases. 'Ich habe vier sie dyevushkoo magnifique.'

The tradition had been broken. The son of a matchmaker, Soloveytshik had modernized, abandoning the old, tried ways for the flare of modernity, and Sholom Aleichem laments: "His father, God rest his soul, used to carry a huge red parasol. But that wasn't good enough for Soloveytshik. He was an aristocrat with a cane and his name was Soloveytshik the Marriage-mediator. If Reb Sholem the Matchmaker would get up and take a look at his son the mediator, he'd turn over in his grave."

Perhaps the single most common phenomenon of this New Kasrilevke is the devisiveness of its inhabitants. There is no sense of mutual trust and assistance any longer. Sholom Aleichem looks around him and sees Jews fighting with Jews. Everywhere there are bitter rivalries. The Orthodox have one newspaper (*The Skullcap*), the progressives another (*The Bowler Hat*); the Hebraists fight the Yiddishists; real estate dealers fight in the streets over renting to summer vacationers from Kasrilevke and Yehupetz. Amidst this turmoil – admittedly, often hysterically funny – Sholom Aleichem is making his social commentary. Kasrilevke – the Jewish people – are in a state of anxiety and tension, he is saying; perhaps the Good Old Days were not so bad, after all. Yet, one senses in this man of the Enlightenment a rejection of this thought, also. What Sholom Aleichem is left with is a dilemma. He is a man in between two worlds, rejecting the narrow-minded traditionalism of one and the tradition-less progressivism of the other.

The story of Kasrilevke is the story of the Jewish people; it is their tale, their allegory, and Sholom Aleichem is their chronicler. In these Kasrilevke stories we see the Jewish writer's unique relationship to his subjects. In the disintegration of the world of Kasrilevke Sholom Aleichem saw the collapse of his own world. In a sense, he was writing his own obituary in the Kasrilevke stories, and we can follow the development of them as one might read a recapitulation of someone's life story, from the sentimentally viewed olden times down to the present days, which of course cannot compare.

In any case, Kasrilevke was doomed. The *Haskalah*, the Enlightenment, Progress, call it whatever you want, had been victorious. The Jew was no longer isolated in his private *shtetl* world; Kasrilevke was broken up. The question to be answered next is: where did it go to, what happened to Kasrilevke and the Kasrilevkites?

IV

„WITH GOD'S HELP, I STARVED TO DEATH": THE TEVYE STORIES

Of the endless stream of characters that were produced by the pen and imagination of Sholom Aleichem, one has come to dominate all others in minds of both readers and non-readers of his works. *Tevye der Milkhiger*, Tevye the Dairyman, is the central figure of nine loosely connected stories written between 1895 and 1916.[1] And although these nine brief tales represent a mere fraction of Sholom Aleichem's works, Tevye stands out from all of his creations as the singularly most unique of all. This position which Tevye enjoys, furthermore, is justified. The Broadway entrepreneurs who singled Tevye out for particular attention in popularizing Sholom Aleichem's works had a fairly penetrating insight into his uniqueness. While still a blood brother to the countless Kasrilevkites of the *shtetl* and a relative by marriage to innumerable others, Tevye is not actually one of them. In geographic fact, he is not a townsman, but rather a villager, a resident of Anatevka, a rural community on the outskirts of Kasrilevke.[2]

But more important than his birthplace is Tevye's character, the essence of the man. Sholom Aleichem develops him in a fashion which exposes facets of his individuality which set him apart from all the other more or less stereotyped Jewish tradesmen, *schlemihls* saints, draft dodgers, and assorted sinners who normally occupy Sholom Aleichem's stage. With Tevye it was as if the author paused for a moment to say: Let me give this Jew an opportunity to show himself. To this, his creator added a most interesting histo-

---

[1] See Mrs. Waife-Goldberg's explanation of the translation, *My Father, Sholom Aleichem*, 144.
[2] In Germany, productions of *Fiddler on the Roof* are called *Anatevka*.

rical component. He placed Tevye at a cross-road in history; Tevye's world is disintegrating around him, and Sholom Aleichem forces Tevye to confront this fact.

Tevye, above all, has his God, and in order to understand him, the reader must understand their relationship, which to be sure was not unique to Tevye among Jews. As Frances Butwin has stated: "God is not a remote Deity to whom one prays on Sabbaths and High Holy Days or in times of great trouble. He is not the Lawgiver to whom Moses spoke amidst thunder and lightening on Mount Sinai. Tevye is on much more intimate terms with God...Tevye himself wages his own war against God and man, and since he believes that man's actions were chiefly inspired by God, God is the chief Adversary."[3] This intimacy has been a hall-mark of the Jewish common man of Eastern Europe for centuries, an intimacy bred out of misery, despair, and the sense that things are not quite in order, therefore let us talk man-to-God. But this easy familiarity with the Divinity in no way effects Tevye's adherence to orthodoxy. Tevye would rather die than miss reciting his daily prayers. "He would much prefer wrestling with a difficult question of Talmudic interpretation than hauling his milk cans from house to house. Indeed, his religion is, ironically, the source of both his great personal inner strength as well as the humor which emanates from his nature. For Tevye considers himself a scholar of sorts, a self-educated and eminently wise scholar-milkman who drops a quotation from a learned book almost at every step, and then follows up with a practical application to the thorniest problem in such a way as to simplify matters for the least learned of men. The humor emerges because Tevye is almost always wrong in his interpretation. What one encounters repeatedly is an elegant and profound Hebrew phrase from Scripture or Talmud, followed by a delightfully incorrect paraphrase into Yiddish which then demonstrates for Tevye's particular situation a singular relevance. He is never at a loss, always ready with an incorrect phrase, always ready to demonstrate the depths of his learning. For Tevye, pride

---

[3] *The Tevye Stories and Others*, trans. Julius and Frances Butwin, introduction by Frances Butwin (New York: Pocket Books, Inc., 1965), xvii.

comes only with learning. Money, property, status in the community, they all have their place in the hierarchy, and Tevye is frank to admit this. But ultimately he has respect only for men with wisdom and erudition, and Tevye at least *thinks* that these qualities represent him most clearly.

Tevye's life is rooted in this traditional, emotional, and personal relationship with the God of Israel and His Law. He is one of the Hassidim, which provides Tevye with the additional latitude of closeness to his Maker which the followers of the Baal Shem Tov enjoyed. Yet, he is rigidly rabbinical in his adherence to the letter of the Law, although none of these strict rules and regulations interfere with Tevye's fundamental humanity and tolerance. He is quite capable of telling a fellow Jew who has fallen away from the Law: "Sit down. You can say grace or not, just as you please. I'm not God's watchman. I won't be punished for your sins."[4] But Tevye can bend only so much, and when one of his daughters flees to marry a gentile youth, Tevye disowns her and no protestations on anyone's part can move him an inch from his resolve.[5] She is dead, and there is no questioning by Tevye. Sholom Aleichem did not create a superman in Tevye; his reactions are always honest and emotional.

Although written over a period of approximately twenty years, there is a distinct unity about the nine stories. They form loosely connected episodes from the same single work, and there can be little doubt, from an analysis of form as well as content, that Sholom Aleichem conceived of the Tevye stories as a single narrative. Each begins with Tevye running into Sholom Aleichem somewhere between Yehupetz, Kasrilevke, Boiberik, and Anatevka. They greet each other warmly, and Tevye, in his rambling fashion, passes the time of day, fills his listener in on peripheral information, past and recent history, and finally gets to the point: his most recent catastrophe. The main point of each of these stories, of all of the Tevye stories for that matter, is how Tevye reacts to these catastrophes and to his times.

---

[4] "Hodel", in *The Tevye Stories and Others*, 43.
[5] "Chava", in *The Tevye Stories and Others*, 61–75.

1. "TEVYE WINS A FORTUNE"

"'All-powerful and All-merciful, great and good, kind and just, how does it happen that to some people you give everything and to others nothing?'"[6] This is the mood in which Tevye confronts his readers in the first of the stories. It is one of skepticism, even though when he meets "Mr. Sholom Aleichem" on the road, Tevye appears as a prosperous butter-and-egg man. Only until recently, he had been "starving with God's help" as a wretched drayman, hauling just enough wood to keep himself, his wife Golde, and his seven daughters in rags. But now things are different: "Take my word for it, the story is worth hearing. I'll sit down for a little while near you here on the grass. Let the horse do a little nibbling meanwhile. After all, even a horse is one of God's living creatures."

Tevye's story is one of despair and continual hope. "A Jew must always hope, must never lose hope. And in the meantime, what if we waste away to a shadow? For that we are Jews – the Chosen People, the envy and admiration of the world." Tevye, in terms of his economic status, had been thoroughly dissatisfied with God's handling of the situation, and had told him so. As he is driving his miserable horse through the woods one morning, he laments his plight, while preparing himself for the morning prayer. Suddenly he encounters two mysterious figures in the forest, who turn out to be young women who are members of a family staying in one of the vacation villas, "one elderly with a silk shawl on her head and the other a younger one with a *sheitel*, both flushed and out of breath".[7] They want to return to Boiberik. Tevye plays the reluctant knight, and grudgingly volunteers to drive the vacationers, who got lost while walking in the woods, back to their summer house. On the journey of a few miles, Tevye ruminates about his fate, about the possibility that the two travelers might be evil spirits, and only far back in his thoughts does there linger the possibility that he might pick up a few kopeks for his troubles.

[6] "Tevye Wins a Fortune", *The Tevye Stories and Others*, 135.
[7] *Sheitel*: a wig worn by orthodox women after marriage.

When he deposits the women at an impressive *dacha* in Boiberik, he is showered with ruble notes by the grateful relatives. As he sweeps the money into his pockets, Tevye exclaims: "May God give you everything you desire ten times over. May you have all that is good, nothing but joy. And now good night, and good luck, and God be with you. With you and your children and grandchildren and all your relatives." As if by magic, Tevye's life has been transformed, thanks to the unexpected generosity of a wealthy family on summer vacation. One of the ladies also contributes a cow which for some reason has gone dry. With his money bulging from his pockets, Tevye leaps into his cart and drives his exhausted nag back to the misery of Tevye's family.

The contrast between Tevye's high spirits and his wife's depression and bitterness are heightened, when Golde thinks that her husband might be drunk. Golde emerges immediately as the fully developed Jewish matriarch, who even in poverty adheres to her role. Her marriage with Tevye had been arranged. Her primary concern is a very pragmatic one: how to provide husbands for seven daughters, no easy task even for a rich man. She has worked as hard as her husband, while not having had the consolation of the Talmud, which traditionally had been closed to Jewish women, and Golde's bitterness can best be understood in respect to this role. For Tevye, his efforts at gathering knowledge and understanding of the Law are admirable in the eyes of the community. A woman who attempts this runs the risk of social condemnation. "A woman is not supposed to have learning, and to the extent that she achieves it her Jewishness may be impaired."[8] So Golde, like thousands of her female counterparts down through the ages of the Jewish communities of Eastern Europe, has had to fulfill a very limited role within the family structure. Strangely enough, this isolation in the home had given her a good deal of strength, in that at least there, she was supreme. She gathered her strength from her home and from her responsibility of keeping a clean, Jewish living place for her family. Her husband might be king in the synagogue, but at home, she was queen. This accounts, in part, for Golde's

---

[8] Zborowski and Herzog, *Life is with People*, 80.

apparent harshness with her husband when he returns from his visit with the *shayne Yidn*, the 'beautiful', i.e. well-to-do, proper Jews of Boiberik. She has never been provided with enough material things by Tevye to do justice to her concept of what a Jewish home should be. All of this disappointment is apparent from the first words they exchange, as Tevye bolts through the door of the wretched hut: "'Good evening!', said I. 'Congratulations, Mazel-tov, Golde!' 'A black and endless mazel-tov to you! What are you so happy about, my beloved bread-winner? Are you coming from a wedding or a circumcision – my goldspinner?' And she lets me have it – all the curses she knows – as only a woman can." The distraught, harassed Golde is metamorphosed by the sight of the money and foodstuffs that Tevye suddenly dumps on the table. Their treasure consists of thirty-seven rubles and a cow, for Tevye more money and possessions than he has ever had in his life. After some deliberations and discussions between the two of them, a decision is reached: Tevye will go into the dairy business. He now brings his listener up-to-date: "So we make a living... May the two of us be blessed by the Lord as often as I am stopped on the road by important people from Yehupetz – even Russians – who beg me to bring them what I can spare. 'We have heard, Tevel, that you are an upright man, even if you are a Jewish dog...' Now, how often does a person get a compliment like that? Do our own people ever praise a man? No, all they ever do is envy him."

And so, Tevye has taken a giant step out of the medievalism of his recent past. As if by magic, he has been transported into the modern day, he has become a man of some prominence in the community, adding the *yikhus* of money to the *yikhus* of learning, which among his peers at least, seemed considerable, in both respects. This first Tevye story is crucial for this reason alone, that Tevye's orientation to his environment is radically changed by his financial situation, and as it improves, his life will become more complicated. Sholom Aleichem puts Tevye within the framework of the *homo economicus*, for the story concerns itself with, for the most part, Tevye's sudden economic prosperity and the accompanying improvement of his family life. The fringe benefits of the story are considerable. Golde, the Jewish wife, frustrated and embittered; the *negidim* of Boiberik, whose table scraps provide Tevye and his family with a treasure, and whose loose change set him up in business and alter his entire life; the central importance of religion in Tevye's life. These are the bits of background on which Sholom Aleichem continued to paint.

2. "THE BUBBLE BURSTS"

Yidishe ashires iz vi shney in merts: Jewish wealth is like snow in March. And so it was with Tevye, as he relates to his friend Sholom Aleichem the reasons for his most recent downfall. They all add up to one thing: Tevye's greed for a fast buck. It seems his dairy business prospered sufficiently for him to save up a few hundred rubles and while contemplating a safe and secure investment, he encounters one day in Yehupetz a man who occupies in Sholom Aleichem's world a place at least as prominent as Tevye:

'Sholom Aleichem, Reb Tevye', I hear a voice right in back of me. I turn around and take a look. I could swear I have seen this man somewhere before. 'Aleichem Sholom', I answer, 'And where do you hail from?' 'Where do I hail from? From Kasrilevke. I am a relative of yours. That is, your wife Golde is my second cousin once removed.' 'Hold on!' I say. 'Aren't you Boruch-Hersh Leah-Dvoshe's son-in-law?' 'You've hit the nail right on the head', he says. 'I am Boruch-Hersh Leah-Dvoshe's son-in-law and my wife is Sheina Sheindel Boruch-Hersh Leah-Dvoshe's daughter. Now do you know who I am?' 'Wait,', I say. 'Your mother-in law's grandmother Sarah-Yenta, and my wife's aunt, Fruma-Zlata, were, I believe, first cousins, and if I am not mistaken, you are the middle son-in-law of Boruch-Hersh Leah-Dvoshe's. But I forgot what they call you. Your name has flown right out of my head. Tell me, what is your name?' 'My name', he says, 'is Menachem-Mendel Boruch-Hersh Leah-Dvoshe's. That's what they call me back home, in Kasrilevke.'[9]

---

[9] "The Bubble Bursts", in *The Tevye Stories and Others*, 3. Jewish family names, until the eighteenth century, derived from the traditional Hebrew custom of taking the father's first name ("son of"). It became so complicated in the Jewish communities of nineteenth-century Russia that it was necessary to drag in as many first names as possible to be able to identify someone, such as Menachem-Mendel in this case.

Enter Menachem-Mendel, the *luftmensh*, the Jewish entrepreneur, who runs his business out of a telephone booth, while keeping one step ahead of the authorities. As *luftmensh* implies, Menachem-Mendel and his kind are made of air, as well as left hanging in mid-air. Maurice Samuel describes him as "the apotheosis of Jewish rootlessness. He lives in the midst of shadows, and of the rumour of reality. He rotates at the centre of a whirlwind of telegrams, combinations, commissions, quotations, fees, and cuts. He talks of sterling, of bonds, of international loans, of wars, of threats of war...He is, if we want to go behind the humour of the presentation, a sick man."[10] Menachem-Mendel is a born loser, but Tevye can only discover this by bitter experience. One thing leads to another, and "after we had eaten and said our benedictions, we began talking, each one naturally talking of what concerned him most. I talked about my business, he of his." Tevye, at this stage of his prosperity, is quite taken up with the prospects of potential wealth. He dreams of becoming a benefactor to the community, of building a new synagogue, or a ritual bath. Menachem-Mendel, with his fantastic stories of 'killings' on the Yehupetz stock exchange, seems a short-cut to the realization of this dream. He sees in Menachem-Mendel a perfect mixture of piety and business sense: "With God's help", says Menachem-Mendel, "the money will come pouring in."

And a partnership is struck, with Tevye's capital and Menachem-Mendel's brains. Months after he had made his investment, Tevye has heard nothing from his second cousin, once-removed. Finally, in despair, he goes to Yehupetz to look for Menachem-Mendel. He wanders into the stock market area and encounters a scene of bedlam:

'I can barely push my way through. People are running around like crazy, shouting, waving their hands, quarreling. I hear shouts of '*Putilov*, shares, stocks... he gave me his word...buy on margin...he owes me a fee...spit in his face... I mutter to myself: 'Get out, Tevye, before you get knocked down.' God is our Father, Tevye the Dairyman is a sinner, Yehupetz is a city, and Menachem-Mendel is a breadwinner. So this is where people make fortunes? So this is how they do their business? May God have mercy on you, Tevye, and on such business.'

[10] *The World of Sholom Aleichem*, 256.

Suddenly, reflected in a window, Tevye sees his long-lost partner: "May our worst enemies look the way Menachem-Mendel looked! A corpse laid out for burial looks cheerful by comparison." The poor wretch tells his story, of lost fortunes, of near-misses, and finally comes to the conclusion: he has lost everything. Tevye's reaction at first is not particularly charitable: "For such a deed, for what you have done to me, you deserve to be stretched out right here in the middle of Yehupetz and flogged so hard that you lose consciousness. How can I face my wife, my children? Tell me, you robber, you murderer, you – The fires of hell, the tortures of *Gehenna* are too good for you." But Tevye's outburst was no more than therapeutic, and soon his humanity wins out: "I look at him standing there, the poor *shlimazl*, leaning against the wall, his head bent, his cap awry. He sighs and he groans and my heart turns over with pity."

As he contemplates his brief period as a near-*nogid*, Tevye's philosophical foundation gives him ample support. He admits that he longed to be a rich man, but God felt that it was more important that Tevye should stay as he was: "'You, Tevye', says God, 'stick to your cheese and butter and forget your dreams'. But what about hope? Naturally, the harder life is, the more you must hope. The poorer you are the more cheerful you must be." He parts from Sholom Aleichem, because it is time to get back to work: "I have to tend to my business." This has been Tevye's only association with his relative Menachem-Mendel, the man "who deals in things you can't put your hands on". As yet, Sholom Aleichem has not projected Tevye against the background of his family directly, only indirectly, in that he wants financial gain in order to provide a better life. But certainly in these first two of the Tevye stories, Sholom Aleichem is suggesting more strongly the economic aspects of Tevye's life, to be sure in a socio-religious framework. It is this unique combination of economics and religion that give the world of Tevye, and even Menachem-Mendel, this peculiar quality. Money is made in God's name. Partnerships are agreed to in the ritual baths.

But Tevye is smart enough to know when he has been burnt, unlike Menachem-Mendel, who will continue to make and lose fortunes "in less time than it takes Tevye to say *Shma Yirosel*".[11] Greed and the possibility of an easy fortune gripped Tevye only this one time. He now turns away from such matters, having discovered for himself what the effects of Capitalism can have on a poor little Jew. Sholom Aleichem makes his point. He exposes Tevye to one of the vices of modern, assimilating civilization, a vice that almost destroyed Sholom Aleichem himself. In his mind, the confrontation between Jew and the stock market could only end in disaster. Tevye discovers this, licks his wounds, and returns to his family for comfort. But Sholom Aleichem is now prepared to extend the forces of civilization into Tevye's home, where he will attempt to make a stand which is doomed to fail.

3. "MODERN CHILDREN"

Sholom Aleichem uses the stories of Tevye's conflicts with his daughters as a representation of Tevye's decreasing control over his world. The problems, the conflicts, increase in their complexities, as well as their seriousness. In "Modern Children" a cherished tradition and a part of Tevye's prerogative as a parent is challenged: the right to arrange his daughters' marriages. One must understand Tevye's responsibility in that marrying off seven daughters is a major task for a man of limited financial means. In terms of the communal ethos, an unmarried girl is just short of a family scandal. Old-maid daughters would be a blight on Tevye's reputation, and with this in mind, one must understand his sense of urgency and excitement when Lazer-Wolf the butcher lets it be known that he is interested in Tevye's daughter Tzeitl.

In spite of the financial tragedy with Menachem-Mendel ("May his name and memory be forever blotted out"), Tevye is still in the butter-and-milk business and remains a person of some eminence in the community. "And besides, with God's help, I'm not the same Tevye I used to be. Now the best match, even in Yehupetz,

---

[11] Frances Butwin, "Introduction", *The Tevye Stories and Others*, xiv. *Shma Yisroel*: the initial words of the Old Testament's most significant confession of faith (Deut. vi. 4), trans. 'Hear, o Israel'.

is not beyond my reach."[12] Tevye has also talked himself into accepting Lazer-Wolf as a son-in-law, even though the butcher is his own contemporary:

> He had children as old as she was. But then I reminded myself: what a lucky thing for her. She'll have everything she wants. And if he is not so good looking? There were other things besides looks. There was only one thing I really had against him: he could barely read his prayers. But then, can everyone be a scholar? There are plenty of wealthy men in Anatevka, in Mazapevka, and even in Yehupetz who don't know one letter from another. Just the same, if it's their luck to have a little money they get all the respect and honor a man could want.

A good match, then, for Tevye is one which provides financial security for his daughter. He admits that ultimately learning is fine, but a silver samovar is better. In the wedding agreement between Tevye and the widowed Lazer-Wolf there are two aspects which dramatize the changeability of the life-style in Tevye's world. The first involves the procedure through which the two men come to an understanding. Lazer-Wolf told Tzeitl directly that she should have her father come by for a talk. Lazer-Wolf himself in passing comments on this unusual method: "You know, Reb Tevye, that I have been a widower for quite a while now. So I thought, why do I have to go looking all over the world, get mixed up with matchmakers, those sons of Satan?" This circumvention of the *shadchen*, the marriage broker and matchmaker, indicates to what extent the classical pattern of the *shtetl* had already changed. Even the older generation seems to be revolting against what had been a fairly rigid social rule. Then, after the marriage had been agreed to, Tevye adds almost in passing, as he suggests that they need not rush: "Besides, there's Tzeitl herself to be asked", to which Lazer-Wolf replies, somewhat in astonishment, "What foolishness! Is this something to ask about? *Tell* her, Reb Tevye. Go home, tell her what is what, and get the wedding canopy ready!" In the traditional arranged Jewish marriage, the bride's consent was never required. It was quite normal for a young man just confirmed, *bar-mitzvahed* at age thirteen, to be told by his parents, "Congra-

---

[12] "Modern Children", in *The Tevye Stories and Others*, 16.

tulations, you're engaged!" to an equally young adolescent whom he had never seen. In Sholom Aleichem, there are some painfully hysterical stories of meetings between such children, where the young groom is tested on the spot by his prospective father-in-law in matters of *Torah*, is found wanting and finds himself shipped back home with a rejection notice in his hand! Quite clearly, Sholom Aleichem found the traditional procedure unsatisfactory. A marriage for love was a privilege only given to the very poor.[13] But Tevye's instincts go beyond the communal into parenthood. Besides being a traditional Jewish patriarch, he is also a loving father. He, unlike many before him, *will* ask his daughter. In fact, he is much more understanding than Golde, who, when she is told of the match by Tevye, immediately sets to work, even before he can finish reciting a passage from the *Talmud*: "Don't bother me with your passages. We've got to get ready for the wedding. First, make a list for Lazer-Wolf of all the things Tzeitl will need. She doesn't have a stitch of underwear, not even a pair of stockings." Golde is happy that Tzeitl will have the material needs taken care of, and she never thinks that Tzeitl might not be satisfied with the match. As we might have expected, Tzeitl throws herself weeping on Tevye and begs him to call off the wedding. He tries the best psychology he knows: the guilt gambit. "So it was not meant that we should have a little joy in our old age, after all our hard work, harnessed, you might say, day and night to a wheelbarrow. No happiness. Only poverty and misery and bad luck over and over..." But Tzeitl's tears are too much for Tevye, and he relents, with some mild bitterness, at the loss for himself as well as for his daughter. But his trouble is compounded by the appearance of another suitor for Tzeitl's hand, Motel Kamzoil, a young impoverished tailor, who happens also to be Tzeitl's choice. He appears before Tevye as a matchmaker, and Tevye listens patiently, until Kamzoil announces who the suitor is – himself: "When he said that I jumped up from the ground as if I had been scalded, and he jumped too, and there we were, facing each other like bristling roosters. 'Either you're crazy', I said to him, 'or simply out of your mind! What are you

---

[13] See Zborowski and Herzog, 271.

everything? The matchmaker, the bridegroom, the ushers all rolled into one? I suppose you'll play the wedding march too! I never heard of such a thing – arranging a match for oneself!'" But this is not all. It seems that Motel and Tzeitl had agreed to their engagement a year earlier. Tevye is crushed on two accounts, one having to do with his *Yikhus*, the other with his pride as head of the family. "How does a stitcher like Motel fit into the picture as my son-in-law?" Later, when Golde is told of the state of things, she responds in the same way as her husband: "A *tailor*! Where does a tailor come into our family?" In terms of the village hierarchy, Motel's profession is very near the bottom. It is an embarassment to Tevye to have his daughter marry a lowly tailor. Secondly, the secret engagement stuns him and his sense of tradition. He challenges Motel: "I ask him bluntly, 'Do I still have the right to say something about my daughter, or doesn't anyone have to ask a father anymore?'" Tevye is puzzled and hurt. "What did they mean – pledging their troth? What kind of world has this become? A boy meets a girl and says to her, 'Let us pledge our troth.' Why, it's just too free-and-easy, that's all?" Yet, Tevye's own attitude is sufficiently different from that of his forefathers, who would have driven Motel out of the village with a cane. Instead, he sighs and begins to figure out a way to convince Golde that the young lovers should have their way. Tevye finally resorts to an old biblical ruse, the interpretation of a dream, in this case, to take advantage of Golde's traditional Jewish sense of superstition. He awakes from an apparent nightmare to gasp out that he had received a visitation from Golde's grandmother and Lazer-Wolf's first wife, urging Tevye, he tells Golde, to break the engagement between Tzeitl and the butcher. This is all Golde has to hear. Tevye's act has been perfectly convincing, and Lazer-Wolf is informed in due course. There could be no criticism of Tevye for his action within the community. After all, such a dream would be considered to be of major significance.

The problem is solved. The ending is happy. Motel and Tzeitl become happily contented young "marrieds" of the village, living in poverty, but joining Tevye and Golde within the traditional structure of the Jewish family. This will be the last time that matters work out satisfactorily for Tevye. His world was challenged, a tradition broken, but no matter. A young Jewish couple nonetheless continued functioning in a world which Tevye could find acceptable. The generation conflict was overcome, Tevye's sense of status in the hierarchy did not negatively affect his choice of a groom for his daughter, and he overcame his need for financial security to permit his daughter to marry for love. Tevye is permitted by Sholom Aleichem a final reprieve before the inevitable catastrophe.

4. "HODEL"

Once again, Sholom Aleichem frames the tragedy of Tevye's world in a love story, this time involving his daughter Hodel, who "can write and can read – Yiddish and Russian both. And books – she swallows like dumplings. You may be wondering how a daughter of Tevye happens to be reading books, while her father deals in butter and cheese? That's what I'd like to know myself..."[14] Tevye then goes off on a diatribe about education for Jews in Czarist Russia. Even though not permitted in schools, Jewish youth wander off to the big cities, finding a place in the schools, in the universities, starving, but educating themselves. He cannot understand this zeal for worldly learning, but underneath is a great admiration for these young people. He is particularly impressed with a young man whom he picks up one day on the road, Pertschik, the son of a local cigarette maker. Pertschik studies at the university, is one of the breed of young radical intellectuals, who, when Tevye humorously compares his dress to that of the Yehupetz rich, explodes angrily: "Don't you dare compare me with them! They can go to hell as far as I care!" This sort of outburst is totally uncharacteristic of Sholom Aleichem's characters, who may have no love for the rich, but are not given to passionate expressions like Pertschik's. Sholom Aleichem, however, deals Tevye a short hand in regard to understanding his young friend. He never permits him to see what he obviously is telling the reader:

---

[14] "Hodel", in *The Tevye Stories and Others*, 41.

There was only one thing I didn't like about him, and that was the way he had of suddenly disappearing... He had the wildest notions, the most peculiar ideas. Everything was upside down, topsy-turvy. For instance, according to his way of thinking, a poor man was far more important than a rich one, and if he happened to be a worker too, then he was really the brightest jewel in the diadem! He who toiled with his hands stood first in his estimation.

Quite clearly, Pertschik is an active revolutionary, one of the countless university students who were involved in subversive activities against the Czarist regime, Tevye, for all his self-proclaiming wisdom, is ignorant of the outside world, unaware of what is going on beyond the walls of his village. He invites Pertschik to help tutor his daughters, and the inevitable happens: Pertschik and Hodel fall in love, and in the 'modern fashion', announce their betrothal to Tevye, who takes the news with some shock, but also tolerance: "When was the contract signed? And why didn't you invite me to the ceremony? Don't you think I have a slight interest in the matter? I joke with them and yet my heart is breaking." As if to really bury the traditional Jewish life, the young couple completely foresake the social ritual of the Jewish wedding and honeymoon. Pertschik is in a rush. He must be off to some mysterious destination. A couple hours after what Tevye, with considerable bitter irony, calls "this wonderful wedding", Pertschik takes the train out of town. For the second time, Tevye must deceive his wife: "She kept plaguing me: what were they in such a hurry about? Go try to explain their haste to a woman. But don't worry – I invented a story, *great, powerful*, and *marvelous*, as the Bible says, about a rich aunt in Yehupetz, an inheritance, all sorts of foolishness." There is something fundamentally disturbing about this relationship between Tevye and Golde, in which the husband is forced into a deception, in order to make the truth acceptable. Meanwhile, Tevye still has no idea as to Pertschik's activities. He suggests to Hodel that perhaps she has fallen in with a band of thieves, and the newly married daughter bursts out laughing. The laughter turns bitter when Hodel tells her father, first that Pertschik has been arrested and sent to jail, and then, that she must join him in exile, probably in Siberia. For Tevye, the loss of a daughter is a tragedy beyond description, even a loss merely to exile in Siberia. At the departure, the family weeps, and Tevye has to ask his listener, Mr. Sholom Aleichem, to forgive him, for shedding a tear even now, in the telling of the story. But Tevye closes the story on a grimly hilarious note: "And now, let's talk about more cheerful things. Tell me, what news is there about the cholera in Odessa?"

For Tevye, the tragedy is twofold. Besides losing his daughter, he betrays his own ignorance of the forces which surround him. He is incapable of understanding youth's commitment, nor the struggle in which they find themselves. Sholom Aleichem, while contending with what is uniquely a Jewish environment, is dealing with an experience which is clearly universal. The generation conflict, for all the misuse and abuse which the term has enjoyed, is never more graphically treated than in this story of Hodel's transcending her father's world. She has moved up and beyond Tevye's frame of reference, out of his religious sphere, into a secular one where the issues are less man's relationship to his God than man's relationship to his fellow man. Without Tevye's assistance (but also without his hindrance), Hodel has educated herself as to the problems of modern Russia. Most tragically, she has done this without her father's awareness, even though he perceives the process of her self-education with some pride. The greatest tragedy for the reader revolves around the nature of the father-daughter alienation even after Hodel joins her husband in exile, for Tevye at the very end cannot understand what has happened to him or to his world. His pride has turned to pain, but pain without understanding.

5. "CHAVA"

It would appear to be no accident that "Chava" stands at the middle of the Tevye stories, for in terms of tension and importance within the social and moral structure of Tevye's world, there can be no more significant theme than that of the child who marries out of Judaism. "To leave the great community of *Klal Isroel* (all of Israel), that is, to renounce the faith of the fathers, is the ultimate sin...It is a social as well as a religious offense, since withdrawal is always felt as a hostile act."[15] Chava's decision to marry the gentile youth Fyedka signifies, in Tevye's understanding of the act, that she is no longer among the living. Indeed, after the decision has been made by Chava, Tevye returns to Golde and informs her, '"Get up, my wife, take off your shoes, and let us sit down and mourn our child as God has commanded'... I told everyone at home to consider Chava dead. There was no more Chava. Her name had been blotted out."[16]

Yet, in none of the other *Tevye* stories is Tevye made to appear as inflexible, as unyielding as in "Chava". Of course, the threat of apostasy, as I have suggested, is perhaps the greatest that can exist in the Jewish community, and Sholom Aleichem is not defending Chava's act. But Tevye's own relationship to Chava's act of conversion, her decision to abandon her family in favor of her husband-to-be, this becomes more significant, as Sholom Aleichem develops the relationships of the characters. "Your child is reaching out for a different world, and you don't understand her, or else you don't wish to understand her", says the priest, to whom Chava has fled. Tevye's fear of this rational priest is mortal, and he replies to the priest's efforts at discussion with rebukes and insults: "'I've never seen his family tree. But I'm sure he must be descended from a long and honorable line. His father must have been either a shepherd or a janitor, or else just a plain drunkard.'" To be sure, all of Tevye's actions in regard to the priest must be seen in the light of a low-yield hysteria, until Chava makes the final decision, at which time Tevye's pent-up frustration explodes on his poor horse: "I found him with one leg twisted around the block of wood. I took a stick and began laying it into him, as if I were going to strip off his skin and break his bones in half. 'May you burn alive, you *shlimazl*. You can starve to death before I give you as much as an oat. Tortures I will give you and anguish and all the ten plagues of Egypt...'" What are the feelings of despair which run through Tevye at that moment? Why would a Jewish parent demonstrate such extraordinary emotion at the betrothal of a child to a gentile?

[15] Zborowski and Herzog, 231.
[16] Tevye is ordering his family to perform the ritual of sitting *shiveh*, the seven days of intensive mourning after the death of a close relative.

Obviously, because of the deep-seated religious experience of Judaism, one intuitively answers. Yet Tevye gives still another reason: "The pain is great, but the disgrace – the disgrace is even greater." Even stronger than the religious implication for Tevye is his own sense of embarrassment – at himself and for the sake of his family reputation. His *Yikhus*, his status in the community, is mortally threatened by her act, and in emphasizing his sense of disgrace, of shame, Tevye places his own image of himself above either the religious importance of Chava's conversion as well as her own happiness.

But the most damaging evidence which Sholom Aleichem presents against Tevye concerns his intellect, which Tevye prides more than anything. For Chava had earlier embarked on a program of self-education, discussing with her father in a theological framework the nature of her feelings. "God created all men equal", she tells her father. Tevye replies with a thoroughly inappropriate quotation, for which he is rebuked by his daughter: "'Marvellous! Unbelievable! You have a quotation for everything! Maybe you also have a quotation which also explains why men have divided themselves up into Jews and gentiles, into lords and slaves, noblemen and beggars?'... And I explained to her that this has been the way of the world since the first day of Creation." Chava's retort: Why has this been the way of the world? Tevye's answer: Because that is the way God created the world. Chava continues: Why did God create the world this way? Tevye tries to cut off the discussion, but Chava persists, until Tevye retreats behind a veil of humor, unable to cope with his daughter's relentless argument: "'But that is why God gave us intellects', she said, 'that we should ask questions.' 'We have an old custom', I told her, 'that when a hen begins to crow like a rooster, we take her away to be slaughtered.'" He dismisses her with a traditional rebuke: the woman's place.

After Chava had taken refuge in the monastery, unable to communicate her feelings to her father, the family goes into mourning for the 'dead' child; but Sholom Aleichem presents his hero with one more opportunity to re-establish some rapport with his fallen-away daughter. While driving his cart along a lonely road outside the village, he looks up and sees Chava: "The same as before, not changed at all, she is even wearing the same dress. My first impulse was to jump off the wagon and take her in my arms. But something held me back. 'What are you, Tevye? A woman? A weakling?' I pulled in my horse's reins. 'Giddap, *shlimazl*.' I tried to go to the right. I look – she is also going to the right. She beckons to me with her hand as though to say, 'Stop a while, I have something to tell you.'" But Tevye does not stop. Chava begs him for a moment of his time, and although the emotions are welling up inside him, he drives his horse on. He leaves her standing there; "Tevye is not a woman", which translates as 'Tevye will not bend to his feelings'. Chava runs after the cart, For a second Tevye is overcome with doubts about his moral position: "And peculiar thoughts came into his mind. What is the meaning of Jew and non-Jew? Why did God create Jews and non-Jews? And since God created Jews and non-Jews why should they be separated from each other, as though one were created by God and the other were not? I regretted that I wasn't as learned as some men so that I could arrive at an answer to the riddle..." But he rides on.

So, Tevye is left with a broken heart and his pride, which gnaw away at him. Even after Chava's final dismissal, and the total rejection which she experiences on the road running after her father, Tevye is unable to reconcile his love for his daughter with the needs of his dignity. There is the smallest edge of guilt in his final remarks to his listener:

Just suppose it should happen – if I tell you this you won't laugh at me? I am afraid you will laugh. But just let us suppose that one fine day I should put on my Sabbath garbardine and stroll over to the railway station as though I was going away on the train, going to see them. I walk up to the ticket window and ask for a ticket. The ticket seller asks me where I want to go. 'To Yehupetz', I tell him. And he says, 'There is no such place.' And I say, 'Well, it's not my fault then'. And I turn myself around and go home again, take off my Sabbath clothes and go back to work.

Tevye almost does not survive this calamity, the worst possible, the loss of a child. At the very end he tells his audience, Sholom Aleichem, "And if you should write, write about something else, not about me. Forget about me. As it is written: '*And he was forgotten*' – No more Tevye the Dairyman!" For Sholom Aleichem's readers, no worse tragedy could befall Tevye than having a child marry out of the faith, so why bother continuing to write about him? It seems that Sholom Aleichem himself must have felt this also, because the conclusion does give the impression of a swan song. Yet, there is little doubt that this is not just the traditional treatment of the age-old Jewish theme of the tragedy of intermarriage. Sholom Aleichem is taking a harder look at the Tevyes, at the older generation, in an effort to comment on their inflexibility. From the treatment, it would seem that Sholom Aleichem, while not making a case in favor of intermarriage and conversion, is however suggesting that the generation conflict is a real factor in the break-up of the traditional Jewish family structure. In Tevye's case, Sholom Aleichem suggests that the father is primarily at fault, not the children. Tevye does not communicate with anyone, certainly not with Golde. In the matter of Chava's marriage to Fyedka, of her expulsion from the family and the community, Tevye does not ask, he instructs. Although he is normally concerned about Golde's fury and anger at him and gives the impression of hen-peckedness, when the crunch actually comes, he assumes the role of dictatorial patriarch. There is no dialogue, no consultation, only Tevye's command.

In the frame of reference of the other stories, "Chava" is the most tragic, because of Tevye's own active role in it. He is a prime mover, not a passive participant, and his decision to reject his daughter is the crucial one. Within the development of almost a thousand years of ghetto existence, Tevye had no other choice. Yet Sholom Aleichem makes us take a good hard look at the problem, and does not suggest that there is any obvious decision or solution.

6. "SCHPRINTZE"

From this point on, the Tevye stories represent an after-thought. Each succeeding tale shows the strain of attempting to continue the role of the character, but there is no longer personal involvement;

the events take over, and Tevye goes along for the ride. In "Schprintze" Sholom Aleichem throws Tevye into the most uncomfortable of Jewish themes: rich Jew versus poor Jew, *shayne Yidn* and *proste yidn*.

Even the times are more uncomfortably out of joint than in the earlier stories. In the wake of the Constitution of 1905 a vigorous wave of anti-Semitism sent the Jews of the Pale into a panic. "And such a panic overtook our rich people that they began leaving Yehupetz in droves, running off abroad, supposedly for their health, for mineral baths, salt water cures, nerves and other such nonsense."[17] This brought them, these Jewish *nouveau riche* who had left the *shtetl*, back to it, to Tevye's environment. What they bring with them, Sholom Aleichem relates, is trouble. One of the children of the rich, Aarontchick, is taken with Tevye's daughter Schprintze. Tevye, who delivers milk to Aarontchick's widowed mother, is flattered by the attention of the young man, and even invites him to his home. Tevye is touched by the mother's plight: what to do with a wild son without a father. Answers and solutions are Tevye's strong point, and he suggests to her that a few biblical quotations could solve the problem of upbringing. Indeed, it was at such a session that Aarontchick met Schprintze. Tevye, unwittingly, had arranged for the forthcoming tragedy. Soon Aarontchick asks Tevye permission to court his daughter. Tevye is perfectly aware of the status problem: "What kind of bridegroom would you make my Schprintze? And what kind of match is she for you? And most important of all, what kind of relative-by-marriage will I be to your mother?" Tevye wavers and hesitates, unable to come to any solution, until he receives a call from the widow to come to her home immediately, where he meets "a short, round barrel of a man, with a sparse little beard and a heavy gold chain around his stomach": Aarontchik's uncle, summoned by telegram to clear the matter up with one question of Tevye: "I am asking you how much this affair will cost us?". The *shayne Yidn*, the status-through-money Jews of the big city, try to buy off Tevye, scorning his pathetic *yikhus* derived from his learning, his erudition which

---

[17] "Schprintze", in *The Tevye Stories and Others*, 76.

to them is meaningless. He is attacked at the very center of his strength, his pride as a Jew. Tevye walks away in silence, unable to speak.

Schprintze's response, within the traditional Judaic sphere of action, is almost inconceivable. She drowns herself. It is difficult to account for her suicide in terms of her personality, for she is the least 'developed' of Tevye's daughters. She never speaks for herself, demonstrates no particularly modern attitudes, and in general remains a shadow figure throughout the brief story. In the other stories of Tevye's daughters, the author's spontaneity of characterization was remarkable. Each of the girls quickly assumed a unique identity which gave the conflict with Tevye the essential edge which was necessary. In the case of Schprintze, however, whose actions more than those of any of her sisters need some definite justification, Sholom Aleichem leaves the reader with a one-dimensional portrait.

Tevye is growing old. He no longer fits into the Jewish community around him. His daughters are marrying and dying. His own tragedy is becoming a burden to the reader, possibly even to his patient listener, Sholom Aleichem. Tevye now sees himself as a modern Job, and constantly reminds God that He is going out of His way to make Tevye suffer. One gets the feeling that perhaps the author is looking for some way to dispose of the old Dairyman. In the next story, a rich son-in-law finds the answer: "Old Jews are always eager to go to Palestine."[18]

7. "TEVYE GOES TO PALESTINE"

"You are looking at me, sir, as though you didn't recognize me. It's me, your faithful old friend, Tevye." This is the greeting with which Tevye meets Sholom Aleichem, as he attempts to explain to his friend his elegant dress and prosperous appearance. It seems Tevye is off to Palestine, which occasions his story of his daughter Beilke.

---

[18] "Tevye Goes to Palestine", in *The Tevye Stories and Others*, 104.

His wife Golde had died, wasted away with the tragedies of her children. Tevye is now alone with his youngest daughter Beilke, "pure goodness all the way through", who cares constantly for Tevye and takes care of his every need. In order to secure a peaceful old age for her father, Beilke is willing to be courted by a prospective candidate of Ephraim the Matchmaker, "a plum, a prize, the pick of the lot. He's a winner, a goldspinner, a rich man, a millionaire. He's a contractor, and his name is Padhatzur." From the beginning Tevye is reluctant to hand his child over to this vulgar businessman, and even after the engagement he urges her to reconsider, knowing that Beilke herself does not love Padhatzur. He reminds her of Hodel, who writes from exile that she is poor but happy. Beilke explodes back: "Don't compare me with Hodel. Hodel grew up in a time when the whole world rocked on its foundations, when it was ready at any moment to turn upside down. In those days people were concerned about the world and forgot about themselves. Now that the world is back to where it was, people think about themselves and forget about the world." Beilke is reflecting the post-Constitution *malaise* of the Russian middle-class who quickly realized that the high-spirited optimism of the Czar's democratic proclamations was a sham, and when the reaction set in soon after 1905, they were crushed. Beilke is a child of this generation, a generation of broken, pessimistic spirits.

The marriage takes place, and the young couple honeymoon in "Nitaly", as Tevye calls it. Padhatzur is indeed a rich man, but he is the epitome of everything that Sholom Aleichem had come to detest in the *nouveau riche* Jew. He is pretentious, a glutton, "makes up his own jokes and laughs at them". Beilke is miserable, but tries to explain her husband to her father; he was the son of a nobody:

Now that he was rich he wanted the honor of entertaining important people in his home, and to that end he was pouring out thousands of rubles, handing out charity in all directions. But money, it seems, isn't everything. You have to have family and background as well. He was willing to go to any length to prove that he wasn't a nobody, he boasted that he was descended from the great Padhatzurs, that his father was a celebrated contractor too. 'Though he knows', she said, 'quite well, and he knows that I know that his father was only a poor fiddler. And on top of that he keeps telling everyone that his wife's father is a millionaire.'

Which is why Padhatzur wants Tevye 'out of the picture', and urges him to go to Palestine, all expenses paid, for the rest of his life. Tevye, in his conversations with Padhatzur, tries to relate his current plight to Talmudic traditions, but the rich man interrupts him: "I will tell you the honest truth. I have never studied *Gamorah* and I wouldn't recognize it if I saw it."[19] He does not care about such traditions, he only knows that he cannot tolerate the presence of his father-in-law as a dairyman when his house is visited by Rothschilds, Brodskys, and other such people.

Tevye turns bitter toward his daughter. He thinks fondly of Hodel: "The one isn't worthy of lighting the oven for the other..." As a final gesture toward his exiled daughter and son-in-law, he makes it a condition of his own exile that Padhatzur arrange for Pertschik's release, which he does under one condition – that they go from Siberia straight to Japan!

And so, Tevye becomes a stranger in his own land. There is a terribly touching parting from his faithful horse, and one final burst of dark humor, as Tevye, shortly before his departure, runs into Ephraim the Matchmaker, who had arranged only recently the marriage of his own daughter, for which Tevye wishes him much rejoicing. "I am rejoicing in it now. My son-in-law turned out to be a crook. He beat up my daughter, took the few guldens away and ran off to America." The matchmaker is also out of place, unable even to practice his profession, a failure to himself and to his loved ones.

There can be no doubt that this was to be still another 'final' Tevye story. There is an emotional ending, with Tevye, an old man, leaving his home, selling his possessions, and saying goodbye to the grave of his wife:

You wonder at the tears in my eyes, Mr. Sholom Aleichem... I am weeping for everybody and everything. I shall miss my horse and my farm, and I shall miss the mayor and the police sergeant, the summer

---

[19] Gamorah: Part of the Talmud which deals with interpretation and discussion of the law as presented in the collection of **Oral Law**.

people of Boiberik, the rich people of Yehupetz, and I shall miss Ephraim the Matchmaker, may a plague take him... When God brings me safely to the place where I am going, I do not know what will finally become of me, but one thing is clear in my mind – that first of all I shall visit the grave of mother Rachel. There I shall offer a prayer for my children whom I shall probably never see again and at the same time I will keep in mind Ephraim the Matchmaker, as well as yourself and all of Israel. Let us shake hands on that, and go your way in good health and give my blessings to everyone and bid everyone a kind farewell for me. And may all go well with you.

Like Tevye, Sholom Aleichem was being driven out of his own land as well. Like Tevye, he experienced the cynicism of the post-1905 world in Czarist Russia and the exploiters like Padhatzur. No doubt Sholom Aleichem felt that this was an opportune time to put Tevye to rest, to have him depart for the Hold Land and for a vague but tranquil death. As Sholom Aleichem bade goodbye to Russia, he said goodbye to Tevye forever – he thought.

8. "GET THEE OUT"

The final two Tevye stories are regrettably commercial sequels which neither do justice to Tevye or his creator. One can only suggest that Sholom Aleichem fell victim to the same pressures that forced other writers to resuscitate a serialized character who would have been better left alone.[20] Even Tevye is a little embarrassed when he meets Mr. Sholom Aleichem again on the streets of some unnamed *shtetl* near Yehupetz: "You seem to be looking at me strangely. You seem to be hesitating and wondering. 'Is it he, or isn't it he?' It is he, Mr. Sholom Aleichem, your old friend. It is he, in person." Tevye's recounting of recent events gives sufficient reason why he never made it to Palestine, for Padhatzur, who made a fortune as a war (Russian—Japanese) profiteer, lost everything, abandoned his creditors, and fled to America with his wife, a fugitive from justice. "In other words, he ran off to America. That's

---

[20] There are numerous anecdotes which deal with Arthur Conan Doyle's efforts to kill off Sherlock Holmes, so that he might go on to other literary subjects. But the popular voice insisted on a living Holmes, not a dead one.

where all the unhappy souls go, and that's where they went."[21] Misery has brought Tevye some responsibility, for Tzeitl's husband Motel Kamzoil, has died from tuberculosis, and Tevye cares for the family. But the story Tevye tells Sholom Aleichem is not one of daughters, or of being treated badly by his fellow Jews. For as Tevye says, "it was in the days of Mendel Beiliss, when Mendel Beiliss became our scapegoat and was made to suffer the punishments of the damned".[22] Tevye is forced to flee his native village as a wave of anti-Semitism sweeps Russia, after the failure of the 1905 revolution to bring about reforms. Certainly this is a more than appropriate theme for Sholom Aleichem to be dealing with, but the refinement with which he dealt with the theme in other stories is missing here. Tevye returns home one day to discover a group of peasants gathering in front of his house. They inform him that "we came here, Tevel, because we want to beat you up". Tevye exchanges some good-natured banter with the mob, and the leader apologetically explains the situation: "Everywhere else your people are being massacred, then why should we let you go? So the village council decided to punish you too. But we haven't decided what to do to you. We don't know whether to break a few of your windowpanes and rip your featherbeds, or to set fire to your house and barn and entire homestead." Tevye discusses the matter with them, and they decide he will be given the chance to sell and to clear out. He liquidates his few possessions, gathers up his daughter and grandchildren, but just before he is about to abandon his ancestral home, Tzeitl reminds him of Chava, who still lives nearby. Tevye turns on her: "Why bring Chava up all of a sudden? How many times have I told you that she is dead?" But in a most improbable fashion Chava has decided to leave her husband and re-join her family, now about to be exiled. Tevye relents, since now he has his grandchildren – "a thousand times dearer and more precious than one's own children" — to think of. Without any word of her husband, Chava leaves the village with her father, the returning prodigal. Once again there is a tearful farewell from his listener, as Tevye makes still another exit into the

[21] "Get Thee Out", in *Tevye's Daughters*, trans. Frances Butwin, 260.
[22] See footnote 18, Chapter II.

setting sun. He has no idea where he is off to, and one suspects that neither did Sholom Aleichem. The story has little relation to the previous tales, and there seems to be no other reason for it other than demonstrating Chava's re-admission into the family and the utter stupidity of the Russian peasant, whose treatment is crudely stereotyped by the author.

9. "TEVYE READS THE PSALMS"

It is difficult to agree with Curt Leviant's appraisal of these last stories as demonstrating the growing artistic maturity of Sholom Aleichem.[23] The writer is now consciously writing for the audience that found in the stupid peasants of *Get Thee Out* an agreeable subject, and for the first time, Sholom Aleichem repeats himself. Once again Tevye is confronted by a band of rampaging peasants determined to burn him out, and using his superior knowledge of the Scripture he outwits them, wins a bet, and is saved.

There is no longer even an effort to justify the encounter between Tevye and Mr. Sholom Aleichem. The writer no doubt was getting somewhat self-conscious about the nature of these meetings, and after the last farewell, simply abandoned the form. The story is framed as usual, but Tevye simply begins with a recounting of the events. The peasants, urged on by the authorities, were rampaging and burning out Jewish homes. Sholom Aleichem's indictment is leveled more against the government's deliberate anti-Semitic policies: "They had to satisfy the authorities. They were afraid, lest some official, or some other minor plague would happen to come by – that's why the local gang wanted to show the authorities that they were no different. That they were the sort who would skip a Jew, just like that, without some hint of a pogrom. For otherwise, they wouldn't be able to look the authorities straight in the eye." Just as the tipsy band of peasants is about to pounce on Tevye's home, he grabs hold of a Russian Psalter out of desperation, and says that the decision whether to beat him up or not will be found in this book, holy to all of them. The peasants agree to a

---

[23] In *Old Country Tales*, 25.

test, which is merely to pronounce a word or two from the book. They are unable to do so, and, aided by Tevye's whiskey supply, decide to let him go.

One feels uncomfortable in accepting the tone of Tevye's explanation of the events which led to his escape from the beating, for Sholom Aleichem appears to be playing to the baser sense of superiority of his reading audience. For Tevye thinks out loud "and no matter how much we rack our brains, and no matter how much we attempt hifalutin explanations, we have to admit that we Jews are basically the finest and the smartest people in the world. Like the prophet says: 'Who is like Israel thy people, a nation on the earth' – in other words, there's no comparison! A gentile is a gentile, and a Jew, after all, is a Jew. Like you yourself say in your stories – you've got to be born a Jew." The story, written between 1914 and 1916, was intended primarily for an audience living in a new world, but not assimilated, and living in considerable hardship. While not particularly appealing to our sensitivities today, the feeling which Tevye is expressing is not far from the "black is beautiful" mystique so current now. For the Jews of the New York ghetto, there was little else to remind them of their former state than an occasional pat of self-congratulation on outsmarting a drunken Russian peasant. But one cannot help but regret that Tevye, after the years of Lear-like suffering, ends his career on such a small-minded, ungracious note.

In spite of the disappointment of the last few stories, we cannot dismiss the Tevye of the earlier years. This grandly humane and robust father desperately fights to hold onto a world which has meaning for him, as he sees a new order creeping right into the midst of his family. As much as Tevye resists, he cannot withstand the onslaught of time and the crumbling values of the Jewish world in the Pale. Although he does not understand what is happening, Tevye watches his world disappear with a consummate sense of dignity, as well as with his ever-present wit and irony. Sometimes Tevye is genuinely gripped by fear as he observes the end of his way of life, but then he thinks, "After all, I am a man, and I have my pride!", and this stout-hearted Jew finds a quote, takes a deep sigh, and moves on.

V

"WHAT DOESN'T A JEW DO FOR A LIVING?": THE LETTERS OF MENACHEM-MENDEL

The story of Menachem-Mendel is actually the economic history of Russian Jewry for over five hundred years. Originally, the Jews had been invited into Eastern Europe not just to escape the ravages of the crusades, but rather to establish those economic structures which had brought prosperity to trade centers in France and Germany.[1] No sooner had the capitalistic structure been erected than the Jews were either driven out or ghettoized. "The best that could be said of them was that they were a hateful necessity: and even where this were admitted, there were some who were ready to forgo the necessity."[2] The Jews did the 'dirty work' of the nobility as administers, tax collectors, stock market operators, and in general, they were soon identified as Europe's middlemen. Even when they attempted to branch out into more traditional areas of occupation, these were closed to them. Laws restricting Jewish trades and employment began appearing as early as the twelfth century in Central Europe. Where they were allowed freedom of activity, Jewish tradesmen flourished and prospered. Jewish goldsmiths, horsetraders, cattlemen, guildmen of all occupations can be found in the economic annals of medieval and post-medieval Jewry. But only on rare occasions were these enterprises permitted to develop without restrictive laws. In city archives all over Europe one discovers specific laws which were intended to drive Jewish tradesmen out of business, or which banned Jewish guilds. Gradually, the Jew was strangled by this legislation until he had no

---

[1] See, among others, Max I. Dimont, *Jews, God and History*, Signet edition (New York: New American Library, 1962), 210–245; 255–265.
[2] *The World of Sholom Aleichem*, 253.

other recourse but to serve the nobility in the often obnoxious tasks of money-making. In Russia, the situation was even more desperate, because the restrictions were almost impossible to work with. The Jew was denied access to the soil, to the professions, to the normal channels of business, to the big cities. He was forced to live only in the middle-sized townlets which we know as *shtetls*, in the Pale. Only on rare occasions could a wealthy Jew, a Brodsky perhaps, acquire a permit to reside in Kiev or Moscow. Otherwise, a Jew who was not content to live out his life in the *shtetl* either as a butcher, or a dairyman, or a tailor, had to undertake an illegal existence in the big cities, in an effort to 'make a living', to hustle, eternally in search of the quick financial killing.

Sholom Aleichem, as has been suggested in Chapter II, was adequately equipped to write about such a life. His own experience as an illegal Jewish trader on the Kiev stock exchange placed him in the midst of one of the most frantic existences imaginable. The Jews themselves describe the activities of the Jewish trader as *dreyen*, going around in a circle. At one point in "The Bubble Bursts" Tevye describes the frenzy of activity as he enters the street where the Jews do business. These *dreyers* never made their way into the bourse (*birzha*) itself. The Jews were contented to stand out in front on the street, and they attained a certain status by acquiring a seat at a table in a café nearby (in Kiev it was Semodenni's, which Menachem-Mendel speaks of).

This is the little man whom Maurice Samuel describes as the tragic misfit of Jewish economics.[3] He is determined to make himself into a man of means, 'with God's help', and to accomplish this he must throw himself into the business of business with the strength of his entire being: "He lives in the midst of shadows, and of the rumour of reality. He rotates at the centre of a whirlwind of telegrams, combinations, commissions, quotations, fees, and cuts. He talks of sterling, of bonds, of international loans, of wars, of threats of wars."[4] This is the picture of Menachem-Mendel, the man left suspended in mid-air by life, the *luftmensh*.

---

[3] *The World of Sholom Aleichem*, 256.
[4] *Ibid.*

It is indeed remarkable that the Menachem-Mendel stories did not turn out to be dark and depressing tragic tales, because the goods of tragedy certainly are present. Menachem-Mendel fails in everything he tries, and at the end, he deserts his wife and children and flees to America, that land of Jewish mythology where all 'no-goodniks' eventually finish. Originally, the stories were independently written anecdotes in epistolary form which Sholom Aleichem began in 1892, a correspondence between Menachem-Mendel and his wife, Sheineh-Sheindel, whose mother is never too far off, ready with a quote. In 1909, Sholom Aleichem prepared a book edition of the stories and what emerged was a full-fledged epistolary novel, a *Briefroman* of several hundred pages, which in the original Yiddish edition of 1917–1925 (*Ale verk fun Sholom Aleichem*), made up volume ten.[5] What keeps these stories from becoming what could be an embarrassing series of disasters is Menachem-Mendel's endless optimism as well as his unfailing assurance that God, any minute, will come to his aid and bring him an accidental windfall. On top of this, there is the delightfully deflating Sheineh-Sheindel, who cannot fathom any of her husband's goings-on, punctures all of his inflated notions and pipe dreams, and has at her finger-tips an endless supply of quotations, sayings, and epigrams supplied by her mother, who never liked her son-in-law in the first place! Menachem-Mendel's relationship with this phantom lady is placed in perspective in the story in which Sholom Aleichem introduces both of his most famous creations, "The Bubble Bursts". Menachem-Mendel tries to explain to Tevye the kind of wife that he has who could write such cutting letters, while poor Menachem-Mendel searches for the golden fleece: "That's what a wife is for – to bury her husband alive. There are worse things than that. I have also, as you know, a mother-in-law. I don't have to go into detail. You have met her."[6] Enough said. Menachem-Mendel's mother-in-law completes the triangle, although we never meet her directly in the letters. She is

---

[5] *Ale verk fun Sholom Aleichem*, published by the Sholom Aleichem Folksfond (New York, 1917–1925), twenty-eight volumes. There has never been a complete edition, and this is also no more than a selection.
[6] In *The Tevye Stories and Others*, 6.

present only in her total domination of her daughter and as a constant reminder to Menachem-Mendel that he is a failure in life.

From the outset, Menachem-Mendel is in conflict with the law, because when he leaves Kasrilevke, from that moment on his presence elsewhere is illegal. He had left Kasrilevke to find fame and fortune in the big-money centers of Russian commerce. His first encounter with Odessa enchants him, and he is convinced that this is where he belongs: "Just picture me with my cane walking along Greek Street (that's the name of the Odessa street where Jews are doing business) and finding twenty thousand little deals awaiting me."[7] He finds himself in Odessa because he left Kishinev, where he had gone from Kasrilevke to pick up a promised dowry left there by an uncle. As always happens with Menachem-Mendel, the dowry disappears into thin air, and he was off to Odessa to trace it down. This first letter sets the form for all subsequent correspondence. First, a formal greeting to his wife (in the original usually in Hebrew), followed immediately by a "firstly...secondly" sequence which emphasizes his physical and mental condition, and then the main body of the letter; in addition, there is almost always a post script ("Just remembered!"), which often contains the most important news of the letter (the last letter ends with "Just remembered! I forgot to tell you where I am going. My dearest wife, I am going to America!") or is completely forgotten: "Just remembered! There was something very important I wanted to tell you, but I forgot what it is. So, God willing, I'll leave it for the next time." At this early stage of his business existence, Menachem-Mendel is already "pressed for time". He demonstrates the characteristics of the harassed, hunted creature, even when things are going relatively well. From the outset, he is *dreying*, running around in circles.

But always Menachem-Mendel runs with what he believes is God's design and good will. No doubt the Victorian businessman of Dickens' day also was certain that the divine hand of The Supreme Being guided his successful business enterprises; the Victorians perfected the concept of metaphysical justification for economic

---

[7] Sholom Aleichem, *The Adventures of Menachem-Mendel*, trans. by Tamara Kahana (New York: G. P. Putnam's Sons, 1969).

success. But the Menachem-Mendels of the Pale had God with them as much as Tevye did. They were, first and foremost, pious Jews who woke up in the morning chafing at the bit to get down to the street to do a little business, but who would never miss their morning prayers. It was only natural that Menachem-Mendel imagined that he walked with God, and that "it must have been written in the books that I am destined to make a fat pile! Wait and hear how the Almighty guides the steps of man." There was no possible way that success could come without God's help, and one had complete assurance that The Almighty was a full partner in all transactions: "I therefore hope to heaven that this business materializes, please God, and then we'll certainly make money, with the Lord's help..." That he has absolutely no idea as to the nature of his business transactions does not phase Menachem Mendel one bit. At the conclusion of his first letter to his wife he confides that he put his entire fortune "in London", British sterling, and that he bought "a whole pack of merchandise – hausses and baisses both – and, praise the Lord, I heard there's a profit already".

From "hausses and baisses", highs and lows, Menachem-Mendel may have barely a glimmer of understanding about the manipulations of the sterling market; but his poor wife back in Kasrilevke is thoroughly mystified, and very suspect. The tone of her first reply to her husband establishes her personality and her state of mind, as well as her dependence on her mother. Most of all, it reveals her feelings about her husband's dealings in abstractions:

Why don't you describe exactly what kind of merchandise you are handling? How much does it cost by the yard? Or maybe it is sold by weight? I still cannot make head or tail of it – how do you eat it, with a spoon or with a fork? And there's another thing I cannot understand: You say you bought merchandise, and it's already bringing in a profit. What kind of merchandise have you got hold of that rises like cake or yeast? 'Even mushrooms', says Mother, God bless her, 'need rain to make them grow.'

Above all, she wants him home. She is afraid of the big city: "As Mother says, God bless her, 'When a cow leaves the herd, she forgets all her good intentions.' If you'll listen to me, you'll sell your goods as quickly as possible."

But Menachem-Mendel cannot return home, because he is totally caught up with the magic of money, the unbelievable frenzy of the chase for wealth which comes across in his letters: "The exchange keeps swinging up and down like mad; telegrams fly back and forth. Jews scramble about like at a fair, buying and selling, rushing, pushing, shouting, making business and getting rich – and me in the middle. There is such a noise and a tumult, it can shatter your eardrums." Sheineh-Sheindel, no matter how impressed her husband seems to be, is in no way taken in by Odessa's attractions or the temptations of the bourse. She wants her husband. She is still subject to the social laws of the *shtetl*, and more and more she is becoming an object of talk. Husbands do not stay away from their families for such a long time:

You know something, Mendel? Listen to me, to your wife – finish off with this Odessa of yours and come home to Kasrilevke!...Does Father, God bless him, give us a place to live in? Are there shops for rent? So what else do you want! Why must I be on the tip of everyone's tongue and have my enemies whisper that you've run away from me to Odessa and abandoned me, may you never live to see that day!

But it all falls on deaf ears. Menachem-Mendel is swimming with success and the thrill of the chase. He has 'graduated' from Greek Street to a table in one of the cafés, where he piles up "hausses and baisses" in "London" – all, of course, on margin. Sheineh-Sheindel switches tactics: "I am writing to say that I am again having trouble with my teeth, may all your wonderful Odessa music makers, big and little, enjoy such a pain! I have to suffer here from toothache and worry myself sick over his children, and he – nothing at all! He is living happily ever after in Odessa..."

Nonetheless, even though Menachem-Mendel sits side by side with all the big speculators at the white marble tables of the Café Franconi, he is still a child of Kasrilevke. He spends his Saturdays in the local synagogue, far away from the other *dreyers* who continue operating even on the Sabbath. The clean-shaven Jews of the big city have fallen away from their God, and Menachem-Mendel is mystified: "I cannot understand the Jews of Odessa – why don't they go to the synagogue to pray? And even those who do go to pray don't pray; they sit like puppets with their fat and shiny puppets; they wear top hats on their heads; their prayer shawls are small and skimpy, and – shsh! – nobody even opens his mouth. And if some Jew should venture to pray a little louder, up comes the beadle with shiny buttons and says, 'Quiet, please!' Funny Jews in Odessa!" But her husband's piety is little consolation to Sheineh-Sheindel. She is still nagged by what to *shtetl* ethics seems an intolerable situation: a woman without a husband; and worse still, a woman without a husband to provide her with symbols of status: "Just imagine, Blumeh-Zlateh finds it necessary to stick her nose up at me. Her head is swollen twice its size with pride, may she swell till she bursts! And for why? Because she is wearing a string of pearls around her neck, may it choke her! Well, she has it sweet with her husband! Some people have all the luck; it's only me that was born in such a dark and miserable hour...As Mother says..." Every letter now ends with the same plea: "And so, my dearest husband, I am writing you to think over carefully what you are doing and to stop frisking around your sweet Odessa, may it burn to an ash, which is the heartfelt wish of your really devoted wife, Sheineh-Sheindel." And as if to parody her husband's style, Sheineh-Sheindel ends also on a postscript occasionally, one usually indicating her complete non-comprehension of events and life in Odessa. Menachem-Mendel had told her that he spends much of his day at a table at Franconi's, failing to explain what Franconi's Café is: "Oh, yes! Please tell me, Mendel, who is Franconi, with whom you seem to be spending all your days and nights? Is it a he or a she?..."

The inevitable happens, and Menachem-Mendel's "London" goes up in smoke, along with his "hausses and baisses": "I got my affairs entangled with little people who were choked by the first squeeze. In a word, this is an earthquake, a disaster, a catastrophe...All the people are scurrying around like poisoned rats...In short, my dearest wife, everything looks dark and bitter...How many brokers made a living around me...and today not even one of them recognizes me." And so, the "Rothschild of Kasrilevke", as he fancied to call himself, is disgraced and prepares to leave for home and the waiting arms of his wife – and mother-in-law.

He seems to be a broken man, disillusioned, distrustful, and cynical: "Without money, one should not be born into this world, and if one does get born, it is better to die..." The Jewish *homo economicus*, the little man, unable to make it in the rat race of the big city. Sheineh-Sheindel comes through, rising to the occasion of her husband's downfall, and after a few deft jabs at his failure, she offers consolation to the stricken man: "Isn't Menachem-Mendel with money the same as Menachem-Mendel without money? Fool, can one defy God? Don't you see, He was against it? So stop squirming. Let the money be your scapegoat forever! The main thing... put your trust in the Eternal One... Come home, and please God, you'll be a welcome guest among your children..."

But Menachem-Mendel is hooked. He cannot escape, cannot break out of the cycle which holds him captive. He is bound to the road that heads toward the big pot of gold at the end of it, and there is nothing which can get him off. Instead of arriving home, Menachem-Mendel posts his next letter from Yehupetz, that mythical Kiev on the same train track as Odessa. He is determined to try his luck on the Yehupetz exchange. The picture of life in Yehupetz holds less of the romance than it did in Odessa. Here life is genuinely dogged, and the Jewish speculators life a marginal existence at best:

Just remembered! When you write me, please address your letters to Boiberik because I'm not allowed to stay in Yehupetz... All day long I traipse along the street called Kreshchatik and around the exchange, and when night falls I hurry off to Boiberik. There in the summer cottages, a whole crowd of speculators spend their time playing cards all night long (males and females together – that's the custom here). And early in the morning everybody rushes off to Yehupetz, and me in the middle.

Menachem-Mendel is indeed "mitten drin", the man in the middle, as he is whirled about the Yehupetz stock market with stunning confusion. He does not understand "papers", shares, has no idea what he is dealing in, but is convinced that he is on the verge of a financial killing. Of course, at the peak of his optimism the market collapses and Menachem-Mendel is once again a ruined and broken man. "It is like the destruction of the Temple!" The collapse is total, but with Menachem-Mendel, "in the middle", there is still the courage, miraculously, to pick up the pieces.

"I want you to know that I am no longer a speculator." Now this Don Quixote of business begins his adventures with an almost incredible variety of activities, in a mad dash for fortune. Menachem-Mendel finds himself among the brokers and bankers of Yehupetz first as a broker. The pre-requisites for such a position are few: "As long as you know how to tell a lie, and on top of it, possess a good stock of impudence, anybody can become a broker. Quite to the contrary, the more lies and the greater the impudence, the better the broker!" Menachem-Mendel's mental state of mind is beginning to lose its resiliency. His own self-esteem dwindles as he realizes the need for dishonesty in order to get ahead, and 'getting ahead' is everything: "A human being is not worth a straw – his origins, his ancestry, have no value at all. You may be anything or nothing – so long as you have money!" Here we see the disintegration of the traditional Jewish world of the *shtetl*. *Yikhus* of the normally acceptable kind count for nothing. Learning, scholarship, ancestry, all are empty. The only criterion in Menachem-Mendel's world is "as long as you have money".

Even the world back home in Kasrilevke seems to feel the strain of Menachem-Mendel's quest. Sheineh-Sheindel's mother, who had stayed until now somewhat in the background, commenting but never actively involving herself in the lives of the people, now steps forward and is indeed a formidable individual. "Why don't you ask what's new at home?", Sheineh-Sheindel asks.

Evidently it doesn't matter to you in the least that my mother has broken up my little sister's engagement. Do you think it was over money – money of course, is a separate matter – but it all started when the young man's father came to visit us on Sabbath, and Mother had some words with him. She hinted that he is descended from butchers and said something to the effect that one can expect nothing but beef from an ox. Poor Nehame-Braindl is for the third time 'a bride no longer and a spinster again'.

Three times the mother has interfered with her daughter's engagement. As we have seen on several previous occasions, Sholom

Aleichem's treatment of his female characters is generally – and there are quite obvious exceptions – unsympathetic. He himself seemed to have particularly good relations with his own mother-in-law, but his writings contribute to the stereotyped myth which is accepted in many cultures, that of the terrible mother-in-law. As for Sheineh-Sheindel herself, her behavior also begins to develop certain hysterical patterns by now. When her infant son complains of a pain in his ear, she reacts somewhat neurotically: "He points to his left ear with his little fingers and screams. I pummel and kiss him, I pinch and I hug him – but he doesn't stop screaming." Jewish family life is collapsing in Kasrilevke, and in Yehupetz Jewish morality is disintegrating. Menachem-Mendel describes Jewish merchants defaulting, crooked business deals, rivers without water, mysterious fires in over-insured buildings. He suffers ruination after ruination by dealing in forests, sugar, refineries and oil. As a moneylender, Menachem-Mendel is a disaster. Finally, he is witness to the ultimate in Jewish moral degradation: wife-swapping! "Here, in Yehupetz, having love affairs is very much in fashion. A young man and a young woman first of all must engage in a love affair, otherwise the match won't be a success. Here, men very often throw their wives over and fall in love with other men's wives, or else the women throw their husbands over and fall in love with other women's husbands. Anyhow, in other words, they change around: what's mine is yours, what's yours is mine..." The tempo of Menachem-Mendel becomes increasingly frenzied. One expects him momentarily to dissolve into hysteria: "*Just remembered*! There was something very important I wanted to tell you, but I forgot what it is. So, God willing, I'll leave it for the next time."

Just as it appears as if Menachem-Mendel has exhausted every possible business opportunity and he seems about to return home, he happens onto a "respectable occupation": as a writer. Sholom Aleichem's ironical view of his own life comes into clear focus throughout the Menachem-Mendel stories, but nowhere clearer than in this chapter of Menachem's life. He finds gazettes which pay by the line and the word, so Menachem-Mendel grinds out hundreds of lines a day, flooding the offices of Yiddish periodicals with anecdotes, romances, autobiographies, and adventures. The fact that Menachem-Mendel sees his name in print, but never receives any financial remuneration is not actually as accurate a picture of Sholom Aleichem's own experience with publishers, but it is not that far from the truth.

"There is only one thing I have passed over, so far: matchmaking. After his expected failure as a writer, Menachem-Mendel accidentally discovers a list of addresses left behind by a crooked matchmaker running away from a hotel bill. He starts wheeling and dealing, discovers his opposite number as a matchmaker, and the two marriage brokers, after considerable manipulating and arranging, perform the amazing feat of matching up a pair of girls!

The reader is not prepared for the postscript to the final letter from Menachem-Mendel:

Just remembered! I forgot to tell you where I am going. My dearest wife, I am going to America! I am not alone. I am traveling with a whole group...Why America all of a sudden? Because they say in America life is good for Jews...Only you are not to worry, my dearest wife, and for mercy's sake, don't think ill of me. Believe me, I shall not forget you, perish the thought, neither you nor our dear little children. ...I'll send steamship tickets for you and the children, and I'll bring you to America ...Only please do not worry and do not take it to heart – for our God is the All-Wise, the All-Merciful, and the All-Powerful!

Like thousands of men before him, Menachem-Mendel has abandoned his family in order to find fortune in America. Like thousands before him, he promises that steamship tickets will soon follow, but if Jewish folklore has any truth to it, America was the land of many a Jewish husband on the run, living on dreams of success that never materialize.

This is Menachem-Mendel: dreamer *par excellence*, optimist unparalleled, rootless, harassed Jew in search of a fortune. Most critics find in Menachem-Mendel perhaps Sholom Aleichem's most consistently comic character. Rather, I might suggest, Maurice Samuel's estimation is more to the point:

Sick men like Menachem Mendel by the thousand, by the tens of thousands, haunted the market-places of Yehupetz and Boiberik and Kasrilevke and Heissin and Bohopolie and Kozodoievka. They were always looking for what the English called a spot of business...And what is most mysterious about the Menachem-Mendels is that they did not become stark, raving lunatics, they did not become criminals, they did not even become neurotics. Menachem-Mendels are not exclusively Jewish, of course; but the Jewish quota has been altogether too high, and the tragedy of their lives has not received the sympathetic attention which is its due.[8]

Like Tevye, Menachem-Mendel embodies in his existence the representation of the collapse of the *shtetl* world. The Jew, Sholom Aleichem seems to be suggesting, had lost his moral fibre, his superiority in adversity which kept him above the world around him, at least in terms of his creed and faith, regardless whether he was economically depressed. When the Jew decided that there was money to be made outside the *shtetl* walls, he sacrificed the protective shell of his traditional values which had shielded him from moral anarchy, to be sure, at the cost of his material well-being. The Jews of Odessa and Yehupetz which Sholom Aleichem parades before us represent the decline and fall of the Jewish world of the Pale, and in a sense, the Menachem-Mendel stories are the most tragic which Sholom Aleichem ever wrote.

[8] *The World of Sholom Aleichem,* 257.

VI

STORIES FOR JEWISH CHILDREN

> "If only you realize what we're doing for you. Do him a favor and he doesn't appreciate it. Don't jump, don't run. Walk like a human being."
> Mother to her child in
> "The Ruined Passover"

1. PORTNOY IN KASRILEVKE

It may seem somewhat strained at this point in our study to make reference to a rather sensational bestseller in America which appeared in 1969, but, for better or worse, there is no denying that Philip Roth's *Portnoy's Complaint*[1] has a certain attraction to the student of Sholom Aleichem who has had the opportunity to consider the image of the Jewish child, particularly the son, in the collected works. Roth's now infamous hero, Alexander Portnoy, is the *ne plus ultra* of Jewish sons, or at least that is his own opinion of his situation. In the novel, Portnoy is going through analysis with a psychiatrist, in an effort to explain his particular neurosis. He has all sorts of problems, some sexual, some social, but all, he claims, have their roots in the same source: his mother. Portnoy (and Roth) analyse what he considers to be the trauma of being the son of a Jewish mother. Now, it would be a self-defeating effort if we were to take a detour and consider the merits of Roth's novel as literature. What *is* of some interest to us is the nature of the characterization of Mrs. Portnoy, her son's relationship to her, and the extent to which Roth's novel is a statement which

---

[1] (New York: Random House, 1969).

has its inspiration from the same taproot which Sholom Aleichem drew upon in creating characters remarkably similar to Mrs. Portnoy.

Roth, in effect, attempts to describe what it is like to be a Jewish child in America. Of the hundreds of stories which Sholom Aleichem wrote, the largest proportion were tales about children, and most interestingly, the majority of these were narrated in 'Portnoy fashion', by an adult seemingly unburdening himself of a particularly important incident in his early life which he only much later comes to recount. Two volumes were entitled *Stories for Jewish Children* (*Mayses far yidishe kinder*), but it is more accurate to say that the majority are stories *about* Jewish children. Sholom Aleichem goes into considerable detail to analyse what it was like to be a Jewish child, and particularly a Jewish child who happened to be a son, born and raised in the *shtetl* atmosphere of Czarist Russia. The Jewish male child of the *shtetl* represented "the family's opportunity to be as good as anybody – our chance to win honor and respect".[2] In theological terms, each male child was a potential Messiah, and was treated accordingly. The upbringing, cultural education, and general welfare of this potentially important little creature was naturally enough the responsibility primarily of his mother. It is at this point, remarkably, that a gap of a chronological century and a thousand years of civilized progress appear to be insignificant, as Roth and Sholom Aleichem converge on a strikingly similar characterized stereotype – or archetype – in the Jewish mother.

The mothers in Sholom Aleichem's stories are variations on a theme, differing in degree, never in kind. Some are brutal, others extraordinarily kind and self-sacrificing, none are indifferent to their children's needs; but all of them are alike in the total belief in the infallability of their techniques of child-rearing, as well as their possession of an instinct which was to guarantee no resistance whatsoever from the young men who were their subjects. It is rare to find such a consistent delineation of character in any one writer's corpus as one does of the mother-matriarch in Sholom

---

[2] *Portnoy's Complaint*, 5.

Aleichem's writings. She displays a singlemindedness and dedication to her task – producing the perfect child – which quite obviously impressed the author. Perfection in the child meant, in terms of the Jewish communal structure, honor for the family, for the parents, and the only certain way, even for the impoverished, of gaining status in the community. It was in terms of the methodology employed to attain this status that Sholom Aleichem makes his criticism.

"'Look at that pair of hands!' And she slapped me smartly across my wrists to make me drop them. 'When you sit at Uncle Hertz's table remember to keep your hands down, do you hear me? And don't let your face get as red as Yadwocha the peasant girl's. And don't roll your eyes like a tomcat. Do you hear what I'm telling you? And sit up like a human being. And the main thing is – your nose. Oh that nose of yours. Come here, let me put your nose in order.'" Throughout this story, "The Purim Feast", a young boy is shoved, pushed, and generally abused by a mother who is "trying to make a *mentsh* out of him".[3] Clearly the author is in a way attempting a subtle characterization. He presents a selfish, domineering, coarse, and thoroughly unsympathetic picture devoid of even a hint of genuine maternal instincts. The boy is abused during preparations for the family Purim festival, at which the young man is to shine, in order to impress Uncle Hertz, the *nogid* of the family circle, and in doing so will shed honor and glory on his mother and father, as well as on himself. Thus, when the party ends in disaster (he was overcome by a fit of uncontrollable laughter and beaten black and blue by his mother for this behavior), he is made to feel an assortment of guilts, having betrayed the larger family, his parents, and himself. Years later, when he discusses the event (the occasion for the story itself), we can sense the extraordinary humiliation which he must have felt on that occasion, as well as the guilt which no doubt marked him for life: "That night I cursed my own bones and I cursed Purim and the Purim feast...and more than anyone else I cursed Uncle Hertz, may he forgive me, for he has long since passed on to his reward. On his grave stands a

---

[3] In "The Tevye Stories and Others", 111–117.

tombstone, the most imposing tombstone on the whole cemetery, and on it in gold letters are engraved the virtues in which he excelled during his life..."

There is one other dimension to this particular type of hard-driving Jewish mother, and that is her relationship with her husband. Before the big event, he asks his wife if Uncle Hertz, who is her brother, has arrived yet from out-of-town:

'"Well, what's the news? Has your Hertz arrived yet?' And she gave him such a fare-thee-well that my father didn't know whether to stand up or to sit down. 'What do you mean by *my* Hertz? What sort of expression!' 'Whose is he if not yours? Is he mine?' said my father trying to do better. But he didn't advance far...My mother attacked him on all sides at once. 'Well, if he is mine, what of it? You don't like it? His ancestry isn't good enough for you? You had to divide your father's inheritance with him, is that it? You never got any favors from him, is that it?' 'Who says I didn't' my father offered in a milder tone, ready to surrender himself. But it didn't do any good. My mother wasn't ready to make a truce yet. 'You have better brothers than I have? Is that it? Finer men, more important, more prosperous, more respectable ones, is that it?' 'Quiet now. Let there be an end to this. Leave me alone', said my father, pulling his cap over his eyes and running out of the house. My father lost the battle and my mother remained the victor. She is always the victor."

Sholom Aleichem is obviously dealing with a situation he finds abnormal, that of a family of emotionally emasculated males, dominated by a female force which is, to the writer, unacceptable within the structure of the Jewish family, with its strict sense of role-playing. In terms of the female liberationists, Jewish family life played into the hands of male chauvinism. Perhaps sensing the fundamental frustrations of the female, Sholom Aleichem created a whole range of basically unhappy Jewish women whose sole gratification derives from the success of their child-rearing. Perhaps this accounts in part for the extraordinary amount of energy which his mother figures generate toward this end.

What is also noteworthy about Sholom Aleichem's matriarchs is that they are almost totally lacking in the sensibility to understand the individual emotional needs and problems of their children. There is *never* any of the modern psychological rhetoric about inhibitions, fixations, sensitivity, and never any understanding of these issues by the mother, although Sholom Aleichem makes it quite clear that the lack of this understanding has caused the narrator – rarely himself in these children's stories – abundant mental stress. The characteristic which Sholom Aleichem finds particularly distressing is the regular use of the device of maternal self-sacrifice in order to create guilt feelings in the young child and a sense of dedication to fulfilling the program which the family has in mind. In "The Dreydl" there is no physical punishment inflicted upon the young child, and the mother is utterly kindhearted and warmly affectionate. The story, like so many others, is in the form of a reminiscence.

The young boy in this case was an orphan, which in the *shtetl* social structure meant without both parents, or also solely without a father. In that case, the education of the child was taken over by a committee of elders, for above all, regardless of status, a Jewish male had to be educated in the Law. Everything was done to stimulate a boy's interest in the Talmud; no single idea dominated the family as much. To have a *talmid khokhem*, a prodigiously bright young scholar, was the ultimate goal of every *shtetl* family. And for an widowed mother, the mandate was the same, the responsibility even greater, perhaps. This explains in part the description of the mother taking her son to *kheder* – elementary school – in "The Dreydl": "'Remember now, study diligently', Mama said, standing by the door. She turned to look at me with a feeling of mingled joy, love, and compassion. I understand Mama's look quite well. She was happy that I was studying in the company of respectable children, but her heart ached that she had to part with me."[4] Yet soon, the narrator detected a pressure which left him as a child puzzled, but which as an adult he has come to understand: "I couldn't understand why Mama always complained that she barely made enough to pay for the store rent and for the *kheder* tuition. Why did she single out tuition? What about food, clothing, shoes, etc? All she thought about was tuition." The psychological offensive by the mother here is non-violent, but very effective.

---

[4] In *Some Laughter Some Tears*, 65–82.

There is no more than the innuendo of self-sacrifice on her part and endurance of hardship, in order that he might get an education. When summer came, our young student had a difficult time concentrating:

Who could even think of praying or studying then? But had you spoken to Mama, she would have told you that her husband, may he rest in peace, was not like that. He was a different sort of person. May he forgive me for saying this, but I don't know what sort of person he was. I only know that Mama constantly badgered and reminded me that I had had a father, threw up to me a dozen times a day that she was paying *kheder* tuition for me, and asked only two things of me: to put my mind to studies and my heart to prayers.

The mother's prime means of motivating the boy is by underlining strongly what she is willing to give up for him, and the effect on the mind of the seven- or eight-year-old boy is predictable, even in retrospect: "She froze, she went hungry, never had sufficient sleep or enough to eat. She suffered all this for my sake. Only for me. Why? Didn't she deserve to have a little pleasure, too? Everyone has his own criterion for joy. For my mother there was no greater pleasure in the world than my chanting the Sabbath and holiday *Kiddush* over the wine for her, or my conducting the Passover Seder, or lighting the Hanuka candles for her." The young man's reaction to his mother's total dedication to her goals is, within the framework of the *shtetl* world, understandable. As an adult he is now puzzled by his guilt feelings, but not particularly resentful or defensive. In terms of the communal structure, his mother's techniques, if we may call them that, have been developed over perhaps centuries, and the young man's cultural memory, within the traditions of the Jewish family and its ritual of child-rearing, allows for a highly developed sense of guilt toward the sacrificing matriarch to have a positive effect on the infant, child, adolescent, and man. The guilt feelings are put to good use, the Jewish child was generally highly motivated towards those goals established by his parents; down through the centuries of the *shtetl*, stability became the keynote of Jewish family life. The son did *not* rebel against his parents, and it was not until the *shtetl* itself was undermined that these tried and true methods of guilt attachment began to cause real emotional problems. The further the disintegration of the secure *shtetl* world proceeds, the more neurotic becomes the reaction of maternal attachment on the part of the child.

The most bizarre, and perhaps ridiculous, expression of this is in Roth's *Portnoy's Complaint*. Since we only experience Portnoy's mother through his own distorted view, we can only be certain of the effect that she has had on the young man, not of what she was really like as a person. What we have here is a *shtetl* mother attempting to use her instinctive equipment for child-rearing, on a young man who no longer has the *shtetl* security to wrap himself in. Alexander Portnoy is no longer a Kasrilevkite. He is two generations removed from Eastern Europe, and his reaction to a mother almost entirely identical to the mother of Sholom Aleichem's "The Dreydl" is to become a neurotic, with a wildly exaggerated mother fixation.

In other Sholom Aleichem stories the lack of psychological compassion takes on an almost unreal dimension. In "Pity for Living Creatures" one is astonished (as is clearly Sholom Aleichem himself) at the adult reaction to what must have been a relatively standard problem: the reaction of a young child to the religious ritual of animal slaughter as proscribed by Jewish Law. A young boy observes a fish swimming in the family bathtub, a carp which is intended for the Friday night Sabbath feast: "The poor thing desperately wanted to return to the river... 'It's a pity', I told Mama, 'a pity for living creatures.' " The mother and cook discover that this compassion comes from discussions with the rabbi, whereupon she bursts out laughing and dismisses her son: "You're a fool, but your rabbi is a bigger one. Just keep grating the horseradish."[5] Later he observes a *shokhet* slitting the throats of chickens and weeps. When he admonishes the cook for beating a cat who stole, she thinks, from the kitchen, she throws him out: "Get out of here, of I'll smack your face. God almighty, where do such foolish children come from?" He is beaten by two gentile boys when he interferes with their killing of fallen birds; then he is beaten by his father for being with gentiles. He is the only person in the

---

[5] In *Some Laughter Some Tears*, 101–106.

village who cares for a terribly ill and deformed little child, who soon dies. Whenever the child's mother sees him, she thinks of her child and weeps "Then Mama chased me away. 'If you wouldn't be underfoot and go where you're not supposed to go, then people wouldn't remember things they ought not to remember.'" Whenever he thinks of the little child, he cries, and his mother replies with laughter: "Did the horseradish get into your eyes? Wipe your eyes, you foolish boy... Wipe your nose, too." In a day and age when we are accustomed to trying to understand the nature of a child's emotional needs and responses, the adult reacton to this young boy's particular fixation – the suffering of animals – seems cruel and unjust. However, there was no room for sentiment and sensitivity which did not conform to the normal, acceptable standards of the *shtetl*, and children – boys in particular – who manifested such feelings received no consideration and, as in the case of our young friend in "Pity for Living Creatures", beatings and scoldings.

If anyone has suffered under the delusion that all of Sholom Aleichem's stories are filled with gentle humor, the few we have so far considered in this chapter should give cause for reconsideration. Clearly, there are aspects of the Jewish "Mutter Gestalt" which Sholom Aleichem did not find appealing. These few stories, and another dozen like them, are not funny, specifically because of an all-consuming mother. Yet, there are others which project the same mother figure, but emphasize the positive rather than the negative. "Gitl Purishkevitch" is the name of one such delightful mother, who is no less forceful in her domination of her son: "He's a good boy, sound as an apple, handsome and plain as can be. He's got all the virtues, but learning he didn't like. What am I saying – didn't like? Beat him, smash him to smithereens, but still he refused to study. 'What's going to be with you, Moishe,' says I, 'if you say no to reading, writing, and praying? You'll only be fit to be a dogcatcher!'" The widowed Gitl does everything she can to give her son respectability, and is fairly satisfied with her efforts. She is a door-to-door *shtetl* saleswomen for Wissotsky's Tea. This hard-working, every-day *mentsh* is given the added positive touch by Sholom Aleichem by being placed in a frame much like that which gave Tevye his opportunity to shine: a meeting with the author: "They told me that there's a writer chap here named Sholom Ilikem. Is that you himself, the Sholom Ilikem that writes?" Old Gitl then relates her tale of woe, which turns out to be a paean for motherhood, and a perfectly convincing one, at that. One day, she suddenly finds her son threatened by the draft. In terms of *shtetl* life, the Jew's relationship to military service was always traumatic. There was no way which could satisfy the Jew's particular needs of daily life and his obligation to serve a government which was openly anti-Semitic. As a result, the Jews did everything they could to avoid military life, and numerous Sholom Aleichem stories deal with this theme, as well as with the theme of Jewish patriotism and bravery in combat for Czarist Russia.[6] In Gitl's case, however, a rank injustice was about to be done:

Draft? What draft? He's a one-and-only child, an only son to his widowed mother that owes everything she is to God and then Wissotsky. Has such a thing ever been heard of? Is there no God? Where's your sense of justice? But when the cards say trouble, you can go knock your head against the wall! It turned out that my Moishe was the exact same age as the three sons of our rich man's three daughters, may three well-placed boils prevent them from being able to stand, lie and sit.

Gitl's son is about to become the scapegoat for the *nogid's* grandsons. Sholom Aleichem, always on the look-out for treacherous *negidim*, now moralizes on how the rich keep their progenies out of the armed forces, while the poor are forced to serve. In Sholom Aleichem's Kasrilevke, there is always a doctor ready to certify a bad back, or a fever which is undiagnosible. She appeals to the draft board and is thrown out. She goes to the regional governor

---

[6] See, for example, "The First Passover Night of the War", in *Old Country Tales*, 259–265. A Jewish soldier says the following: "Just three things are enough to make me happy. That a Jew like me is equal to everyone else; that a Jew like me is one of the Czar's men; that a Jew like me can show his loyalty to the entire world. Let our enemies see that a Jew too can serve faithfully and well, and that a Jew also can hold his head high with honor of the land where his ancestors' bones lie buried, and where his bones too will lie." "Gitl Perushkevitch", is to be found in *Old Country Tales*, 139–148.

and is thrown out. Then, as she describes it, "she straight off sold everything she had and set out to seek the truth right in Petersburg itself...and if I had to get hold of the Czar himself, don't you think I could have found him? When it comes to the truth I could even reach God himself." What it has come to is her son, Moishe, and Gitl will not give him up, not even to the army. She enters the chambers of the Duma, Russia's parliament, to hear the debate on the draft laws, which turn out to be strongly anti-Jewish, but worse still, discriminatory against the poor. It is suggested that Jews be permitted to buy their way out of the army, all of which is too much for Gitl: "Expect me to keep still? So I called out from the gallery and screamed loud enough for the entire Duma to hear: 'What about Moishe?' The police throw her out, but a sympathetic deputy hears her case, and miracle of miracles, Moishe is released from his military obligation, which, by the way, he was enjoying.

In this story, a mother's dogged determination to find justice and her belief in a righteous cause finally triumph. Ironically, Sholom Aleichem subtly suggests that perhaps the young man would have been better off had he accepted military duty. Still, he revels in Gitl's victory and does not harshly undermine the triumph of motherhood.

Sholom Aleichem had a particular spot of affection for the widowed woman who, like Gitl, sacrifices and saves for her son. "The Little Pot", like "Gitl Purishkevitch", is in the form of a Chekhovian monologue in which the central character is permitted to reveal herself in her own words, in this case, to her rabbi. Yenta the Poultrywoman is one of Sholom Aleichem's most stereotyped and yet most extraordinary character. She embodies almost all the clichés which have been associated with, in a larger sense, motherhood in general even in America. She is the type of caricatured matriarch favored by mass media humorists: doting, kind but singleminded, and inevitably associated with chicken soup:

So every day I make him a chicken soup out of a quarter of a chicken, and every night when he comes home from *cheder* he eats it. And I sit across the table from him with some work in my hands and rejoice at the sight. I pray to God that He should help me so that tomorrow I should be able to make him another soup out of another quarter of a chicken. 'Mother', he asks me, 'why don't you eat with me?' 'Eat', I said, 'eat all you want. I ate already.' 'What did you eat?' 'What did I eat? What difference does it make what I ate, as long as I ate?' And when he is through reading or studying, I take a couple of baked potatoes out of the oven, or rub a slice of bread with onion and make myself a feast. And I swear to you by all that is holy, that I get more enjoyment and satisfaction out of that onion than I would out of the finest roast or the richest soup, because I remember that my Dovidl, may the evil eye spare him, had some chicken soup and that tomorrow he will have chicken soup again.[7]

In the above passage one senses a balanced harmony, an understanding between mother and son which has a heritage as old as the *shtetl*. There is a distinct ritualization to the mother-son relationship which in the Old World provided a framework which proved to be acceptable to all parties. However, the structure proved to be non-adaptable. The very same mother, with the same expectations and hopes, when transferred to a suburb of Newark, New Jersey and doting over a son with an Ivy League education, becomes, at least in the eyes of this son, a figure who totally dominates his existence and inculcates such extraordinary guilt feelings that only psychoanalysis can relieve the oppression from his psyche. This is the problem of Alexander Portnoy, who represents in every respect the traditional Jewish son, but now lacking one major and totally determining factor: the cultural memory of the *shtetl*. Along with Portnoy's emancipation came the loss of a certain part of his Jewish identity which permitted the male youth to accept somewhat benignly the feelings of total immersion in the matriarchal will which Sholom Aleichem's male children somehow accept, with more or less resignation. The mother of Alexander Portnoy is no different from the mother of the young man in "The Little Pot". Her reactions, her instincts are exactly the same as her *shtetl* antecedent. What has changed is the world in which she had operated over the centuries, the world of the accepted norms of mother-son relationships within the tight confines of the Jewish family.

---

[7] "The Little Pot", in *Tevye's Daughters*, 180–191.

Yet, Portnoy cannot break loose cleanly, without a residue. Although he has moved to suburbia and appears totally Americanized, there lingers in him this five-hundred-year-old accumulation of Jewish consciousness, a faint remembrance, a reflex action which unfortunately manifests itself as an abnormality of behavior which fixates him. He is a typical Sholom Aleichem character, but living in another time and in another world.

2. THE BRUTALIZATION OF THE CHILD

One extremely unexpected aspect of the child in Sholom Aleichem – and by extrapolation in the *shtetl* itself – is his brutalization by parents, peers, and particularly teachers. The young man of the story "The Flag" experiences general mockery and physical punishment because of a speech impediment: "Everyone under the sun thought it a good deed to beat me: my father, my mother, my sisters, my teacher, my classmates. They all tried to get me to talk properly."[8] Furthermore, it was the birthright of the rich child to beat up the poor or orphaned child.[9] Any young boy could expect a whipping if he expressed interest in an occupation or activity which was not in keeping with the *yikhus*, the status of his parents.[10]

But in general, the great sadism was demonstrated by the elementary school teachers. Study for the Jewish child began at age three, when he was carried off by the *belfer*, the teaching assistant, to the *dardeki melamed*, the elementary teacher, who enjoyed absolutely no status in the community, because he "lives by selling what he should be giving."[11] Goaded by this lack of respect from his peers, the teacher traditionally lashed out at his young pupils, who were, moreover, the victims of some of the most antiquated teaching methods conceived of by men. Three-year-old children were forced to memorize the Hebrew letters, then by rote learn

---

[8] "The Flag", in *Old Country Tales*, 73–84.
[9] See "The Esrog" in *Some Laughter Some Tears*, 26–36.
[10] See "Methuseleh, A Jewish Horse", in *Old Country Tales*, 87–97; and "From the Riviera", in *Stories and Satires*, 303–307; also, "*The Fiddle*", in *Selected Stories of Sholom Aleichem*, 307–323.
[11] Zborowski and Herzog, 89.

passages of the Bible, which were recited endlessly, while the *melamed* marched up and down the aisles, with whip in hand.

In Sholom Aleichem's writings, these teachers are without exception misfits and failures who vent their frustration by "beating, flogging, and crippling Jewish children".[12] None is more devastating than "Boaz the Teacher".[13] The narrator remembers "the day Mama took me by the hand and brought me to Boaz's *cheder* for the first time; I felt like a young chicken on its way to the *shokhet*. It flutters with fright, poor thing – not comprehending, but sensing that the future isn't all chicken feed." The teacher himself is as demonic as the child had sensed and as the adult could reflect on: the only pedagogic device was the whip." A child must fear – God, the rebbi, his parents, sins, and evil thoughts. In order for a child to be imbued with the correct amount of fear, he must be laid down properly, with pants lowered, and given two dozen lashes." Sholom Aleichem underscores a sense of genuine perversion beyond this apparent morality of abuse: "He was never in a rage when he dispensed the whippings. Boaz was not the sort to get angry... He considered laughing something terrible. Boaz had never laughed in his life and hated to see others laughing...Sometimes we got a whipping just for the fun of it. 'Let's see how a little boy lets himself be whipped.'" Nowhere is there justice, nowhere reason. In "Robbers!" the teacher Mazeppa, a small, thin tyrant, "hated lengthy chitchats. Even for the slightest incident – whether you were guilty or not – he ordered you to lie down for a whipping. 'Rebbi, Yosl-Yakov hit me.' 'Lie down.' 'Rebbi, that's a lie. He kicked me first.' 'Lie down.' 'Rebbi, Chaim-Berl stuck his tongue out at me.' 'Lie down.' 'Rebbi, that's a downright lie. It was *he* who thumbed his nose at *me*.' 'Lie down...' " Everyone was whipped, the poor more than the rich, the small more than the big. It was no wonder that the children themselves turned brutal to one another and to other things. In "Methuseleh, a Jewish Horse", Ruvele, a ruthless, cynical Jewish youth, gets his pleasure out of

---

[12] "The Little Redheaded Jews", in *Some Laughter Some Tears*, 191–230. This is one of Sholom Aleichem's hardest-hitting satires on Jewish obstinacy in accepting Zionism."
[13] "Boaz the Teacher", in *Some Laughter Some Tears*, 161–168.

tormenting a horse. Sholom Aleichem, in an effort to justify this distorted vision of a Jewish boy, informs us that Ruvele himself was beaten by his parents because he had the temerity to want to be a violinist.

Although the poor suffered more than the rich, the *nogid*'s son did not escape. In the Purim story "Visiting with King Ahasuerus", Sholom Aleichem plays with the prince and the pauper theme. The rich lad, who tells the story, is the traditional have-not: He cannot participate in the Purim play "because I came from a rich and prominent family".[14] The object of his regret is the poorest child of the village: "But most of all I was jealous of Feivel the orphan who would don a red shirt and masquerade as Joseph the Righteousness for the troupe's performance of *The Sale of Joseph*." But he was the grandson of Reb Meir, the richest man in town and has "his own personal Angel of Death" to guard over his morality: Reb Itzi, his tutor. For a moment he escapes the family's net and joins the troupe of actors, until his Angel of Death catches him and turns him over to his father:

Once outside, my father stopped, took one look at me, and briskly slapped me twice. 'That's just a prelude. Once we get home, your tutor will really give it to you. Now listen here, Reb Itzi, I'm turning him over to you, and I want you to whip the daylights out of him. Til he's black and blue. A boy going on nine! Let him remember what it is to run off with the Purim players, those low-down, low-class, third-rate clowns, those down-at-the-heel tramps. Let him remember what it means to ruin everyone's holiday.

Clearly nothing outraged Sholom Aleichem so much as this brutalization of children. He dedicated the two volumes of children's stories to them, while hoping that the adults might at least become enlightened as to their responsibilities as parents. Yet in spite of the apparent hopelessness of the plight of these children, they somehow manage to survive. After all, they all narrate their own stories, and these narrations take on a quality of reminiscence which is strangely devoid of bitterness or resentment.

---

[14] In *Old Country Tales*, 51–64.

In fact, although he clearly marks 'the good guys and the bad guys' in these children's stories, Sholom Aleichem at least tacitly stresses the durability of the Jewish child 'to make it' while growing up in what normally might be described as a psychologically debilitating environment. And as if to re-assure us completely, he permits us to follow the history of one of these children from his earliest years until young manhood (in that world, somewhere around twelve!), and shows him triumphant in spite of every possible disruption and lack of consideration. It is only fitting that Sholom Aleichem's most durable, even most honest creation should be such a child, Mottel, the orphaned son of an impoverished cantor.

3. "HOORAH, I'M AN ORPHAN"

For Sholom Aleichem, Mottel was someone special. A draft of a Mottel-story was on the table next to his deathbed, and over a period of almost twenty-five years spanning two continents, Mottel remained at the center of Sholom Aleichem's thoughts. More than Tevye, more than Menachem-Mendel, he represents the Jewish spirit as Sholom Aleichem saw it, both in Europe and in America. Of his three major characters, only Mottel is described in The New World. He belongs in America, and is as much at home on the East Side of New York as he was back in Kasrilevke. Fortunate for us, Mottel is an excellent observer of his surroundings, for he tells his own story, a Jewish picaro who gets himself involved in every enterprise of his family, grows up through the forced feeding of events which shook Europe, travels across half the world, and comes out underneath the Delancey Street Bridge as stable as one could hope for.[15]

Mottel's adventures constitute thirty-nine interrelated chapters, a perpetual serialization in episodic form which involves, besides Mottel, his widowed mother ("She's doing what she always

---

[15] The English title is *Adventures of Mottel the Cantor's Son*, translated by Tamara Kahana (New York: Collier Books, 1961). The original Yiddish mentions Mottel's father in the title: *Motl Peyse dem khazns*, in two volumes of the *Ale verk* twenty-eight volumes of 1917–25 (vols. 17 and 18).

does – she's crying"); his brother Eli, a serious, responsible young man who inherits the role of head of the family and who invests in a series of outrageously funny business enterprises; his wife, pock-marked Brocha with the bass voice; Eli's best friend Pinney, always with a cuff rolled up, or a sock falling down, Pinney with the long, skinny body, a *schlimazl* who somehow manages in a world not made for *schlimazls*. The adventures of Mottel present the most comprehensive chronicle of Jewish life at the turn of the century. After experiencing little success in a variety of legal and illegal business ventures, the group, a sort of Jewish commune at that point, decides that they have had enough of Europe, and that the land of the future is America. So, amidst total confusion and mother's wailing over the grave of her husband, the families (there are Eli's and Pinney's) head for an illegal border crossing at the frontier of Russia and the Austro-Hungarian Empire. Confrontations with Austrians, Germans, Jews of all descriptions telling hair-raising stories ("If you compare her bad luck with my bad luck, you'll realize that she's lucky!"). As they travel closer and closer to the western coast of Europe for the hoped-for trip to America, their problems become more complex and Mottel's mother's tears more copious, until her crying becomes a cause for serious concern: it could keep them out of the United States, if she develops trachoma from crying. When she hears this, of course she bursts out crying. In Antwerp they wait for mother's condition to improve, and pass the time observing the German Jews who also are waiting for the boat: "All Jews on 'the other side' hate Yiddish, and love German. Even beggars talk German. They're ready to die of starvation, as long as they do it in German." Finally, they manage to get to London, and Brocha, who hates the city, wails from one end of town to the other: "London, why don't you burn?"

But by far the most exciting part of their exodus involves the trip across the ocean and their arrival in New York. There is a most moving description of the *Yom Kippur* services on the high seas, as the elegant Jews of first class come down to steerage to mourn and to worship with the common Jews. Ad for Mottel's mother, on the saddest of all the days of the Jewish year, "Mother is happy – this is *her* day!"

Everything comes to a near disaster on Ellis Island, as the travellers wait to go through the immigration process. Sholom Aleichem's description of the situation is perhaps the most definitive statement ever made in literature on the subject of Ellis Island, now a relic of history and a permanent part of the Age of Immigration. Pinney, who is a rabid pro-American throughout the book, is crushed by "Elie's Island" and its inhumanity. Families are permanently separated, people are locked up, deported, there are pitiful scenes of desperate peasants, unable to communicate in English, making futile efforts to join their loved ones. Sholom Aleichem in a rare departure includes peoples from all lands in these Ellis Island scenes and condemns the whole system out of hand.

But in spite of these vicissitudes, they finally plant themselves on the piers of New York, and Pinney turns to Europe for the extraordinary speech which was quoted earlier, addressed to a decadent Old World which will someday regret the loss of its Jews. Not everywhere is the image of America so overwhelmingly positive as it is in Pinney's speech on the banks of the Hudson River, and certainly Sholom Aleichem's own experiences had a great deal to do with this mixed reaction.[16] But Pinney's message ("You murderers, we have to thank you for having reached this haven, this refuge, this great and blessed land") is clear; for the *proste Yidn* of Kasrilevke, for the Jewish down-and-outers, America was indeed the land of the free.

America works wonders on 'the gang'. Feivel soon becomes Philip; Mendel is called Mike, and everybody is 'making a living'. Furthermore, they are not even strangers in a strange land, for soon after their departure, Kasrilevke burned to the ground, and the survivors came to America. Former *negidim* now find themselves working on pushcarts on Second Avenue. Others work in factories, take part in workers' rallies, go out on strike, and

---

[16] Besides being a haven where the Menachem-Mendels flee to, America is the setting for several non-Mottel stories, with a definite bias on the part of the author evident. See "Mr. Green has a Job" in *Some Laughter Some Tears*, 233–236; and the devastating "Story of a Greenhorn", 243–248 in the same volume.

participate in the tremendous excitement of life on the Lower East Side of New York around the turn of the century.[17] All of this is seen through the eyes of a delightfully realistic young boy growing up in the midst of a world teeming with new experiences. At this point, with Mottel's life still before him and an unfinished story on his bed table, Sholom Aleichem died.

The direction he would have taken, had he lived to continue Mottel's adventures, was clear. He had a definite problem in mind for future stories: how would the Jew face Americanization, the threat of assimilation in a land which gave the Jew relative freedom of choice. Although he himself did not live to confront this challenge, Sholom Aleichem left a rich enough heritage, so that others, some far removed from Kasrilevke, were able to continue. But clearly, Sholom Aleichem the realist recognized the way of the future for the Jew. Kasrilevke was no more. Sholom Aleichem, the town's architect, benefactor, and major citizen, burned it to the ground in a symbolic gesture of finality. It is somewhat foreboding to note how, almost twenty years before Adolf Hitler's rise to power, Sholom Aleichem signaled the end of European Jewry.

---

[17] See, most notably, Hutchins Hapgood, *The Spirit of the Ghetto*, Paperback edition (New York: Schocken Books, 1966).

VII

OUTSIDE OF KASRILEVKE

The conflicting forces at work in Sholom Aleichem's mind make it almost impossible for the critic to categorically state Sholom Aleichem's world view. Clearly, in regard to certain types of individuals, he had his prejudices, his likes and dislikes. His criticism of the *shtetl* world and its antique civilization, often his impatience with the hesitancy of the Kasrilevkites to move out of the past might be expected from an educated, moderately assimilated big-city Jew, which Sholom Aleichem most definitely was.

Yet, whatever criticism we find in the Kasrilevke stories about small-minded Jews and the pettiness of their ways measures up in no way to the complete disdain he showed for the Jews who left Kasrilevke, abandoned the *shtetl*, and became big-city folk. The satire of Kasrilevke modernizing turns to tragedy when the Jew pulls up his roots, leaves his hereditary home, and moves to the industrialized, mechanized world of the city. We were offered a preview in the Menachem-Mendel stories, but the humor of the characterization overshadowed in part Sholom Aleichem's genuine feeling about the destruction of Menachem-Mendel by the city.

Sholom Aleichem even goes beyond condemnation of the city to include what seems to be, in his time of *Haskalah*, of enlightenment, a difficult concept to accept: he attacks non-Jewish, secular education for Jews, often a by-product of city life.

1. BUZIE AND SHIMEK

Almost as if to chronicle the impact of the outside world on a Kasrilevkite, Sholom Aleichem created a four-part romance entitled "A Page from the Song of Songs", a unique phenomenon not only in Sholom Aleichem, but in Yiddish Literature as well: a tender love story.[1] The stories are narrated by Shimek as an adult, as he recounts his life with his drowned older brother's daughter Buzie, with whom he grew up, loved, and lost. The narration is filled with flowering passages taken from the biblical *Song of Songs*, as Shimek describes the beauty and tenderness of his beloved. As children the two enjoyed pleasures that few Jewish children experienced, such as romps through the open and green fields of the countryside. The country and nature were not the preserves of Jewish children, and only on rare occasions could a Buzie or a Shimek indulge in such things. One such occasion was *Shevuous*, a festival harvest holiday which called for copious amounts of greenery taken from the woods. In the second of these stories, "Another Page from the Song of Songs", we discover the children racing through the fields, in a very un-Jewish fashion: hand-in-hand, arm-in-arm, as they search gaily for the holiday greens before *Shevuous*.[2] In orthodox families, boys and girls were not permitted any sort of physical contact from a very early age; indeed, they were forbidden each other's company, so strong were the taboos against any sort of excessive sexuality in the *shtetl*.[3] In spite of the familial relationship – uncle and niece – , this did not dismiss the possibility of marriage, and at the conclusion of this story, the children are together, admired by Shimek's parents who look at each other with knowing glances of approval.

But by the third part, obviously written some time later, the entire picture had changed. "Pages from the Song of Songs: This

---

[1] "A Page from The Song of Songs", in *A Treasury of Yiddish Stories*, ed. Greenberg and Howe, 421–427.
[2] "Another Page from The Song of Songs", in *Tevye's Daughters*, 46–52
[3] See Zborowski and Herzog, for attitudes towards sex in the *shtetl*, 128–139 and 270–295.

Night" takes place many years after the tender scenes in the woods. Shimek had gone out into the world, against the wishes of his father: "I had disobeyed him and gone my own way to seek a secular education. At first he was angry. He said he would never forgive me. Perhaps only on his deathbed. But later he forgave me. Then he began to send money, accompanied by short, dispassionate letters..."[4] Shimek, in search of knowledge, a Jewish Faustus, had abandoned his home and his "Song of Songs world of long ago". Now he hears that Buzie is engaged and his elderly parents urge him to return for a visit, and the prodigal finds himself once again contemplating his village:

I found my home exactly the same as I had left it years before. It had not changed at all. Father was the same as ever. Except that his silvery beard had become whiter, and worries, apparently, had set more wrinkles into his broad, white brow. Mama, too, was exactly the same. Except that her ruddy face had become somewhat yellowish. I fancied that she had become smaller. But perhaps it only seemed so because she was stooped over now. And her eyes were red, puffy, and swollen. Was it from weeping? Why had Mama been crying? Was it because of me, her only son? Was it because I had not obeyed father, disregarded his wishes, gone my own way to seek a secular education, and not been home in years?

The story is embarrassingly sentimental and cloying, and represents Sholom Aleichem at his commercial weakest. He is obviously exploiting the techniques and themes of the very writers he condemned so outright years before. What is interesting, however, is that Sholom Aleichem, son of the Enlightenment, appears to be advocating a philosophy of "There's no place like home", which is not exactly consistent with the spirit of intellectual curiosity upon which the Jewish Age of Reason was founded. Shimek is consumed by a nearly hysterical sense of error in his life: "A tempest stormed in my head, and in my heart a fire directed at no one but myself alone. At myself and at those young and foolish dreams of mine, for the sake of which I had left my parents and forgotten about Buzie. Dreams for which I had sacrificed a part of my life and lost my chance for happiness forever." Sholom Aleichem uses a litany

---

[4] "Pages from The Song of Songs: This Night", in *Some Laughter Some Tears*, 47–62.

of self-reproach, repeating phrases which lacerate Shimek's conscience: "I had disobeyed him, refused to follow his ways but pursued my own instead". Also, Shimek sees everywhere "the beautiful clear white hands of Mama" lighting the sabbath candles, preparing the holiday food, or covering her face while she sobs silently. Shimek appears to be teetering on the edge of a complete emotional collapse caused by these endless regrets at having ruined his life as well as the lives of his parents. A visit to the town synagogue during the holiday almost proves too much for him to take:

Years ago, I remember, I was happy there, infinitely blissful. Years ago, in this miniature holy temple, my childish soul had once hovered with the angels beneath the painted ceiling. I had prayed in zestful devotion with father and all the other Jews...Now I once again sat in my old *shul*, praying with the old congregants. I listened to the old cantor singing the melodies of long ago. The congregation prayed with zest...I wanted to pray with everyone, as I used to long ago, but I could not pray.

All the anger and regret finally overwhelms Shimek, as he tearfully contemplates the waste of his innocence, spent searching for knowledge when happiness was to be found at home all the while.

In these Buzie-Shimek stories Sholom Aleichem appears as an unqualified anti-intellectual and defender of *shtetl* life, even more than *shtetl* values. The point is driven home as forcefully in the last of the installments, "Final Pages from the Song of Songs".[5] What Curt Leviant calls "a product of Sholom Aleichem's most creative period" is a re-hash of the material in the previous story.[6] As in the Tevye stories, we find Sholom Aleichem, when the need suited him, hanging on to material which no doubt found a significant response in his readers, in this case, the fallen-away son, the knowledge-seeker who deserts his parents and abandons his home. Sholom Aleichem deals with the material as if he had never written the third part: "Years past I went away from home against the will of my parents. I disregarded their wishes, refused to follow their ways, pursued my own path instead, and went to seek a secular education...Thus I forfeited happiness." In this final chapter,

---

[5] "Final Pages from The Song of Songs", in *Old Country Tales*, 35–48.
[6] "Introduction", *Old Country Tales*, 33.

however, Buzie emerges as a somewhat more significant figure, and she too, although ironically, lowers a moralizing boom against Shimek. On a walk which the former childhood sweethearts take together she confesses to the narrator

> that she couldn't measure up to me. How could a provincial Jewish girl like her measure up to me. No, she should have realized that she couldn't measure up to me. How could a provincial Jewish girl like her be compared to me. She should have foreseen that since I had disobeyed my parents, disregarded their wishes, refused to follow their ways but pursued my own instead, I would surely travel far and become so high and mighty that I wouldn't want to see anyone or know anyone.

The "Song of Songs" stories, because of the singularity of the characters and motifs, present in a concentrated form what is a most uncomfortable theme to have to deal with in Sholom Aleichem, that happiness can best be found in the bosom of traditional ways of life. There is no sense at all that Shimek has done anything right in seeking to liberate himself, in gaining an education in the outside world, in attempting in any way to adjust to a world advancing both intellectually and technically. One is thoroughly prepared, to be sure, to accept the notion of discovering one's roots in own's own soil. However, it is the implication which Sholom Aleichem makes in addressing himself to this theme which strikes the reader as out of touch and inconsistent with what we know were his progressivism in both secular and religious matters. He was, after all, not only a part of the *Haskalah*, he was a spearhead of the fight to bring a breath of modernity to the *shtetl*. But there is no doubt that in "The Song of Songs" stories, as in many others, he turns on progress and somewhat nostalgically returns to his origins – or what he romantically conceives of as his origins. He was as we know a big-city Jew, many years removed from contact with the *shtetl* world, and in this, the last phase of his life, it is not inconceivable that Sholom Aleichem might indeed envision a *shtetl* which gradually became a refuge of his mind from the hustle-bustle and frenzied confusion of his travels from Europe to America. It is not unlike the image of the *shtetl* as perceived in the popularization of Sholom Aleichem, *Fiddler on the Roof*, by the hundreds of thousands of Jews and non-Jews who carry away the notion that the hamlets of Eastern Europe were filled with people singing and dancing in brightly colored silken shirts.

The Buzie-Shimek stories are not isolated cases. Sholom Aleichem continually made strong indictments against the outside world, and always in terms of the Jew searching for knowledge beyond the boundaries of his home. "The Lottery Ticket" is the story of an old synagogue sexton, Yisroel, and his son Benyomchick, his "lottery ticket", his sure bet on a winner.[7] Yisroel is determined to provide his son with the best possible education, even though he is too poor to hire a tutor. He urges the lad to study, and the old man undertakes all sorts of tasks in order to have additional income for the boy's training. Yisroel is not disappointed, as Benyomshick develops into a first-rate scholar and seems destined to fulfill his father's dreams. But once again, Sholom Aleichem presses a heavy hand on the narrative to make his point, and does so without any trace of irony:

But something happened: in the last forty or fifty years a ray of worldly light has stolen into our corner of the earth and has reached into our very synagogues, even there, where the impoverished lads sit with their tomes. There you found them secretly snatching their first taste of secular food, some rhetoric as an appetizer, then swallowing – or choking over – a Russian grammar, with maybe a few chapters of a novel for dessert. From studies like these, naturally, no *Talmudic* scholars or rabbis emerged. Instead, Jewish youths wandered off into the world and were ruined, became doctors, lawyers, writers of prose and verse, teachers – and plain non-believers. Not a single rabbi who was worth anything.

Benyomchick then proceeds to act out a version of Sholom Aleichem's picture of assimilation. With considerable pride Yisroel watches his "lottery ticket" study incessantly, until he finally passes his exam to enter the secular *gymnasium*, the pre-college high school which took very few Jews.[8] Yisroel's joy and pride

---

[7] "The Lottery Ticket", in *Selected Stories of Sholom Aleichem*, 350–371.
[8] The most famous of Sholom Aleichem's stories dealing with the trials of getting a young Jewish boy into the secular high school is "Gy-Ma-Na-Si-A", in *Tevye's Daughters*, 225–238, which in recent years has been dramatized for national educational television, starring Gertrude Berg as the mother devoting her life to her son's education; and Morris Carnovsky, as the distraught but willing father.

seem justified, since his son's letters inevitably mention his "faith in the Eternal" and re-affirm his Jewishness. But, Yisroel fails to note the more foreboding hints which appear, as when the boy writes: "There is only one thing wrong: we have so far not been able to correct our accent altogether. But that will be done in time." The assimilation process, Sholom Aleichem would have us note, was already underway. Yet, when young Benjamin – so he was called at school – visits the town over vacation, dressed in his uniform, his father's pride is boundless, as is the envy of the community, particularly that of Reb Hersh, the *nogid*. When Benjamin leaves to return to his studies, old Yisroel's joy is complete.

But Benjamin encounters problems, particularly those associated with being a Jew. The quota system keeps him out of the university. His letters become melancholy, and then he stops writing altogether. Then word comes to the town registrar: Benjamin is to be taken off the roster of the Jewish community, by official decree – he has converted. Yisroel had lost his son to the quest for learning, and Sholom Aleichem is unequivocal in his feelings: "What happened afterward? What became of Benjamin? Did he write any more letters? Don't press me with questions. I'll tell you only that as far as Yisroel was concerned, there was no Benjamin anymore anywhere. Benjamin was dead. In the lottery, Yisroel had drawn a blank." Sholom Aleichem, who is his own narrator in this story is bitter at two actions: that of Benjamin for having fallen away from Judaism; second, at the community for rejoicing in Yisroel's fall: "There are people who love to watch a person in agony, who stare at him when he weeps, look after him when he follows a corpse at a funeral, stand by when he wrings his hands. Say what you will, I don't like mournful pictures. My muse does not wear a black veil on her face. My muse is a poor – but cheerful one..." Sholom Aleichem then details the *Schadenfreude* of the town, and of the *nogid* in particular. "'A *shammes*, a ne'er-do-well, a pauper – and he wants to be better than anyone else. He has a son, so what does he have to become? A doctor. Nothing less. I'd like to hear what our *shammes* has to say now. He had it coming', said Reb Hersh, with his peculiar double-cough and stroked his paunch comfortably. 'It should be a lesson for people. A pauper should be careful how he jumps in your face. A doctor he had to have...'" Yisroel's humiliation is total; he is ridiculed by the town for having had the audacity to transcend the measure of *yikhus* he had coming to him; and as a Jew he is destroyed because of his son's conversion, for the crime of the son falls to the father (for Tevye, remember that Chava's marriage to a gentile reflected mostly on him). On top of this, Sholom Aleichem, whose "muse does not wear a black veil on her face", describes the most tragic aspect of Yisroel's fall from grace, the loss of his son: "It was dusk when he turned in at his cottage, looking like a ghost. Entering without a word, he sat down on the ground, took off his boots, tore his shirt at the heart as one does for the dead, and prepared to sit in mourning for an hour, as one does at a time like that. Simma did the same, and so did the three sisters. Together they sat on the ground moaning and weeping for the one they had lost."

In "The Lottery Ticket", Sholom Aleichem concentrates on the effect of the act of assimilation on the *shtetl*, but he does not offer a picture of the assimilated Jew himself, other than the brief return of Benjamin over the holidays. In several stories he singles out the Jew who has broken away, and in each case, without exception, the picture is devastatingly critical. In "Competitors", Sholom Aleichem describes the hilarious encounter of two fruit venders on a train as they vie for the same customers. They abuse each other, each other's goods, and finally, when they begin pushing each other around, one of them loses all of her possessions. The compassionate Jews in the car take up a collection for her, and all give, until they come to a "young intellectual with well-nourished plump cheeks, a small yellow pointed beard, and golden pince-nez. One of these fellows with rich parents, rich parents-in-law and plenty in his own pocket", who refuses to contribute "out of principle", since he considers the whole bunch of bearded Jews and common venders "impudent, vulgar, and ignorant". Although it is not mentioned by Sholom Aleichem, this type of individual in his stories often makes every effort to hide his Jewish identity, and the crisis of this identity Sholom Aleichem inevitably places within the framework of the railroad car, where Jew mingled with Jew and gentile. In "The Tenth Man", a Jew in such a railroad car is trying to gather a *minyan* to say the prayer for his dead son, and for his wife, who died of a broken heart after the son passed away.[9] They found nine willing Jews, but the last person refused to say anything, apparently not understanding the request made in Yiddish:

A quiet beardless man with gold-rimmed pince-nez, he had a small freckled face, a Jewish nose, a mustache with a most un-Jewish upward swirl, protruding ears, and a red neck. Throughout the trip he kept aloof...He was hatless, of course, held a Russian newspaper on his lap, and did not say a word. An honest-to-goodness gentile. An authentic Russky. But then again – was that really a gentile sitting there? He didn't look like a gentile. And furthermore, no Jew could ever fool another Jew. A Jew can recognize a fellow Jew a mile away, even on a moonless night.... We decided it was the same old story all over again. The poor fellow wanted to pass for a gentile.

One of the Jews finally asks him to join them, and the young man, astonishing all with his Yiddish answer, refuses: "I am a Jew, but I don't believe in these things." The father of the dead son is the only one able to reply, and then with a series of anecdotes; the first about a simple Jewish peasant whose wife has a baby in the middle of a gentile village. The Jew lacks a tenth for the *minyan* until a drayman comes along: moral, so many gentiles but only a Jew could help. Then he tells of a fire on a Sabbath eve in a Jewish town. Luckily, along came a gentile, who was able to work on the Sabbath eve, and he put out the fire: moral, so many Jews and only a gentile could help. Finally, he narrates the story of a rabbi's son who got drafted, in spite of bribes and every possible subterfuge, but at the last moment he was rejected because of scurvy hair. After completing the stories, the mourning father turns to the beardless Jew and says, "I ask you now, my dear young man: What good are *you*? A Jew is what you are, a gentile is what you'd

---

[9] Both "Competitors", in *Tevye's Daughters*, 38–45, and "The Tenth Man", in *Some Laughter Some Tears*, 153–157, represent an art form which was peculiar to Sholom Aleichem, the railroad story. Volume XXVIII of the *Collected Works*, in Yiddish, is entitled *Ayznban-geshikhtes, Railroad Stories*. Jewish types spent so much of their time on trains, going and coming, that it was a perfectly natural setting for Jewish stories .

like to be, but most of all you're a scurvy lout!" At the next station the tenth man disappeared.

Yet, like the young emancipated Jew of "The Tenth Man", Sholom Aleichem insists that it is indeed senseless to even try to escape from one's Jewishness, that a Jew is a Jew in spite of himself. Max Berliyant, a traveling salesman by profession, is a lobster-eating, pork chop-devouring Jew who reads the most violently anti-Semitic newspaper available at the station, *The Besserabian*. Sholom Aleichem dates the story for us, because Berliyant is upset about the pogrom at Keshinev, which took place in 1903; but he does not know what he can do about such things, especially since he is now taken for a gentile. In fact, in order to keep other Jews away while on the train, he covers himself with *The Besserabian* while he naps. Upon awakening he discovers the compartment of the train is occupied by another traveler, also covered with pages from *The Besserabian*, a man who like Max, looks peculiarly Jewish. Out of curiosity, Max innocently begins whistling a Jewish folk song, and when the stranger stirs beneath his anti-Semitic newspaper and likewise whistles a few chords of the same tune, the two of them burst out singing the song in Yiddish, joyfully asserting their Jewish identity. The name of the story: "Two Anti-Semites".[10]

Worse off than all the others who abandon the *shtetl* is the *prosteh yid*, the ordinary Jewish workingman who had nothing in the *shtetl*, but has less in the big city. At least, this is what Sholom Aleichem suggests rather all too obviously in "Three Little Heads".[11] Unlike Sholom Asch, Sholom Aleichem did not deal too often with the Jewish proletariat of the big city, but whenever he did, as in this story and two or three others, the point was the same. The city destroys Judaism. The three little heads belong to the children of Peiseh the boxmaker – Avremchik, Moisechik, and Dvorka. The children are called in the Russian manner rather than by their Jewish names, because Peiseh is a Marxist and when he came to the city he wanted to identify himself as a Russian rather

---

[10] "Two-Anti Semites", in *Old Country Tales*, 206–213.
[11] "Three Little Heads", *Selected Stories of Sholom Aleichem*, 333–338.

than a Jew. He would change his own name, except that he was afraid of his wife, who forbade it. He stands all day cutting boxes, singing songs which are not Jewish, and for which his wife reproaches him: "Will you ever stop singing those outlandish songs. You must have fallen in love with them! Since you have come to the big city you are not a Jew anymore." They live in a wretched basement apartment, with a single window that permits only the reflection of the sun to enter. It is *Shevuos*, the holiday most closely associated with nature and the outdoors, but there is no outdoors in Sholom Aleichem's image of the city: "For on their street there is no field, no garden, there are no trees, there's not a blade of grass! On their street there are only tall buildings, gray walls, high chimneys pouring smoke, and every building is covered with windowpanes, thousands of little windowpanes, and inside the buildings are machines that run by themselves, and carts that move without horses. And aside from that, there is nothing, nothing... Born and brought up in the great city, in the large buildings, in crowded quarters, the three children never had a chance to see anything alive – a hen, a cow, or any other creature except a cat." This is an extraordinary anti-city statement, one which advocates quite obviously a return to a natural, romanticized *shtetl* which is in total contrast to anything which Sholom Aleichem ever described or which actually ever existed. What is remarkable is that he ever could have advocated such an anti-progressive, anti-modern viewpoint, considering that he abandoned the *shtetl* as an adolescent and never remotely returned, except on summer vacations with the rest of the big-city tourists. All his life he was a 'fallen-away' Jew, at least in terms of orthodoxy; he was an *Apikoyres*, a modified free-thinker who did not keep even to the kosher dietary regulations, according to his daughter.[12] Yet here we find him painting a dismal picture of city life for the lower-class Jews, who cannot find a bit of greenery to celebrate the *Shevuos* holiday.

[12] Moreover, Sholom Aleichem admitted that Darwin, Spencer, and Buckle were among the most influential thinkers who affected his own writing. As for the dietary laws, his daughter describes in her biography of her father how all the children were permitted to eat ham in the house! See *My Father, Sholom Aleichem* 117–118.

Peiseh, almost in spite of himself and his emancipation, goes to the market place and finds some greens, which he brings back to his hovel: "And when the parents' backs are turned for a moment, the children throw themselves on the floor, bury their heads in the fragrant grasses, fondle and kiss the rough blades that are called greens... There are so many things that Jews must have, and they get them. Even greens... Even greens..." And so the story ends, with Jewish children reaching out for their heritage which was left back at some idealized *shtetl* where nature and the Jewish people were, in Sholom Aleichem's mind, somehow in harmony. What is even stranger is that in this story with a city setting he attempts something of a nature description, while in the vast majority of his *shtetl*-based narratives no such thing ever appears. He describes the *shtetl* in most realistic terms, as a series of mudfilled alleys along which run dilapidated shacks inhabited by hungry Jews.[13]

And yet, it is difficult to see Sholom Aleichem reproaching anyone else but himself. He was much too much a realist to advocate genuinely a return to the *shtetl* life. What he might be suggesting in such a story as "Three Little Heads" is that the Jew, no matter how far he wanders, remains a Jew, and that the cultural heritage of the *shtetl*, for all of its parochialism, is still that unique something which binds all of Eastern Jewry together. This would appear the only acceptable apology from the moral point of view which he advocates in this story, for admittedly, the *shtetl* itself was, in terms of a dignified and satisfactory level of existence, a poor excuse for a community.

2. ON TO SUBURBIA!

It is only proper that the last story we consider in this brief introduction to Sholom Aleichem should look on the *shtetl* with an elegiacal, sentimental, and longing expression. For this has been, remarkably, the attitude of the vast majority of Jews who have

---

[13] The only consistent exception being the Buzie-Shimek stories, which uncharacteristically abound in nature descriptions.

abandoned that life of bondage and suppression back in the Pale. With the possible exception of the former ghetto inhabitants who settled in Israel, there has been a tendency to hold onto the ties which were made with 'the old country' in a way which can still be translated into English. *Yiddishkeit* still has a warm ring for Jews whose roots go back to the Pale of Settlement. For those millions who crossed the ocean to America, there was at least a brief period when they could re-create Kasrilevke beneath the Delancey Street Bridge in New York, without having to give up any part of the old world. The *shtetl* was moved in toto to America's East Coast, as Hutchins Hapgood has so ably pointed out, with the *shayne* and the *proste yidn*, with the *negidim*, with the market places and pushcarts.

But it took only one generation of total freedom which the New World afforded to wreck the *shtetl* structure in a way which the Czar never could accomplish. To the world of the *shtetl*, with its traditional suspicions of the outside, its forced isolation in the face of the hatred around it, acceptance of the Jew as an equal signified the end of the ghetto. It took only one generation for the children of these New York Kasrilevkites, who at first attended New York's city colleges, then Columbia and New York University, and even an occasional non-city Ivy League school, to burst out of the self-imposed isolation of the East Side and to spread out into the split-levels of the suburbs. It took one generation only to almost totally obliterate the *shtetl* fact of life. Maurice Schwartz' Yiddish Art Theatre is now a garage; the 2,000,000 daily readers of the Yiddish newspapers of 1917 are down to a few hundred thousand today; Yiddish is still spoken on the East Side, but now heavily laced with Spanish. A new type of ghetto is emerging under the Delancey Street Bridge.

Yet, the Jewish suburbanites have made their own peculiar arrangement with the Old World. They, along with their children, who attend universities all over the country now, still relate somehow to the *shtetl*. The older generation, which broke out of the American *shtetl* and perhaps still has some affinity to the language of Eastern European Jewry, finds a cultural memory in literary events such as Paddy Chayevsky's *The Tenth Man* or

Fiddler on the Roof. Chayevsky's play uses as its point of departure the theme of the *dybbuk*, the disembodied spirit of a dead person which can find no rest until it takes possession of the mind of a living human being. The theme was popularized on the serious Yiddish stage by what is generally recognized as the greatest achievement of Yiddish drama, Solomon Anski's play *The Dybbuk*. Chayevsky modernizes the language (English), the setting (Long Island), and even the evil spirit itself (now a neurosis), but in spite of the apparent metamorphosis, *The Tenth Man* remains a fundamentally Jewish play, about the exorcizing of an evil spirit, which is particularly identifiable to a Jewish audience, even one two generations removed from such rituals.

Fiddler is an even more graphic case of cultural identification. Of course, the adaptation of Sholom Aleichem's Tevye stories appeals to people of all backgrounds and religions, but undeniably it is American Jewry one generation removed from the East Coast ghettoes which has responded particularly, urging on its children, so that they might discover 'what it was like back in the old country'. For most of the parents and some of the children, Sholom Aleichem is the creator of Tevye, a wise and devoted Jew who sings Jewish melodies with very catchy English lyrics for three hours on an American stage. They can look back on scenes of Golde lighting the *Shabbes* candles and think of a mother or a grandmother. The appeal is emotional, cultural-ethnic, and sure of success. At this writing, after literally thousands of performances of *Fiddler on the Roof* all over America, Europe, and the world, a New York company is preparing a musical adaptation of one of I. B. Singer's most sentimental stories, "The Little Shoemakers", a tale which begins in a Polish *shtetl* and ends up in a split-level ranch house in an American suburb, where five middle-aged Jewish businessmen have set up a replica of their father's old shoe shop, so that the six might still work together as they had done in 'the old country'.

The real Sholom Aleichem lies buried today in Mount Nebo Cemetery in the Cypress Hills section of Brooklyn. On his tombstone is written: "Let me be near the common Jews". This wish was granted him, because his *proste yidn* came by the millions to the shores of America, and he came with them. In a sense, he was not buried in exile, but rather at home, with his fellow Kasrilevkites. If he were alive today, he would no doubt find ample material for his pen in the laughter and tears of his fellow Jews as they act out their unique role in their new homeland. Yet it is uncertain whether he could have coped with the Jew's extraordinary assimilation and the forms that this assimilation took. For the Jew was, generally, welcomed in America, and suffered only slight indignations which in no way compared to his treatment back in Europe. As a result, the *shtetl* world in America disappeared, or is about to disappear. Already beneath the Delancey Street Bridge the language is a peculiar blend of Yiddish and Spanish, as new immigrant waves crowd into the tenements of New York's East Side. But Sholom Aleichem was spared this task of dealing with the subtle problems of the American Jew. He left this to others, and it is to these others that we briefly turn now.

VIII

THE AMERICAN-JEWISH WRITER: AN EPILOGUE

Sholom Aleichem was not the only Yiddish writer to come to America after the turn of the century. Yiddish literature, even in exile, did not die with him. With Kasrilevke's moving to New York, the intellectual center of Yiddish culture shifted westward, away from Russia and Poland, and many Yiddish writers likewise followed Sholom Aleichem to America, where they flourished in the not unfamiliar environment of The East Side. I. J. and I. B. Singer, Mordecai Spector, Abraham Reisen, Lamed Shapiro, Joseph Opatoshu, Itzik Manger, and Jacob Glatstein are just a few of the Yiddish writers who in the years after Sholom Aleichem's death kept up the tradition of Yiddish literature on American soil.

Ironically, the one who demonstrated the least affinity with Sholom Aleichem's writings has attained the greatest fame, to be sure in English translation. Isaac Bashevis Singer's approach to the traditional Yiddish world is so radically different from that of Sholom Aleichem's that it is at times difficult to conceive that both were thoroughly rooted in the Hassidic tradition and drew their inspiration from it.[1] It was Singer who identified Yiddish literature with the irrational and supernatural, with the darker vision of the Jewish world and the conflict between good and evil,

---

[1] See Michael Fixler's article, "The Redeemers: Themes in the Fiction of Isaac Bashevis Singer", *Kenyon Review*, XXVI, no. 2 (Spring, 1964), 371-386.

between devil and God.[2] Singer's work reflects an atmosphere of gothic strangeness which draws chiefly on the kabbalistic side of the Jewish experience. The *shtetl* becomes the setting for a type of struggle almost unknown to Yiddish literature. Still, in spite of such atypical confrontations and conflicts, Singer is capable of sliding into a sentimentality as cloying as any found in the less artistically successful stories of Sholom Aleichem or any other of the above-mentioned Yiddish writers. But, in general Singer's style and themes represent a departure from the main pre-occupations of Yiddish literature as it came to be written by Jews in American 'exile'. For the most part, these young contemporaries of Sholom Aleichem lived in New York, were active in the same circles as Sholom Aleichem, and after he died, carried on the traditions of Yiddish literature, to be sure in a more American vein. Their stories were set now, in the 1920s and 1930s, in the Kasrilevke of The East Side, a world equally humorous and depressing as that of Sholom Aleichem.[3] Writing still in Yiddish for the Jewish millions, serialized and circulated through the Jewish newspapers of New York, these literary figures represented the last burst of energy which the culture of the ghetto was able to muster before the rise of National Socialism. Late in the thirties Jewish immigration stopped; the process of assimilation had begun almost immediately around the turn of the century for those with the energy and the will to do so. Today, with the exception of I. B. Singer, one would be hard-pressed to establish the literary reputation of a Yiddish writer in The United States, or even in New York, for that matter. With extraordinary suddenness, yet consistent with the meteoric rise of the literary traditions of Yiddish, Yiddish

[2] Sholom Aleichem's sense of fantasy is something quite different from that of Singer. Typical is "The Malicious Matzoh", in which the Czar's ministers suggest a ban on the production of *matzoh*, the Jews' unleavened bread. The Czar eats a piece out of curiousity, becomes violently ill, and the physicians discover a Jew in the Czar's stomach; he was hiding in the piece of matzoh! The Jew now forces the monarch to retract all anti-Jewish decrees, whereupon "the Jew squeezes himself out through the Czar's little finger and goes off looking for a spot of business". *Old Country Tales*, 278–280.

[3] The most comprehensive anthology of Yiddish writers who wrote while in America can be found in *A Treasury of Yiddish Stories*, edited by Howe and Greenberg, Viking Compass Book (New York: Viking Press, 1965).

literature, as an identifiable cultural and linguistic entity, has nearly disappeared. It reached its peak shortly before World War One, had the greatest reading public in the pre-Depression years in America and the post-Czarist euphoria in Soviet Russia; and is very near extinction now.

It is the fact of this process of extinction which makes the prominence of Yiddish literature, and Sholom Aleichem in particular, all the more extraordinary. For at a time when the number of Yiddish speakers in the world is rapidly decreasing, when all indicators point to the erosion of the cultural ground soil of *Yiddishkeit*, this minor and highly personal nationalistic literary tradition is exerting a cultural force in exile equal to its impact at its most influential point on those Jews of the Pale for whom the literature was originally intended. The result is that aspect of American literature which has produced the American-Jewish writer.

Why should almost an entire generation of writers who happen to be Jewish almost without exception focus their attention on the nature of their Jewish identity? One is tempted to talk in terms of the 'ethnicizing' of American life and letters over the past two decades since the revolution in black American literature has gotten underway. Indeed, since that revolution commenced there has been an ever-growing tendency on the part of other ethnic groups to participate. On college campuses Black Studies are giving ground to American Indian Studies, Chinese-American Studies, language classes in Armenian for Armenian-Americans, even Yiddish for non-native speakers. There is a clear and conscious re-awakening on the part of Americans, particularly the young, in the cultural past, in the ethnic roots and traditions of two generations or more before them. The reasons for this development are too complicated to consider in any detail at this point and in this study. One would have to start with the quality of life in America, the ability of American culture to provide cultural roots, the nature of ethnic memory, and the need for a folk heritage. Along with the growing awareness of blacks which is now manifest in almost every aspect of American life, the identifiable phenomenon of Jewish self-awareness is the most striking incident of this 'return to the sources', mainly because it has played such a conspicuous role in contemporary American fiction. And in no other instance can these sources be so clearly traced. For without exception the inspiration, indeed the characterization, can be found in the insecure *shtetl* world of the Pale, and in the writings particularly of Sholom Aleichem.

Although there are a dozen writers currently drawing their literary energies from this world which no longer exists, for my purposes I shall focus on three who demonstrate in varying degrees the nature of the relationship between Yiddish literature and American fiction today: Bernard Malamud, Saul Bellow, and Philip Roth.[4] They represent the two generations of post-Sholom Aleichem Jews who came to The New World. Malamud, born in 1914, Bellow in 1915, and Roth in 1932, effectively bridge the gap between the Jewish child of the American ghetto and the Jewish child of suburbia. They chronicle the process of assimilation of the Jewish American and the nature of the Jewish experience in America.

Of the three writers, Bernard Malamud's sense of Yiddishkeit is by far the most visible. The opening of his short story "The Magic Barrel" is as follows:

Not long ago there lived in uptown New York, in a small, almost meagre room, though crowded with books, Leo Finkle, a rabbinical student at the Yeshivah University. Finkle, after six years of study, was to be ordained in June and had been advised by an acquaintance that he might find it easier to win himself a congregation if he were married. Since he had no present prospects of marriage, after two tormented days of turning it over in his mind, he called in Pinye Salzman, a marriage broker whose two-line advertisement he had read in the *Forward*.[5]

With Salzman's appearance we are carried back centuries into a past which Malamud somehow carried in his veins. The marriage broker is a ghost from the world of Sholom Aleichem:

---

[4] Also suggested are the writings of Henry Roth, Herbert Gold, Daniel Fuchs, Bruce Jay Friedman, Mark Harris, Harvey Swados, Chaim Potok, J. D. Salinger, and Edward Lewis Wallant.
[5] In *The Magic Barrel* (New York: Farrar, Straus & Giroux, 1959), 193.

He smelled frankly of fish, which he loved to eat, and although he was missing a few teeth, his presence was not displeasing, because of an amiable manner curiously contrasted with mournful eyes. His voice, his lips, his wisp of a beard, his bony fingers were animated...He fumbled with the portfolio straps and took out of the leather case an oily paper bag, from which he extracted a hard, seeded roll and a small, smoked white fish. With a quick motion of his hand he stripped the fish out of its skin and began ravenously to chew. 'All day in a rush,' he muttered.[6]

Finkle, the insecure rabbinical student who calls in a matchmaker, and Salzman, harried, "all day in a rush", the Jewish "dreher" trying to create a living out of air are both parts of the same past, the world of the *shtetl luftmensh*. The only difference in Malamud's vision of the two men is that he describes them in English rather than in Yiddish. However their cultural identity is in no way American, and the inspiration which created them and which makes them breathe can only be traced back to the talmudic students of the Pale who prayed for a Friday night meal from some *nogid* and to the Menachem Mendels, a *shadchan* who once arranged a marriage between two men!

However, it cannot be denied that Malamud clearly transcends this *shtetl* experience once he concentrates on the inter-action of his characters and provides an intellectual frame of reference which is more complicated than anything written by Sholom Aleichem. The problem of Finkle's redemption in "The Magic Barrel" is much beyond anything attempted by Malamud's predecessors, but after all, the Yiddish audience of the Pale was considerably different from Malamud's somewhat more sophisticated American readers, and one might expect this. But the essential nature of the characters of Malamud's fiction is undeniably Yiddish: their inflection, their attitude, their suffering, even their humor. This is all apparent in the brief exchange between Finkle, who is desperately searching for the marriage-broker, and Mrs. Salzman, the ever-suffering Jewish wife, as they stand before the door of her Bronx apartment:

[6] *The Magic Barrel*, 193–200.

'Salzman – does he live here? Pinye Salzman,' he said, 'the matchmaker?'
She stared at him a long minute. 'Of course.'
He felt embarrassed. 'Is he in?'
'No.' Her mouth though left open, offered nothing more.
'The matter is urgent. Can you tell me where his office is?'
'In the air.' She pointed upward.
'You mean he has no office'? Leo asked.
'In his socks...' At length she answered, 'So who knows where he is? Everytime he thinks a new thought he runs to a different place. Go home, he will find you.'
'Tell him Leo Finkle.'
She gave no sign she had heard. He walked downstairs, depressed. But Salzmann, breathless, stood waiting at his door. Leo was astounded and overjoyed. 'How did you get here before me?' 'I rushed.'[7]

In the end, Leo Finkle discovers those missing ingredients which had eluded him and had caused his great despair: true love, both of man and of God, discoveries for which Sholom Aleichem's struggling Jews would have merely shrugged a shoulder. After all, who in the *shtetl* had time for such redemptive luxuries? Leo Finkle, in terms of his heritage, his attitudes, his general cultural base, is a Kasrilevkite; his inner turmoil, however, has its source in Malamud's vision. His novels and short stories are Dostoyevskian in their singular attention to the problems of guilt, expiation, and salvation. Malamud thus represents the perfect synthesis of Old World inhabitants with New World anxieties. Malamud's *shlemihls, shlimazls*, and *luftmenshen* are different from their *shtetl* counterparts only insofar as their creator has penetrated deeper into their minds. Sholom Aleichem never permits himself to intrude upon the privacy of Tevye, Menachem-Mendel, or Mottel. We see them functioning in their environment, but we are never taken into the more subtle regions of their psychic thoughts. If he had been born to another generation, to one of Yiddish writers of the old country, Malamud might have been Yiddish literature's first 'psychological' writer.

It has already been mentioned that Malamud writes exclusively in English. However, the quality of his language is so affected by the Yiddish idiom that often it seems that one is dealing with an

[7] *The Magic Barrel*, 210–211.

English translation. Nowhere is this more apparent than in *The Assistant* (1957). Morris Bober, a sixty-year-old failure in a grocery store in a dying neighborhood of Brooklyn, waits for his bitterly suffering wife Ida to come downstairs. Breitbart, the bulb salesman with an idiot son, has just finished reading the Jewish paper and has had his glass of tea in the back of the store:

> After ten minutes he got up, scratched all over, lifted across his thin shoulders the two large cartons tied together with clothesline and left. Morris watched him go. The world suffers. *He* felt every schmerz. At lunchtime Ida came down. She had cleaned the whole house. Morris was standing before the faded couch, looking out of the rear window at the back yards. He had been thinking of Ephraim. His wife saw his wet eyes. 'So stop sometimes, please.' Her own grew wet. He went to the sink, caught cold water in his cupped palms and dipped his face into it. 'The Italyener', he said, drying himself, 'bought this morning across the street.' She was irritated. 'Give him for twenty-nine dollars five rooms so he should spit in your face.' 'A cold water flat,' he reminded her. 'You put in gas radiators.' 'Who says he spits? This I didn't say.' 'You said something to him not nice?' 'Me?' 'Then why he went across the street?'[8]

These remarks fairly well define Morris Bober's world and point out the similarity to that of Tevye's. The futile struggle for financial security, the suffering wife, the Jew surrounded by gentiles, a beloved son prematurely dead, all these themes are ones familiar to the *shtetl*. Besides these, Morris' other preoccupation is with his only daughter Helen, who is being courted by the grocer's gentile assistant, Frankie Alpine. The sense of foreboding which Ida experiences could only be greeted by Tevye with a knowing nod:

> She spoke to Morris and cautiously asked if he had noticed anything developing between Helen and the clerk. 'Don't be foolish,' the grocer replied. He had thought about the possibility, at times felt concerned, but after pondering how different they were, had put the idea out of his head.
> 'Morris, I'm afraid.'
> 'You are afraid of everything, even when it doesn't exist.'
> 'Tell him to leave now – business is better.'
> 'So is better', he muttered, 'but who knows how will be next week.

[8] *The Assistant* (New York: Farrar, Straus and Cudahy, 1957), 7.

We decide he will stay till summer.'
'Morris, he will make trouble.'
'What kind trouble will he make?'
'Wait,' she said, clasping her hands, 'a tragedy will happen.'
Her remark at first annoyed, then worried him.[9]

The "tragedy", that a Jewish girl should marry "the Italyener", perfectly represents the smaller world of Malamud's vision and underlines the relationship to the *shtetl*. Of course, the qualities which make Malamud artistically superior to Sholom Aleichem are not within the province of this study. His concern with the mythic journeys of his protagonist "to test the stuff of his heroism", as Jonathan Baumbach suggests, puts Malamud's fiction, at least in terms of its intellectual goals, in a different class than that of Sholom Aleichem's.[10] But our concern is not with this 'larger world' of Malamud. What is relevant is the fact that in building a superior device, Malamud has started with the old, traditional materials of Yiddish literature.

Most of the former *shtetl* inhabitants of Malamud's fiction actually were born in the old country. They are predominantly older men, unlike Leo Finkle, but in the tradition of Pinye Salzman: Feld, the shoemaker; Kessler, formerly an egg-candler; Manischeitz, a tailor. They are all *proste yidn*, the little people of Kasrilevke, all unfortunate *shlimazls*; in Malamud's terms, jinxed men who in their twilight years have nothing to look forward to other than more bad fortune. It is in this state of affairs that Malamud confronts them and the failure of their lives, and by means of his own kind of peculiar literary magic, converts these Jewish sufferers into mythic heroes, who go far beyond their *shtetl* origins in the significance of their salvation.

But in his more recent novel, *The Fixer* (1966), Malamud reaches back to the *shtetl*, and away from a New World integration, so that the suffering, redemption, and ultimate salvation of Jakov Bok has much more meaning in terms of Kasrilevke than any of his

---

[9] *The Assistant*, 223.
[10] See Jonathan Baumbach, "All Men Are Jews" in *The Landscape of Nightmare*: Studies in the Contemporary American Novel (New York: New York University Press, 1965), 106.

previous writings. The work is a fictionalizing of the events of the Beiliss Case of 1911 referred to earlier, when a Jew in Kiev was arrested and accused of the ritual murder of a Russian child, in order to provide blood for the preparation of Passover matzohs. Malamud's hero, Jakov Bok, is a miserable failure in the *shtetl*, an unemployed fixer: "I have to dig with my fingernails for a living...In the shtetl everything is falling apart. Who bothers with leaks in his roof when he's peaking through cracks in his roof to spy on God? Opportunity here is born dead."[11] He finds the village in which he has grown up a prison, his Judaism a dead weight around his neck, and he is determined to abandon both. Bok, cursing his state in life, his Jewishness, and everything about his life, runs to the big city, to Kiev, where he tries to pass for a gentile. He succeeds for a time, but the deception is discovered just in time to make him the perfect fall-guy for the murder of a gentile boy. He is arrested, imprisoned, and forced to face the most terrible physical and mental abuse, all because he belonged to a faith which he detests and shuns. In the depths of his prison despair, Jakov Bok, the Jew in spite of himself, laments: "His fate nauseated him. Escaping from the Pale he had at once been entrapped in prison. From birth a black horse had followed him, a Jewish nightmare. What was being a Jew but an everlasting curse? He was sick of their history, destiny, blood guilt."[12] But the endless months in a solitary jail cell gives Jakov, the eternal *shlimazl*, an integrity he was unaware of. The authorities promise to let him go free if he will admit that he was used as a tool of Jewish religious circles, although they are perfectly aware of his innocence. Bok has become a political pawn of the Czarist authorities who hope to whip up public hatred of the Jews in order to take attention away from official corruption and the people's misery. Jakov is aware that his confession will bring down a reign of terror against his fellow Jews. So Jakov Bok, who keeps asking "why me?", a little Jew with no stomach for heroism or martyrdom, indeed, with no desire to be a Jew, ceases to run from his fate: "So for a Jew it was the same wherever he went, he carried

---

[11] *The Fixer*, Dell Edition (New York: Dell Publishing Company, 1966), 12.
[12] Ibid., 187. *The Fixer*.

a remembrance pack on his back... No, there was no need to go to Kiev, or Moscow or any place else. You could stay in the shtetl and trade in air and beans... but a Jew wasn't free."[13]

Thus, Malamud forces upon a reluctant Jew his inescapable past. No matter if one tries to run from the *shtetl*, it will follow him. In the ordeal of Jakov Bok Malamud asserts the unalterability of the Jewish experience. Like Sholom Aleichem's "two anti-Semites", it is this realization that sustains Bok and permits him to triumph.

If Malamud's sense of *Yiddishkeit*, in terms of theme, characterization, even tone of language, seems quite apparent, one must look more closely at the works of Saul Bellow to determine the nature of the cultural connection. Bellow is not the same sort of 'overt' Jewish writer: his language is uniquely his own and hardly bears a hint of the traditional Yiddish inflections which one encounters throughout Malamud's prose; his settings are exclusively American, and with the exception of *The Adventures of Augie March* (1953), avoid even the East Side atmosphere of Malamud or the Jewish suburban world of Philip Roth. Moreover, Bellow is a supremely intellectual, even philosophical writer, who deals with problems in a way which one never encountered in the relatively simplistic world of Sholom Aleichem. The fact that all of his protagonists outside of Eugene Henderson (*Henderson the Rain King*, 1959) are Jewish is not sufficient reason of itself to identify Bellow as being part of the same tradition as Sholom Aleichem. Even the treatment of the theme of anti-Semitism in *The Victim* (1947) is uniquely part of Bellow's conception and not necessarily within the frame of reference of 'traditional' antagonism towards Jews.

One has to consider all of Bellow's heroes side-by-side to see in his conception of them the relationship of them to, say, a Menachem-Mendel. Although they scarcely speak the same language, they share a common fate: they are all *luftmenshen*, and even more so, *shlemihls*. The very title of his first novel, *The Dangling Man* (1944), suggests the image of a helpless figure suspended in mid-air, searching for a footing in life. Joseph Cohn is not a traditional

---

[13] Ibid., 255. *The Fixer*.

shtetl dreher, hustling for a living. He is sensitive, intelligent, a modern man. But he is no less 'detached' from existence than his European prototypes. Like Sholom Aleichem, Bellow permits Joseph to tell his own story, in the form of a journal. Thus, in the manner of Menachem-Mendel, Joseph explores his own lack of substance and uselessness. In *The Victim*, Asa Leventhal, living alone, is confronted by Allbee and accused of ruining his life by causing Allbee to lose his job. Leventhal's sense of inadequacy, Allbee's accusations, and the confrontation between sensitive Jew and debauched anti-Semite heighten in Leventhal the realization that he has no personal identification, that he too is, like all of Bellow's heroes, a dangling man.

But Bellow's characters are dangling men of mind, and not so much of matter. They are mental *luftmenshen*, unable to function and causing themselves great psychic pain because of their complex and problematic states of mind. Nowhere is this more apparent than in the case of Moses Herzog, the compulsive, letter-writing (once again Menachem-Mendel!) academician who is the hero of Bellow's novel *Herzog* (1964). Moses, twice divorced, with psychiatrists in both Chicago and New York, painfully comes to grips with his past in an effort to save his future. He has been a meek 'receiver', humiliated and betrayed by friends now identified as enemies. In a depersonalized society devoid of love, Moses is unable to find a footing, and so he too dangles. He tries to find in his intellectual activities a foot-hold, but upon honest re-examination, he realizes that this can provide no solution to his problems. Now Bellow suggests for Herzog a means to his salvation which had not been offered in any of the previous works: a return to the past, to the family. In his reveries about the old Jewish ghetto in Montreal, where he (and Bellow) was raised, Moses gradually begins to discover a source of strength. He is at his calmest when he makes a sort of pilgrimage to the old family home in Chicago where his parents moved after coming down from Canada, and Moses emerges with a new resolution. With financial and mental support from his brother, Moses, the brilliant *shlemihl* finds peace of mind finally in his own little *shtetl* in Western Massachusetts farm country.

If *Herzog* seems to point to perhaps a growing sense of more traditional *Yiddishkeit* in Bellow, one finds in his latest novel, *Mr. Sammler's Planet* (1970), a further development. Sammler himself is saved from the gas chambers by his own wits, and then later he and his daughter are rescued from an internment camp when a highly family-oriented relative discovers their names on a roster of displaced persons. This relative, Dr. Gruner, enjoys spending hours chatting with Sammler about relatives in the old country, and his death forces upon Sammler the realization that he has lost his only genuine relative. For those younger American Jews who surround Sammler are all misfits of one kind or another. Besides finding in Gruner a compassionate soul, Mr. Sammler also experiences a similar reaction during the six-day Arab–Israeli War of 1967. Driven by an inner urge, although nearly seventy years old, Sammler, a former journalist, manages to make his way to the front almost immediately after hostilities had begun. His sense of the matter was: where else should a Jew be but here? For Bellow, this is no less than an extraordinary direction. There is a certain militant ethnic quality about the novel which is hinted at in *Herzog* and develops full-blown in *Mr. Sammler's Planet*. Clearly Sammler laments the passing of the qualities which could be found in the traditions honored by his benefactor Dr. Gruner. And more than this, he is horrified by and disgusted with the values of the young, with their bad manners and their total rejection of the Jewish experience as Sammler understands its. The novel is filled with what Alfred Kazin calls "the punitive moral outrage" of Bellow as he invokes the civilized past of Jewish traditions as opposed to the irrationality of the world as Sammler (and Bellow) now see it.[14] As a result, this "least Jewish" and most consistently intellectual of the American-Jewish writers seems to be re-establishing his identity more clearly within the ethical and moral frame of reference of Judaism. With *Mr. Sammler's Planet*, Bellow places himself solidly in the ranks of the Yiddish didactic moralists of a century earlier, these such as Mendele Mocher Sforim, who looked at

---

[14] See Kazin's review of *Mr. Sammler's Planet* in *New York Review of Books*, Vol. XV, No. 10 (December 3, 1970), 3.

the 'modern' Jew with contempt, and with literary jeremiads not unlike Sammler's portrayed a world of misfits, quacks, and decadent Jewish types who had lost their way.

The last of the Jewish writers to be discussed here is no doubt the most sensational. Philip Roth, born in 1932, is not of either Bellow's or Malamud's generation. His familiarity with Yiddish is limited to a few catch phrases picked up from listening to his parents' conversations (Bellow is himself an expert translator from the Yiddish). His fictive world hardly bears any resemblance to Malamud's East Side, or to the more American ghetto experience of Bellow in *Herzog* or *Augie March*. Roth is most at home in the assimilated Jewish world of the elegant suburb. Or perhaps one should say least at home. For of these three writers, and perhaps among all of the American-Jewish writers, Roth is the most caustic, the most critical, and ironically, the most Jewish, in a literary sense. His writings have embarrassed Jewish communities and their spiritual leaders, brought down on Roth the accusation of anti-Semitism, and in general caused a great deal of consternation. Had Sholom Aleichem written in Russian, he might have caused the same reaction. For Sholom Aleichem was no less a social satirist than Roth. He exposed the Jews to their own frailties and could cut deeply with the pen. This, of course, is Roth's strength as well. He specializes in depicting the shallowness of Jewish social existence in America; his works are filled with hypocritical rabbis, inconsiderate parents, indifferent *negidim* who squander their money to acquire more *yichus*, social climbing wives, and brutalized children. The themes are quite familiar to us by now: they are the stuff of Yiddish literature, the very same ideas which the great Yiddishists of the nineteenth-century faced. But this time, it was not only for Jewish eyes. Roth writes in English, and this is the major difference. His unflattering picture of American Jewry takes precedent over his moralistically admirable purpose, at least in the eyes of his detractors. They view his critical vision as a device which exposes American Jewry, which makes it vulnerable by depicting it as made up of a wholly unattractive, materialistic, and morally vacant mass of people. And he is read by non-Jews.

Sholom Aleichem wrote only for Jews; but Philip Roth writes

for anyone who reads English. This is the reason, one might suggest, that Roth finds himself under such rigorous attack by Jewish groups. The irony is that he is accused of being "un-Jewish", while actually he is, in terms of themes and traditions of Yiddish literature, utterly Jewish.

The collection of shorter pieces entitled *Goodbye, Columbus* (1959) reveals all of Roth's varied thematic stuff as well as his 'gripes'. The title story is a catalog of the American-Jew's romance with American anti-culture. In depicting the life and times of an upward-mobile Jewish family which has escaped the lower-class Jewish world of downtown Newark, New Jersey and now enjoys all the pleasures and comforts of suburban Short Hills, Roth takes us through a world of Andre Kostalanetz, Montovani, Wildroot Cream Oil, Bit Ten Football, Senior Proms, fraternity skits, Margaret Sanger Clinics, Hadassah, backyard basketball courts, and "Radcliffies". It is an utterly American family, totally absorbed in the devastatingly banal and trivial business of getting ahead. Yet, what strikes home is the obvious similarity between the style of life of Roth's Jews of the suburbs and Sholom Aleichem's Nouveau Riche Jews with their delightfully overstated pretenses. Both writers, by means of a delicious sense of social satire, permit their subjects to reveal their own shallowness. In "Goodbye, Columbus" Mrs. Patimkin, the wealthy wife and mother, is gently cross-examining her daughter's current suitor, in an effort to find out if he is 'the right' sort of young man. She is attempting to determine which of the three branches of Judaism Neil advocates:

'We're all going to Temple Friday night. Why don't you come with us? I mean, are you orthodox or conservative?' I considered. 'Well, I haven't gone in a long time...I sort of switch...I'm just *Jewish*', I said well-meaningly, but that too sent Mrs. Patimkin back to her Hadassah work. Finally I asked: 'Do you know Martin Buber's work?'
'Buber...Buber', she said, looking at her Hadassah list, 'is he orthodox or conservative?', she asked.
'...He's a philosopher.'
'Is he *reformed*?', she asked, piqued either at my evasiveness or at the possibility that Buber attended Friday night services without a hat, and Mrs. Buber had only one set of dishes in her kitchen.

'Orthodox', I said faintly.
'That's very nice'. she said.[15]

Neil, who tells his own story throughout, comments bitingly on the values and conceptions of the Patimkins. He looks at Mr. Patimkin, prosperous owner of Patimkin Bathroom and Kitchen Sinks, a good-hearted war-profiteer who wants nothing else out of life other than to provide for his family. Neil mocks him, and would give everything at the same time to be taken into the family and the company, so that he too might escape the world of 'the downtown Jews' and move to the suburbs. Mrs. Patimkin, for whom Roth reserves particular treatment, is the re-incarnation of the *shtetl* mother-Gestalt, bereft of any sympathetic qualities. She actively dislikes her daughter Brenda, stuffs her son and husband with food, and commutes in a whirlwind of activity between the Hadassah and Temple.

The Patimkins have not completely escaped from Newark. In the basement of their suburban ranch house is the old refrigerator, and Brenda and Neil make love in an old attic room stuffed with ancient furniture of the Patimkin's former existence, a scene which amply demonstrates Roth's point while not being artistically satisfactory, however. There are other vestiges of the existence they would prefer to forget. Ben's half-brother Leo is a Malamudian *shlimazl* who embarrasses the more prosperous members of the family at the wedding of the Patimkin's son Ronald. Yet he strikes a very familiar chord, as he confides to Neil:

'Look at me', Leo said, splashing his suit front with champagne, 'I sell a good bulb. You can't get the kind of bulb I sell in the drugstores. It's a quality bulb. But I'm the little guy. I don't even own a car. His brother, and I don't even own an automobile. I take a train wherever I go. I'm the only guy I know who wears out three pairs of rubbers every winter. Most guys get new ones when they lose the old ones. I wear them out, like shoes.[16]

In each of the following stories Roth holds up for consideration another of his 'Jewish types'. In "The Conversion of the Jews" it

---

[15] *Goodbye, Columbus*, (New York: Bantam Books, Inc., 1963), 62–63.
[16] *Goodbye Columbus*, 80.

is the hypocritical Rabbi Binder, a supposedly enlightened, 'modern' American rabbi who permits during the afternoon of religious instruction a free-discussion: "feel free to talk about any Jewish matter at all – religion, family, politics, sport –".[17] In this apparently open discussion little Ozzie Freedman, a pre-Bar Mitzvoh, perfectly normal but curious Jewish boy, posed three questions to the rabbi: First, if God could do anything, why could he not have a baby produced without intercourse, thereby acknowledging the possibility of the divine birth of Jesus? Secondly, why does his mother pick out only the Jewish names when reading about some tragedy in the newspapers; and finally, if the Declaration of Independence says that all men are created equal, how can the Jews be the Chosen People? Each time Rabbi Binder's enlightened reply was to invite Mrs. Freedman, a widow, down for a little chat. Everywhere Roth underlines the stupidity of the spiritual leader. Ozzie likes to read Hebrew slowly, so as to comprehend better. The rabbi insists that he read the Hebrew for speed, regardless of comprehension. Finally, after having been hit by his mother because of the rabbi's complaints about Ozzie's questions, the young boy explodes one day at his teacher "You don't know! You don't know anything about God!", and when Binder in rage strikes Ozzie across the face, the boy flees from the world which apparently is oppressing his genuine inquiries. The themes are once again classically Yiddish: the ignorant *malamed* brutalizing Jewish children and frustrating their creativity; the widowed Jewish mother hovering over the only male child, alternating kisses and blows. The hesitating steps toward intelligent questioning, which Binder spuriously advocates, are halted when the questioning becomes too complicated, indeed are met with violence.

"Defender of the Faith" falls into that category of story which Sholom Aleichem consciously cultivated at times, the Jewish war story, and the attitudes of the Jew toward his military obligations. Again in this story Roth is relentlessly critical, as three young Jewish recruits toward the end of World War One attempt to take advantage of a crusty Jewish top sergeant and combat veteran who

---

[17] "The Conversion of the Jews", in *Goodbye, Columbus*, 104.

is first puzzled when the Jewish recruits clearly expect preferential treatment from him, because "he is one of them". Roth's Sergeant Marx emerges with a newly found sense of Jewish identity to be sure, but after arranging for the shipping out to the Pacific Theatre of war of Grossbart, along with Fishbein and Halpern (they had hoped for a local assignment), Marx is accused of being an anti-Semite by Grossbart and is left to contemplate his actions. But in the figure of Sheldon Grossbart Roth has created the most negative image of the Jewish soldier since the draft-dodging days of Sholom Aleichem.

In many ways the most interesting story of the collection is "Eli the Fanatic", in which a progressive and totally assimilated Jewish community on Long Island is shocked to discover one morning soon after the end of the war that a group of displaced Jewish children have been moved into a mansion in town which is to become The Yeshivah of Woodenton, New York. The sight of a *Hassid* running through the streets of this modern, commuting upper-middle class Jewish community, with his long black caftan and broad-brimmed hat, sends the "young moderns" flocking to their friend, townsman, and lawyer, Eli Peck. The question is how to get rid of these Jews with skullcaps, "these goddam fanatics", as the modern Jews call the new residents. The experience of dealing with these long-suffering immigrants is both traumatic and enlightening for Eli, who has already suffered a nervous breakdown and has been a patient of Dr. Eckman, his psychiatrist, for some time. Now this, and the experience produces one of Roth's most funny, exhilarating, and mordantly critical stories.

But none of his writings has caused as much furor as has the appearance of the novel *Portnoy's Complaint* in 1969. Using Sholom Aleichem's favorite method of the first-person narrative, Roth permits Alexander Portnoy to explain to his psychiatrist what it is like to be a Jewish son. The major difference between Roth and Sholom Aleichem in the application of this narrative technique is that within the American experience one tells one's problems to a psychiatrist. Sholom Aleichem's narrators are often no less emotionally disturbed young men, but, unlike Alexander Portnoy, such was not their fate to have a Dr. Spielvogel around! In all other respects, however, the problems of Roth's hero are remarkably similar to those encountered in the mature Jewish men who tell their life-stories to the unseen listener in the collection *Stories for Jewish Children* of Sholom Aleichem.

There is one further footnote which might be mentioned that further draws these three American writers back to the *shtetl* world of Sholom Aleichem. Each deals with a theme which was also of particular concern to the Yiddish writer, namely the Jew's relationship with the Russian peasants immediately sharing their misery and hardship. To the American writers, this translates into the tensions existing between the Jew, and the class of American with whom he has shared the ghetto, the black. The writings themselves make it abundantly clear that the conflict between Jew and black is of major concern to these three men: Malamud in "The Angel Levine" and "Black is my Favorite Color", Roth in "Goodbye, Columbus", and Bellow most recently in *Mr. Sammler's Planet* hint at a major literary and social confrontation in this theme still to come.[18]

We come to the end of this modest introduction. Yiddish literature has exchanged the black caftan and the peasant's blouse for the Brooks Brothers suit. Tevye's hut has become the split-level on Long Island; and even the *mama loshen* has had to give way to the articulate breeding of literate English. But, somehow, the quality of Yiddish life, with all its complications and problems which seem in terms of sensibility and distance so thoroughly removed from American life in the 1970s, this near-dead world is unquestionably exerting an extraordinary influence on American literature today. Like so many of the ironies present in Sholom Aleichem, Yiddish literature and *Yiddishkeit*, the culture of the *shtetl*, suggest the most ironical of all: they have risen from the ashes of Eastern Europe to come alive once again, and in the minds of a group of American writers have been given a sort of immortality which points to an even greater significance in the future for the world of Sholom Aleichem.

[18] See also Malamud's latest novel, *The Tenants* (New York: Farrar, Straus, and Giroux, 1971).

APPENDIX: SHOLOM ALEICHEM IN YIDDISH

This appendix is intended as an introduction to the Yiddish material available to the student of Sholom Aleichem who might have a reading knowledge of that language. For a definitive bibliography, a reading knowledge of Russian would be essential. All material listed may be found in the YIVO library collection in New York City.

1. GENERAL

For studies in Yiddish Literature, the most fundamental research tool is *Leksikon fun der yidisher literature, prese nu filologye*, ed. Zalmen Reyzen (Vilna, 1929) (2nd edition); the article on Sholom Aleichem is extremely useful, in vol. 4, 573–736.
Dos Sholom Aleichem-bukh, ed. Y. D. Berkowitz (New York, 1926). The editor was Sholom Aleichem's son-in-law and his first translator into Hebrew. Berkowitz was an intimate associate of Sholom Aleichem during the last decade of the writer's life. This volume contains a great deal of correspondence, literary vignettes, and other useful information not available elsewhere.

2. COLLECTIONS OF WORKS

There is no authoritative or definitive bibliography of Sholom Aleichem's works, either in Yiddish, English, or any other language. The nature of his writing makes such an undertaking formidable. He published in a variety of Yiddish newspapers and journals, and it is difficult enough to determine how many works he wrote. As for a *Complete Works*, this might be an impossible task, given the state of newspaper collections in Soviet Russia today. Searching out individual stories in Yiddish newspapers long gone conceivably could be out of the question. In 1954 Uriel Weinreich wrote in *The Field of Yiddish*: "The publication of a complete collection of Sholom Aleichem's works was undertaken at least three times, but two attempts were not completed; a third is in progress. So far, all series entitled *Ale verk* ('All Works') are, in fact, selections only. The basic edition, planned for about forty volumes, only got as far as volume 28." *Publications of the Linguistic Circle of New York*, Number 3 (Columbia University).

Ale verk fun Sholom Aleichem, 28 volumes (New York: Sholom Aleichem Folksfond, 1917–25). The following are the titles of each of the twenty-eight volumes of this most complete edition in Yiddish:

>Vol. I: *Fun Kasrilevke* (contains "Kasrilevker progres")
>Vol. II: *Fun peysakh biz peysakh* (mostly stories of the holidays)
>Vol. III: *Mayses un fantazyes* (fantasies and more imaginative stories)
>Vol. IV: *Dramatishe shriftn* (several, but not all, plays)
>Vol. V: *Tevye der milkhiker* (contains all but the last of the Tevye stories)
>Vol. VI: *Kleyne mentshelekh mit kleyne hasoges* (contains many of the great Kasrilevke stories: "Di shtot fun kleyne mentshelekh", "Drayfus in Kasrilevke", "Tsvey shalakh-monesn" "Ven ikh bin Roytshild")
>Vol. VII: *In shturem* (a novel of the city in picaresque tradition)
>Vol. VIII: *Mayses far yidishe kinder I* (contains Sholom Aleichem's first major story "Dos meserl")
>Vol. IX: *Mayses far yidishe kinder II* ("Grins oyf shvues", "Dos dreydl", the rest of the non-Mottel children stories)
>Vol. X: *Menakhem-Mendel*

Vol. XI: *Yidishe romanen* (*Stempenyu* complete)
Vol. XII: *Zumer-lebn* (contains satires and vacation stories)
Vol. XIII: *Alt-nay Kasrilevke* (contains the material for *Inside Kasrilevke*, as well as the story "A peysakhike ekspropriatsye")
Vol. XIV: *Yosele Solovey* (a novel)
Vol. XV: *Yidishe shrayber*
Vol. XVI: *Oreme un freylekhe I* (contains "A vigrishne bilet")
Vol. XVII: *Oreme un freylekhe II* (contains many of the sketches of Kasrilevke types: "Elik der mekhanik", "Kopl balmoyakh", "Mendel der blekhener")
Vol. XVIII: *Motl Peyse dem khazns I* (Part One of the Mottel stories)
Vol. XIX: *Motl Peyse dem khazns II* (Part Two of the Mottel stories)
Vol. XX: *Yugnt-romanen* (the earlier long prose works)
Vol. XXI: *Monologn*
Vol. XXII: *Lekoved yontev I* (contains holiday stories and some marginal holiday tales, such as "Knortn" [Cnards])
Vol. XXIII: *Lekoved yontev II* (city stories and village stories of holidays)
Vol. XXIV: *Komedyes* (dramatizations)
Vol. XXV: *Fun tsvey veltn* (dramatizations)
Vol. XXVI: *Funim yarid I* (first part of autobiography)
Vol. XXVII: *Funim yarid II* (second part of autobiography)
Vol. XXVIII: *Ayznban-geshikhtes* (almost all of the "Railroad Stories")

There are several other editions described as *Complete*, but in no case is this the fact:

Ale verk fun Sholom Aleichem, Morgn-frayhayt edition, 28 volumes (New York, 1937). Identical with previous edition, with the exception of the ordering of the volumes.

Sholom Aleichem, ale verk, ed. Oyslender and Frumkin (Moscow, 1948). This represents three volumes of a projected twenty-volume edition in Yiddish to be published in the Soviet Union. It was the first attempt at serious editing and variant study. No other volumes are forthcoming.

Ale verk fun Sholom Aleichem, thirty volumes planned, by Ikuf (Buenos Aires, Argentina, 1952–). Thus far, five volumes have appeared.

Some important works have appeared only in individual volumes, not connected with editions:

Dos Sholom Aleichem-bukh (see page 1 of appendix).

Shomers mishpot (Barditshev, 1888). Never re-printed.

Blondznde Shtern (New York, 1912). His only significant novel.

3. SELECTED SECONDARY SOURCES IN YIDDISH

Niger, S. *Sholom Aleichem: zayne vikhtikste verk, zayn humor, und sayn ort in der yidisher literatur* (New York- 1928).

Nusinov, Y. Untitled article on Sholom Aleichem's Early Style, *Di royte velt* (Kharkov, 1926), nos. 5–6, 104–125.

Trunk, Y. Y., *Tevye un Menakhem-Mendel in yidishn veltgoyrl* (New York, 1944). The most perceptive study of these two types in Sholom Aleichem, tying them to the breakdown of the *shtetl* world.

Oyslender, N., *Grundshtrikhn fun yidishn realizm* (Kiev, 1920). A second edition appeared in Vilna, 1928. Analysis of characters, children's stories, and development of ideas in Yiddish literature from Mendele through Sholom Aleichem. Special treatment of Tevye and Menakhem-Mendel.

In Reyzen's bibliography there are hundreds of items on Sholom Aleichem which appeared in journals, newspapers, and periodicals.

SELECTED BIBLIOGRAPHY

1. WORKS IN ENGLLISH

There is no complete edition of Sholom Aleichem in English. The following is a selection of the more available titles:
1. *The Great Fair: Scenes from my Childhood*, translated by Tamara Kahana, Noonday Paperback (New York: Noonday Press, 1958).
2. *Adventures of Mottel, The Cantor's Son*, translated by Tamara Kahana, Collier Paperback (New York: Collier Books, 1961).
3. *The Tevye Stories and Others*, translated by Julius and Frances Butwin, Pocketbook Paperback (New York: Pocket Books, Inc., 1965).
4. *Some Laughter, Some Tears*, translated by Curt Leviant (New York: G. P. Putnam's Sons, 1968).
5. *Old Country Tales*, translated by Curt Leviant (New York: G. P. Putnam's Sons, 1966).
6. *Stories and Satires*, translated by Curt Leviant (New York: Thomas Yoseloff, 1959).
7. *The Adventures of Menahem-Mendl*, translated by Tamara Kahana (New York: G. P. Putnam's Sons, 1969).
8. *Tevye's Daughters*, translated by Frances Butwin (New York: Crown Publishers, 1949).
9. *The Old Country*, translated by Julius and Frances Butwin (New York: Crown Publishers, 1946).
10. *Selected Stories of Sholom Aleichem*, introduction by Alfred Kazin, Modern Library Edition (New York: Random House, 1956).
11. *Inside Kasrilevke*, translated by Isadore Goldshtick (New York: Schocken Books, 1948).
12. There is a generous selection in *A Treasury of Yiddish Stories*, edited by Irving Howe and Eliezer Greenberg. Viking Paperback (New York: Viking Press, 1965).

2. IMPORTANT SECONDARY SOURCES IN ENGLISH

1. Marie Waife-Goldberg, *My Father, Sholom Aleichem* (New York: Simon & Schuster, 1968). Best available biography.
2. Maurice Samuel, *The World of Sholom Aleichem*, Schocken Paperback (New York: Schocken Books, 1965).
3. Hutchins Hapgood, *The Spirit of the Ghetto*, drawings by Jacob Epstein, notes by Harry Golden, Schocken Paperback (New York: Schocken Books, 1966).
4. Max I. Dimont, *Jews, God and History*, Signet Edition (New York: New American Library, 1962).
5. Mark Zborowski and Elizabeth Herzog, *Life is With People: The Culture of the Shtetl*, Schocken Paperback (New York: Schocken Books, 1962).
6. Salcia Landmann, *Jiddisch: Abenteuer einer Sprache* (Munich: Deutscher Taschenbuch Verlag, 1964).
7. *The Field of Yiddish*: Studies in Yiddish Language, Folklore, and Literature, edited by Uriel Weinreich (New York, Columbia University, 1954). Contains valuable bibliographical information on Sholom Aleichem in Yiddish and English.
8. David S. Lifson, *The Yiddish Theatre in America* (New York: Thomas Yoseloff, 1963).
9. Sol Liptzin, *The Flowering of Yiddish Literature* (New York: Thomas Yoseloff, 1963).
10. *The Encyclopedia of Jewish Knowledge*, edited by Jacob de Haas (New York: Behrman's Jewish Book House, 1934).
11. *The Encyclopedia of the Jewish Religion*, general editors: R. J. Zwi Werblowsky and Geoffrey Wigoder (New York: Holt, Rinehart & Winston, 1965).
12. Rhoda S. Kachuck, "Sholom Aleichem's Humor in English Translation", *YIVO Annual of Jewish Social Science*, vol. XIII (New York, 1965).
13. Michael Fixler, "The Redeemers: Themes in the Fiction of Isaac Bashevis Singer", *The Kenyon Review*, vol. XXVI, no. 2 (Spring, 1964), 371–386.

INDEX

Abramowitch, Sholom Yakob, *see* Mendele Mocher Sforim
Adler, Jacob, 45–46
Andreyev, Leonid, 37
Arendt, Hannah, 81
Asch, Sholem, 40–41, 81
   "Kola Street", 40, 81
Ashkenazi, 12–14
Auerbach, Berthold, 27

Baal Shem Tov, 15, 94
Balzac, Honoré de, 21
Beiliss, Mendel, 38, 128, 185
Bellow, Saul, 186–194
   The Adventures of Augie March, 186, 189
   Dangling Man, 186
   Henderson the Rain King, 186
   Herzog, 187, 189
   Mr. Sammler's Planet, 188, 194
   The Victim, 186–187
Ben-Ami, Jacob, 46
Brodsky, family of, 74, 99–100, 132
Buckle, Henry, 27
   History of Civilization, 27

Cahan, Abraham, 47
Canterbury Tales, 66
Chayevsky, Paddy, 173–174
   The Tenth Man, 173–174
Chekhov, Anton, 21, 37, 49, 53, 70
   "On the Harmfulness of Tobacco", 70

Defoe, Daniel, 27
   Robinson Crusoe, 27

Dick, I. M., 16
Dickens, Charles, 19, 21, 28, 134
Dostoyevsky, Fyodor, 18, 182
Dreyfus, Alfred, 74–77

Faulkner, William, 21
Fiddler on the Roof, 52, 165, 174
Flaubert, Gustave, 19
Forverts, 45, 47, 51
Freytag, Gustav, 77
Friedman, Bruce Jay, 180
Fuchs, Daniel, 180

Garfield, John, 46
Glatstein, Jacob, 177
Goethe, J. W., 28
Gogol, N. V., 28, 53
Gold, Herbert, 180
Gorki, or Gorky, Maxim, 37, 49, 71
Gudrun, 13

Ha-Melitz, 23, 29, 30
Hapgood, Hutchins, 173
Harris, Mark, 180
Hauptmann, Gerhart, 18
Ha-Zefirah, 23
Heine, Heinrich, 21
Hemingway, Ernest, 21
Herzl, Theodor, 37
Hesse, Hermann, 70
Hitler, Adolf, 11, 52, 160

Kafka, Franz, 53
Kazin, Alfred, 11, 31
Kuprin, Alexander, 37, 49

Ladino, 12
Lamed vav, 17, 60
Landmann, Salcia, 13
Leviant, Curt, 129, 164
Lord of the Flies, 25
Loyeff, Elimelech, 27, 28, 30, 31

Malamud, Bernard, 180–186, 194
  "The Angel Levine", 194
  The Assistant, 183–184
  "Black is my Favorite Color", 194
  The Fixer, 184–186
  "The Magic Barrel", 180–182
  The Tenants, 194
Manger, Itzig, 177
Mann, Thomas, 21, 33, 46, 70
Mapu, Abraham, 22, 23, 24, 26
  Love of Zion, 23, 24, 26
Mendele Mocher Sforim, 16–19, 37 55, 82
  Fishke der Krumer (Fishke the Lame), 17
  Die Klatshe (The Old Nag), 17
  Dos Kleine Menshele (The Little Man), 16, 17
  Masoes Beniamin Haslishi (The Wanderings of Benjamin the Third), 18
  Der Vinshfingerl (The Wishing Ring), 18
  Die Takse (The Meat-tax), 17
Mendelssohn, Moses, 15
Mill, John Stuart, 27
  Essay on Liberty, 27
Morgen Journal, 45

Nibelungenlied, Das, 13

Opatoshu, Joseph, 177

Peretz, I. L., 18, 37
  "Bontsha the Silent", 18
Potok, Chaim, 180

Quixote, Don, 18, 139

Raabe, Wilhelm, 77
Rabinowitz, Nahum, 23–27

Rabinowitz, Olga Loyeff, 27–30
Rabinowitz, Sholom, *see* Sholom Aleichem
Rashi, 14
Reisen, Abraham, 177
Roth, Henry, 180
Roth, Philip, 143, 149, 153–154, 189–194
  "The Conversion of the Jews", 191–192
  "Defender of the Faith", 192
  "Eli the Fanatic", 193
  "Goodbye, Columbus", 190–191
  Portnoy's Complaint, 143, 149, 153–154, 193–194
Rothschild, family of, 72–73, 79, 99–100, 137

Salinger, J. D., 180
Samuel, Maurice, 51, 132, 141
Schiller, Friedrich, 28
Schwartz, Maurice, 46, 173
Schwartz-Bart, André, 60
  The Last of the Just, 60
Sephardim, 12
Shakespeare, William, 28
Shapiro, Lamed, 177
Sholom Aleichem
  as dramatist, 44–48
  early Hebrew writings, 26–27
  and his father, 23–25
  image of America, 42, 43, 88–89, 133, 141–142, 157–160, 164, 173–175, 178–180
  readings in world literature, 27–28
  and Socialism, 83–88
  and Zionism, 18, 23, 37, 50, 51, 57, 83
  Works:
  Autobiography: *From the Fair*, 51
  Hebrew Writings: *The Daughter of Zion*, 26; *The Jewish Robinson Crusoe*, 27; *Shomer's Mishpot*, 34
  Novels: *Sender Blank*, 33; *Stempenyu*, 33; *Yosele Solovey*, 33
  Plays: *Samuel Pasternak*, 46; *Stempenyu*, 46
  Short Stories and Vignettes:

INDEX

Sholom *(cont.)*
 "Another Page from the Song of Songs", 162
 "Boaz the Teacher", 155
 "Cnards", 94–95
 "Competitors", 169–170
 "The Dreydl", 147–148
 "An Easy Feast", 83
 "The Esrog", 154
 "The Fiddle", 154
 "Final Pages from the Song of Songs", 164–165
 "The First Passover Night of The War", 38, 151
 "The Flag", 154
 "From the Riviera", 154
 "Gitl Purishkevitch", 150–152
 "The Great Panic of the Little People", 76, 82
 "Homesick", 83
 "The Inheritors", 65
 Inside Kasrilevke, 86–102
 "The Little Pot", 152–153
 "The Little Redheaded Jews", 155
 "The Lottery Ticket", 166–168
 "The Malicious Matzoh", 178
 "Merrymakers: Sketches of Disappearing Types", 58
 "Methusaleh, a Jewish Horse", 154–155
 Mottel, The Cantor's Son, 42, 48, 49, 157–160
 "My First Love Affair", 97
 "On America", 42
 "A Page from the Song of Songs", 162, 166
 "Pages from the Song of Songs: This Night", 163
 "The Passover Expropriation", 84–86
 "The Penknife", 32–33, 36
 "Pity for Living Creatures", 149–150
 "A Predestined Disaster", 42
 "The Purim Feast", 145–146
 "The Search", 66
 "Someone to Envy", 66
 "The Story of a Greenhorn", 42
 "Summer Romances", 99
 "The Tenth Man" 168–170
 The Tevye Stories, 36, 60, 103, 135, 164
 "The Bubble Bursts", 109–112
 "Chava", 71, 118–122
 "Get Thee Out", 39, 127–129
 "Hodel", 71, 116–118
 "Modern Children", 112–116
 "Shprintze", 122–124
 "Tevye Goes to Palestine", 124–127
 "Tevye Reads the Psalms", 129–130
 "Tevye Wins a Fortune", 106–109
 "The Town of the Little People", 57
 "Three Little Heads", 170–171
 "Two Anti-Semites", 170–171
 "Two Dead Men", 72
 "Two Shalachmones", 62–63
 "Two Stones", 30
 "Visiting with King Ahasuerus", 156
Shomer (N. M. Shykevich), 34
Singer, I. B., 18, 25, 45, 177
 "Gimpel the Fool", 18
 In My Father's Court, 25
Singer, I. J., 177
Slonimsky, H. S., 22, 23
Spector, Mordecai, 177
Spielhagen, Friedrich, 27, 33
Süsskind von Trimberg, 13
Swados, Harvey, 180
Swift, Jonathan, 17, 21

Tageblatt, 45
Tog, 45, 51
Tolstoy, L. N., 19, 28, 37
Tomashevsky, Boris, 45–46
Turgenev, I. S., 21, 27

Wahrheit, 45, 51
Waife-Goldberg, Marie, 47
Wallant, Edward Lewis, 180
Weizmann, Moishe, 49
World, New York, 48, 51

Yiddish, language, 11–19
Yidishe Folks Bibliothek, Di, 34

Zederbaum, A. O., 22, 23
Zola, Emile, 21